THE DEVELOPMENTAL COURSE OF GENDER DIFFERENTIATION: CONCEPTUALIZING, MEASURING, AND EVALUATING CONSTRUCTS AND PATHWAYS

Lynn S. Liben
Rebecca S. Bigler

WITH COMMENTARIES BY
Diane N. Ruble and Carol Lynn Martin
Kimberly K. Powlishta

D1526805

Willis F. Overton
Series Editor

MONOGRAPHS OF THE SOCIETY FOR RESEARCH IN CHILD DEVELOPMENT
Serial No. 269, Vol. 67, No. 2, 2002

Blackwell
Publishing

Boston, Massachusetts   Oxford, United Kingdom

EDITOR
WILLIS F. OVERTON
Temple University

EDITORIAL ASSISTANT
DANIELLE L. HORVATH
Temple University

CONSULTING EDITORS FOR THE MONOGRAPHS (2002)

THE DEVELOPMENTAL COURSE OF GENDER DIFFERENTIATION: CONCEPTUALIZING, MEASURING, AND EVALUATING CONSTRUCTS AND PATHWAYS

CONTENTS

ABSTRACT

Liben, Lynn S.; Bigler, Rebecca S. The Developmental Course of Gender Differentiation: Conceptualizing, Measuring, and Evaluating Constructs and Pathways. *Monographs of the Society for Research in Child Development*, 2002, **67** (2, Serial No. 269).

Gender differentiation is pervasive, and understanding how and why it develops is important for both theoretical and practical reasons. The work described here is rooted in constructivist accounts of gender differentiation. Past research provides considerable support for constructivist predictions concerning (a) developmental changes in gender attitudes and (b) the relation between gender attitudes and information processing. Little work, however, has addressed the more fundamental question of how children's developing gender attitudes about others are related to developing gender characterizations of self. The focus of the current *Monograph* is on this other-self relation during middle childhood.

A brief review of past theory and empirical work on gender differentiation is provided. It is argued that a major explanation of the limitations and inconsistencies evident in earlier work may be traced to restrictions in the measures available to assess key constructs. A conceptual analysis of the specific limitations of past measures is presented. The *Monograph* then offers alternative models of the developmental relation between attitudes toward others and characterization of self (the *attitudinal* and the *personal pathway models*), and identifies conditions expected to influence the strength of the observed other-self relation.

Four studies establish the reliability and validity of a suite of measures that provides comparable methods for assessing attitudes toward others (attitude measures, or AM) and sex typing of self (personal measures, or PM) in three domains: occupations, activities, and traits (or OAT). Parallel forms are provided for adults (the OAT-AM and OAT-PM) and for children of middle-school age, roughly 11–13 years old (the COAT-AM and COAT-PM). A fifth study provides longitudinal data from children tested at four times, beginning at the start of grade 6 (approximately age 11 years) and ending at the close of grade 7 (approximately age 13 years). These data are used to examine the developmental relation between children's sex typing of others and sex typing of the self, and to test the predictions concerning the factors hypothesized to affect the strength of the relation between the two types of sex typing.

Overall, the data supported the conceptual distinctions among individuals' (a) gender attitudes toward others, (b) feminine self, and (c) masculine self, and, additionally, revealed some intriguing differences across domains. Interestingly, the data concerning the other-self relation differed by sex of participant. Among girls, analyses of concurrent relations showed that those girls who held fewer stereotypes of masculine activities for others showed greater endorsement of masculine items for self, a finding compatible with both the other-to-self attitudinal pathway model and the self-to-other personal pathway model. The prospective regression analyses, however, showed no effects. That is, preadolescent girls' gender attitudes about others did not predict their later self-endorsements, nor did self-endorsements predict later attitudes. Data from boys showed a strikingly different pattern, one consistent with the self-to-other personal pathway model: There was no evidence of concurrent other-self relations, but prospective analyses indicated that preadolescent boys who endorsed greater numbers of feminine traits as self-descriptive early in grade 6 developed increasingly egalitarian gender attitudes by the end of grade 7. The *Monograph* closes with discussions of additional implications of the empirical data, of preliminary work on developing parallel measures for younger children, and of the need to design research that illuminates the cognitive-developmental mechanisms underlying age-related changes in sex typing.

I. INTRODUCTION

The shelves of our bookstores and the entries on our best-seller lists are replete with titles such as *Men are from Mars: Women are from Venus* (Gray, 1992), *Why Men Don't Listen & Women Can't Read Maps: How We're Different and What to Do about It* (Pease & Pease, 2000), and *Opposite Sides of the Bed: A Lively Guide to the Differences Between Women and Men* (Evatt, 1993). Our clothing stores and sports pages are divided into separate sections for men and women, boys and girls. Television commercials and magazine advertisements (and the products they hawk) are targeted for either males or females. In short, popular American culture is filled with evidence that gender is a common and pervasive dimension on which human experience differs.

Our scholarly literatures, too, provide extensive evidence of the varied and robust nature of gender differentiation. Anthropologists have a long history of interest in gender. Margaret Mead's (1928) work examining the sexual lives of adolescent girls in Samoa is a classic example. Contemporary anthropologists have studied gender differentiation in many aspects of daily life—for example, differentiating between women's importance in the private sphere of home and men's importance in the public sphere of politics (e.g., Rosaldo, 1974; see also reviews in Morgen, 1989; Sanday & Goodenough, 1990). Sociologists have examined gender differentiation in a host of domains, including occupational roles (e.g., Reskin & Hartmann, 1986; Williams, 1993), household work (e.g., Hochschild, 1989), communication and interaction (Ridgeway, 1991), and parenting (e.g., Hewlett, 1991). Educators have been concerned with the genesis of and the effects of gender-differentiated patterns of academic interests and achievement (AAUW, 1992), and have studied how outcomes are affected by coeducational versus single-sex educational environments (AAUW, 1998; Signorella, Frieze, & Hershey, 1996). And, as documented throughout the remainder of this *Monograph*, psychologists have made the study of gender differences a major focus of the discipline.

1

WHY STUDY THE DEVELOPMENT OF GENDER DIFFERENTIATION?

The ubiquity of gender differentiation alone makes it a topic of interest. When, why, and how do pervasive gender-differentiated qualities, interests, and beliefs develop? Such questions are, by definition, the focus of scholars who explicitly study sex and gender. But for at least three reasons, gender differentiation should be of interest even to developmental scientists whose substantive interests lie elsewhere.

First, next to chronological age, the child's sex has probably been the participant factor most predictive of outcomes in many cognitive and social realms (e.g., see Golombok & Fivush, 1994; Halpern, 2000; Ruble & Martin, 1998). To be fair, one reason for its predictive power may be that sex has been so routinely included as a variable in empirical work. For example, under the editorship of Boyd McCandless, *Developmental Psychology* required that all authors conduct and report analyses of sex differences (McCandless, 1969). Perhaps if other participant variables (such as socioeconomic status, racial/ethnic membership, geographic origins) were as routinely identified and as adequately sampled, they would prove even more important. Nevertheless, sex would undoubtedly remain among the important predictors of developmental outcomes, and thus investigators working on a wide range of substantive areas must be concerned with understanding its role.

Second, the exploration of how sex-related differences emerge, persist, and change over the course of human development should be of interest to any developmental scientist because it confronts a core goal of the field: understanding the interplay of biology and the environment during development. There can be no argument that at least in some ways the biology of males and females differs. So, too, there can be no doubt that the life experiences of males and females differ. The domain thus provides a fascinating arena to address the age-old nature-nurture debate. Although the discipline has fortunately moved beyond conceptualizing nature and nurture as separable, additive influences on development (see especially Gottlieb, 1997; Gottlieb, Wahlsten, & Lickliter, 1998; 1998; Lerner, 1998; Overton, 1998), the general question of the reciprocal, transactional nature of biological and experiential processes remains of contemporary interest.

Third, insofar as we are scientists who are concerned with the policy implications of our discipline, it is important to understand how gender differentiation unfolds. Gender stereotyping may, for example, limit the expression of individuals' aptitudes and interests. If so, it is important to implement social policies and programs that combat gender stereotyping. Past work has documented the difficulty of designing effective intervention programs to reduce children's stereotyped beliefs and behaviors (e.g., see Katz, 1986; Liben & Bigler, 1987; Serbin & Unger, 1986). Thus, better understanding of the mechanisms by which gender differentiation occurs is needed if we are to develop more successful interventions.

DESCRIPTIVE PREMISES AND DESCRIPTIVE UNKNOWNS

Before beginning to explore the developmental mechanisms that may account for the pervasive gender differences evident in popular culture and documented in scholarly literatures, it is imperative to acknowledge variability within the gender differentiation described in the opening paragraphs. Gender differentiation is not monolithic across cultures or history. That is, despite the pervasiveness of gender differences, there is marked variation among cultures and across historical periods with respect to the degree to which they occur, and with respect to the specific arenas in which they occur. A striking illustration is the sex-differentiated nature of occupations. For example, in the United States, women currently comprise approximately one-quarter of all physicians (American Medical Association, 2001), whereas in Finland, they comprise approximately one-half (Riska, 2001). Such distributions also undergo dramatic historical change. Again, taking the same two countries as illustrations, in the United States the percentage of women doctors has increased steadily over the past few decades, rising from about 8% in 1970 to about 23% in 1998 (AMA, 2001); in Finland over the identical time period the change was from 27% to 49% (Riska, 2001). Change may occur in the opposite direction as well and with far more rapidity, as in Afghanistan where just prior to the ascent of the Taliban in 1996, women made up 40% of the country's doctors. Once the Taliban declared it illegal for women to work outside the home, the percentage of practicing women doctors dropped to 0%. Numerous other illustrations from a wide range of arenas (e.g., athletics, child care, household duties, incidence of risky behaviors) could also be cited to demonstrate cultural differences and historical change.

In addition, gender differentiation is not monolithic within those identified as male or female. That is, despite the descriptively accurate characterization that, on average, groups of boys and men differ from groups of girls and women, it is equally true that on virtually any variable of interest, there is widespread distribution *within* each sex (see Halpern, 2000, in press, for particularly clear discussions). A good example is found in the domain of spatial ability. Although sex differences favoring males consistently appear at the level of group analysis (e.g., Halpern, 2000, in press; Kimura, 1999; Liben, 1991, in press; Linn & Petersen, 1985), the large and overlapping distributions mean that many girls and women will have better spatial abilities than particular boys and men.

There is another important way in which gender differentiation may—or may not—be monolithic, and that is the degree to which there is consistency within individuals. As we discuss later in far more detail, we are especially interested in two potential kinds of within-individual consistency. One concerns *domains*. Given that a particular individual is highly gendered in relation to one domain (e.g., with respect to personality traits), is that same individual necessarily also highly gendered in relation to other domains (e.g., with respect to work or leisure)? The second kind of consistency concerns *targets*. Given that a particular individual is highly gendered in relation to his or her *own* identity and behaviors, is that individual necessarily highly gendered in relation to his or her attitudes and behaviors toward *others*?

Scholars of gender, social psychologists, and others interested in the structure of human identity find the descriptive question about individual consistency of interest in and of itself. But developmental scholars must be concerned with understanding how the ultimate configurations (monolithic or not) come about. Consider, for example, a hypothetical conclusion that individual adults are highly consistent with respect to gendering across domains. Such an outcome might be reached by a variety of developmental pathways. For example, children might first develop a set of relatively isolated modules of beliefs about toys, traits, and jobs; note similarities among them; and ultimately integrate them into one overarching, superordinate gender structure. Alternatively, children might begin with some general concept of maleness and femaleness, and, by mechanisms that themselves must eventually be specified, gradually come to apply these overarching concepts to a larger and larger number of domains.

Similar alternatives exist with respect to targets. From a developmental perspective, gender conceptions of self and other could come about via separate and independent sources and mechanisms. Alternatively, there could be causal relations, and these could be in either direction. It is possible, for example, that children enact gender-differentiated behaviors, and then, in turn, take the cognitions they have constructed from their own behaviors and apply them to others. Alternatively, children might first construct generalized cultural beliefs about what is appropriate for boys and girls, and then, in turn, apply those general beliefs to themselves.

We are not the first developmentalists to recognize the importance of identifying varied domains, targets, and the developmental pathways by which gender-related beliefs and behaviors emerge and are applied. Indeed, a number of theories have been proposed to explain the development of children's gender-related behaviors, beliefs, and characteristics. However, what differentiates our work from past efforts is our focus on the conceptualization and measurement of key constructs and the relations among them. We argue that before it is possible to investigate these constructs and explore how they are related to gender differentiation, and before it is possible to draw conclusions about structural relations among these constructs, it is critical to have valid and reliable ways to measure them. Further, we argue for the importance of evaluating alternative pathways of developmental effects such as those described earlier. This *Monograph* is thus addressed to analyzing measurement problems, describing a suite of assessment scales designed to overcome them, offering hypotheses about relations between and among constructs that should be observed when measurement problems are minimized, proposing alternative developmental pathways, and reporting empirical data relevant to evaluating the proposed structural relations and pathways.

We close this introductory chapter with a note about terminology and an overview of the remaining portions of this *Monograph*.

MONOGRAPH OVERVIEW

The topic of this *Monograph* is what we have called *gender differentiation*. More specifically, we are interested in the relations between children's conceptions of gender and their own patterns of gender differentiation. We use the term *sex typing* to refer to the mapping of objects, activities, roles, and traits onto biological sex such that they follow prescriptive cultural stereotypes of gender. The term is useful because it can be applied broadly. First, it may be used to refer to individuals' conceptions of gender—that is, the extent to which objects, activities, roles, and traits are viewed as appropriate for only one gender (i.e., *sex typing of others*). Sex typing of others is used here synonymously with the terms *gender attitudes* and *gender stereotyping*. Second, it may be used to refer to individuals' identities, personal preferences, and behaviors—that is, the extent to which these self qualities conform to cultural gender stereotypes (i.e., *sex typing of self*). Although we interpret the term *behaviors* to refer to actual actions in real time, the work discussed in this *Monograph* relies on participants' self reports of their own behaviors. In the closing section, we return to a brief discussion of the importance of examining actual behaviors in future research.

Chapter II is devoted to discussions of past work on the development of sex typing. We begin by providing very brief descriptions of the three major kinds of explanations that have been offered to account for the development of sex typing—what we have termed *gender essentialism, gender environmentalism*, and *gender constructivism*. Because our own perspective is most compatible with the third of these, we then turn to a more detailed discussion of constructs and predictions from constructivist accounts, highlighting contributions as well as lacunae in past work. We next provide a review of empirical work that has been addressed to predictions derived from constructivist theories. Finally, we provide an analysis of the measures that have been used in past work to study the development of sex typing.

Motivated by our analysis of the limitations in existing sex-typing measures, in Chapter III we lay out the methodological and theoretical rationale for our empirical work. First, we highlight the characteristics that we judged to be desirable for measures. Second, and still working within the constructivist approach, we explicate pathways that may be operating to develop children's sex typing of themselves and others during middle childhood. Third, we describe the patterns that we expected to observe in empirical studies using scales that meet the identified methodological desiderata. We discuss expectations both with respect to the concurrent relations among constructs as well as with respect to prospective relations.

In Chapter IV we report four empirical studies focused on the development of a suite of measures that offers parallel scales along several dimensions. First, the scales address three domains, specifically occupations, activities, and traits (hence OAT). Second, the scales are directed toward two targets, with one scale assessing attitudes toward others (attitude measure, or AM) and the other assessing sex typing of self (personal measure, or PM). Third, the scales include parallel forms for adults and children. Given the domains, targets, and populations to which the scales are addressed, the resulting adult scales are referred to as the OAT-AM and OAT-PM, and the parallel children's scales are referred to as the COAT-AM and COAT-PM. Studies 1–4 provide data that establish the reliability and validity of the measures themselves, and address concurrent relations among the measured constructs.

In Chapter V we describe a fifth empirical study that provides longitudinal data relevant to evaluating the viability of alternative pathways. Specifically, we use these longitudinal data to explore the relations between developing sex typing of others and developing sex typing the self, and the direction of that influence.

In Chapter VI, we offer concluding comments about methodology and gender constructivism, discuss how the current empirical findings bear upon hypothesized developmental pathways, and consider the relevance of our work for educational interventions. We close by discussing the need for future work to study the cognitive-developmental mechanisms that underlie observed age-linked changes in sex typing of others and self.

II. REVIEW OF PAST WORK

FAMILIES OF EXPLANATORY APPROACHES

At the broadest level, the explanations that have been offered for why gender differentiation develops at all may be grouped into three families. This typology of explanatory mechanisms includes approaches that emphasize inherent, biologically driven sex differences; those that emphasize environmental, learning mechanisms; and those that emphasize individuals' own constructive processes in the creation and use of gender concepts and behaviors. We have labeled these, respectively, gender essentialism, gender environmentalism, and gender constructivism. Despite the seemingly unidimensional implications of the labels, we note that in actuality, most contemporary theories are inclusive with respect to mechanisms. That is, most theories differ with respect to which mechanisms are viewed as most powerful in initiating or sustaining gender differentiation rather than with respect to which mechanisms are operative at all, and many theories may reasonably be discussed under more than one heading. Thus, the seemingly sharp divisions and labels are employed here primarily for the rhetorical purpose of clarifying alternatives. More complete discussions of theories of gender development may be found in earlier reviews (e.g., see Golombok & Fivush, 1994; Halpern, 2000; Huston, 1983; Liben & Signorella, 1987; Maccoby, 1998; Ruble & Martin, 1998; Stangor & Ruble, 1987).

Gender Essentialism

We refer to the family of approaches that assigns a strong role to the physical, material qualities of boys and girls as gender essentialism. Within this family, theories vary markedly with respect to the specific mechanisms that are explored (e.g., sex-linked genes, prenatal hormones, sex steroids at puberty) and in the degree to which environmental factors are taken into account when studying outcomes (e.g., environmental factors that affect gene expression, experiential factors that may moderate outcomes).

7

A theoretical approach to gender differentiation falling squarely within this family of explanatory approaches is evolutionary psychology (e.g., Cosmides & Tooby, 1994; Geary, 2002). In this view, some abilities, physical structures, and traits are hypothesized to have had differential survival value for males and females. For example, good spatial skills are hypothesized to have had survival value for men who traveled to hunt (thus privileging reproduction of men who had the high spatial skills needed for wayfinding and aiming) but not for women who stayed home to tend the children and fields. Over millennia, genetic selection through differential levels of survival and reproduction would eventually lead to sex-differentiated distributions of spatial skills in the gene pool, thereby accounting for the sex difference in spatial skills observed in our time (e.g., see Gaulin, 1993).

A somewhat different example is provided by developmental neuropsychologists who also focus on biological differences between males and females. Illustrative are investigators who study how different levels of exposure to testosterone and estrogen during the prenatal period affect brain development and, in turn, link these differences to later sex-differentiated social behaviors or cognitive skills (e.g., see Berenbaum & Hines, 1992; Collaer & Hines, 1995; Hines, 2000; Resnick, Berenbaum, Gottesman, & Bouchard, 1986).

Some research is aimed specifically at trying to understand the interactive contributions of biological and experiential factors. A particularly good illustration is the research program by Casey (1996) which draws on the "bent twig" model of individual differences suggested by Sherman (1978). Casey has focused her work on females with different patterns of brain organization (assessed by familial patterns of handedness) that are thought to be differentially conducive to developing strong spatial skills. Of interest is whether spatial skills (performance on mental rotation tasks) show an effect of biology alone or are also influenced by environmental experience. Consistent with her interactive hypothesis, Casey (1996) found that environmental factors interact with biological differences in determining women's spatial skills. Additional examples of recent relevant theory and research related to biological factors may be found in Fitch and Bimonte (2002), Halpern (2000), Hines (2000), Kimura (1999), and Liben, Susman, et al. (2002).

Gender Environmentalism

The second family of approaches, labeled gender environmentalism, emphasizes the role of societal practices in generating and maintaining gender differentiation. Again, this general view includes a large range of specific theories that vary in important ways. Traditional learning theorists, for example, posited that reinforcement and punishment shape sex-role behavior (Bandura, 1977; Mischel, 1970). Environmental theories have generated a large body of data consistent with the notion that males and females are, in fact, treated differently by parents, teachers, and peers (e.g., Fagot & Hagan, 1991; Langlois & Downs, 1980; Snow, Jacklin, & Maccoby, 1983). Recent work has been revealing increasingly subtle differences. Leaper (2000), for example, showed that differential treatment of males and females by parents is complex and sometimes subtle, occurring within particular types of settings.

Social learning theorists have argued that observational learning is a primary means through which children learn "appropriate" gender role behaviors (Bandura, 1977; Mischel, 1970). Studies on the relation of gender and imitation have generally indicated that children are more likely to imitate behaviors performed by same-sex rather than by other-sex individuals (e.g., Bandura, Ross & Ross, 1961; Bussey & Perry, 1982; Perry & Bussey, 1979), and that children are more likely to model behaviors that the culture defines as "gender appropriate" for the child (e.g., Barkley, Ullman, Otto, & Bracht, 1977). Many contemporary theorists continue to argue that such processes are important in maintaining the gender differentiation of a culture (e.g., see Bussey & Bandura, 1999).

Another line of research falling within the tradition of environmentalism—although lacking an emphasis on mechanisms derived from traditional learning theories—examines how the use of gender-based organizational strategies and linguistic markers used by authority figures may have an impact on gender differentiation. Researchers have shown that particularly strong gender differentiation occurs in environments in which gender is emphasized functionally or linguistically. Fagot and Leinbach (1989), for example, reported that pre-school children whose parents were more attentive to sex-typed toy play showed earlier labeling of gender and increased levels of sex-typed play than did children whose parents were less attentive to such play. Relatedly, Bigler (1995) found that young children placed in summer school classrooms in which gender was used to label children and to organize activities (e.g., "Good morning, boys and girls") had higher levels of gender stereotyping than did children placed in classrooms in which gender was ignored. There is also evidence that the kind of language (e.g., Bem & Bem, 1973; Hyde, 1984; Liben, Bigler, & Krogh, 2002) and media portrayals (e.g., Calvert & Huston, 1987; Signorielli & Bacue, 1999) that more generally surround children may play a role in their developing beliefs about the sex-differentiated nature of various roles such as occupations.

In short, and as evidenced in the findings of individual studies as well as the outcomes of both traditional and meta-analytic reviews, there is strong evidence that environmental factors play a powerful role in children's gender differentiation (for fuller discussions, see Bussey & Bandura, 1999; Golombok & Fivush, 1994; Huston, 1983; Leaper, Anderson, & Sanders, 1998; Lytton & Romney, 1991; Maccoby, 1998; Ruble & Martin, 1998; Stangor & Ruble, 1987).

Gender Constructivism

Constructivist theories reject the position that children simply receive and then enact messages delivered to them either by biology or by the environment. Instead, children are viewed as active agents who develop the schemata that underlie their gender beliefs and behaviors, and then apply these schemata generatively for further processing. Kohlberg's theory of sex-role development, rooted in Piagetian theory, is a particularly clear illustration. Kohlberg (1966) conceptualized the child as an embodied agent who actively assimilates environmental experience: "At any given point, the child uses . . . experiences of . . . body and . . . social environment to form basic sex-role concepts and values, but at any given point environmental experiences also stimulate restructuring of these concepts and values" (p. 85).

Three prominent, contemporary theories of sex-role development—those of Martin and Halverson (1981), Bussey and Bandura (1999), and Bem (1981)—may also be grouped within the constructivist family. Similar to Kohlberg, these theorists suggested that gender cognitions (or gender schemata) play a critical role in processing (and hence assimilating) new information. These approaches differ from Kohlberg, however, in assigning far more weight to the environment in the initial shaping of gender schemata, and thus may be characterized as exemplars of "social constructivism" (see Overton, 1998). We review these three constructivist positions very briefly here, discussing some of their implications in more detail in the literature review that follows.

Martin and Halverson (1981) argued that children categorize and organize information on the basis of sex, both as a result of the characteristics of gender (e.g., its stability) and environmental variables. Two kinds of schemata are formed. First, children's perception of gender as a dichotomous category leads to the formation of an overall, gender-based "in-group/outgroup schema." This schema contains information about which behaviors, characteristics, and objects are for males and which are for females. In addition, children develop an "own-sex schema." This is a narrower, more detailed schema that is specific to the characteristics and behaviors of the child's *own* sex. To use an example offered by Martin and Halverson (1981), as a result of hearing adults, peers, or media label what is for boys and what is for girls, children acquire schemata about girls and boys in general—for example, that girls sew and boys fix cars. Girls will thus be motivated to learn more about sewing, but not about fixing cars, resulting in an own-sex schema that is detailed about sewing, but not about cars. Boys will be motivated in the reverse direction so that a boy's own-sex schema will be detailed about fixing cars but not about sewing. These cognitive representations are then used by children to interpret new information and structure their behavior. Thus, according to Martin and Halverson's theory, children (a) categorize information according to gender, (b) are assumed to internalize stereotypes of males and females, and (c) approach activities that are viewed by society and the child as gender appropriate, and avoid those that are not.

In a similar vein, Bussey and Bandura (1999) argued that children notice sex differences in their environment and internalize them as rules that they then apply to themselves via "self-sanctions." The initial stages of sex typing in this theory are thus based on traditional social learning principles, including (a) effects of reinforcement and punishment, respectively, of gender "appropriate" and "inappropriate" behaviors and (b) observational learning that takes place via modeling of different roles, traits, and behaviors by males and females. Indeed, given the important role played by learning, their theory could have been discussed under gender environmentalism above. We have placed it under social constructivism, however, because, over time, children are hypothesized to develop internalized cognitions that guide further behavior. Specifically, children are said to develop inner "self-sanctions" as a consequence of internalizing the sanctions against gender inappropriate behavior that had previously been encountered in the environment. In addition, children develop sex-typed notions of self efficacy: They come to believe themselves more competent in gender "appropriate" than in gender "inappropriate" domains.

Bem (1981) also incorporated social constructivist processes in her theory. Specifically, she argued that children come to view gender as central because of two different environmental mechanisms. First, Bem suggested that sex typing develops among children because of the broad functional significance that gender is accorded in society. That is, she argued that adults' use of gender to organize and label the world causes children to view gender as a salient social category. Second, sex typing is thought to develop among children because the environment provides explicit (e.g., direct teaching) and implicit (e.g., modeling) links between gender and a host of physical and social attributes. As a result of these two factors, children become "schematic" for gender, seeing much of the world as sex typed. Under this view, children's gender schemata are believed to drive children to acquire those attributes that are viewed as "appropriate" for their gender.

11

Overall, constructivist accounts of gender differentiation have several qualities that distinguish them from those of other families of theories. First, constructivist accounts argue that sex differentiation in the environment does not serve as an accurate proxy for children's sex typing. That is, because children actively *construct* their beliefs about gender, children may show more—or less—gender differentiation in their beliefs and behavior than might be evident in their environment.

Second, once the child has established gender cognitions of particular kinds, these cognitions are expected to influence the development of other gender cognitions and behaviors. As noted earlier, most contemporary theories (e.g., Bussey & Bandura, 1999) begin with children's cognitions about others, positing that these influence the child's development of cognitions about self, and in turn influence the child's adoption of gendered self-interests and behaviors. As explained in more detail later, we propose that a parallel effect may work in the reverse direction as well. That is, we suggest that self-relevant behaviors and beliefs may play a causal role in shaping cognitions about others.

Third, constructivist approaches that are strongly identified with an embodied, active agent position (i.e., "phenomenological constructivism"; see Overton, 1998) also use cognitive-developmental mechanisms for characterizing the initial establishment of these gender cognitions, be they directed at self or other targets. Kohlberg (1966), for example, argued that "Sex-role concepts and attitudes change with age in universal ways because of universal age changes in basic modes of cognitive organization" (p. 83). From this theoretical perspective, a major goal of research is to study coordination between gender development and general cognitive-development progression.

Constructivist accounts of the development of sex typing have flourished and gained popularity over the past 30 years. Some facets of these theories have been well supported by empirical research. Descriptive studies indicate that sex typing undergoes developmental change (see Huston, 1983; Ruble & Martin, 1998). For example, sex typing of others declines after the age of 6 or 7 years, largely as a consequence of the development of more sophisticated cognitive skills (e.g., Bigler & Liben, 1992; Signorella, Bigler, & Liben, 1993; Trautner, Helbing, Sahm, & Lohaus, 1989). Gender attitudes have also been shown to be related to information processing (e.g., Cordua, McGraw, & Drabman, 1979; Levy, 1989; Liben & Signorella, 1980, 1993; Martin & Halverson, 1983; Signorella & Liben, 1984) such that children generally remember gender-stereotypic information better than counterstereotypic information. Further, age-related progressions in logical thinking have been shown to be linked to changes in children's gender concepts and behaviors (e.g., Bigler & Liben, 1992; DeVries, 1974; Liben & Bigler, 1987; Marcus & Overton, 1978; Szkrybalo & Ruble, 1999).

Unfortunately, however, the accumulation of empirical data concerning the developmental and interactive role of children's conceptions of gender in others and self has lagged behind. Why might this be the case?

First, and as alluded to earlier, we propose that the field has been seriously hampered by limitations in the measurement of those constructs that are thought to play a critical role in the development of sex typing. Overton (1998) has persuasively argued that measurement issues cannot be isolated from conceptual frameworks, and that methodologies are too often ignored in developmental research in general. Gender researchers have raised concerns about gender-related measures in particular (e.g., Beere, 1990; Downs & Langlois, 1988; Serbin, Powlishta, & Gulko, 1993; Spence, 1984; Szkrybalo & Ruble, 1999). Later we identify several specific limitations that have plagued earlier measures, and describe the development of a suite of measures designed to reduce these problems.

Second, perhaps for the usual pragmatic concerns that make it more difficult to employ longitudinal than cross-sectional designs (including not only the demands on time, but also the need for developmentally equivalent measures for different age groups), there has been relatively little longitudinal research bearing on the directional hypotheses that are implicated by past constructivist theories. That is, most evidence concerning the relation between sex typing of others and sex typing of self is based on data collected at a single point in time. When longitudinal data have been collected (e.g., Serbin et al., 1993), the purpose has generally been to address the issue of the stability of sex-typing constructs rather than the issue of developmental relations among sex-typing constructs.

Evidence that self- and other-directed gender constructs are related at a single time is perfectly consistent with the developmental prediction that sex typing of others shapes sex typing of self. However, such data are equally consistent with the alternative possibility that it is the child's sex typing of self that shapes the child's sex typing of others. Later in this *Monograph* we discuss these two alternative developmental pathways in detail. In addition, we present longitudinal data relevant to these directional hypotheses.

Third, although past work has described broad mechanisms by which sex typing initially occurs (e.g., assimilation of cultural norms), it has not yet offered detailed hypotheses about what factors should be expected to influence the application or the further development of gender schemata. That is, little work has addressed whether gender attitudes about others (be they highly stereotyped or egalitarian) guide behavior equivalently across children or across situations, or whether, once established,

13

gender schemata about others influence sex typing of self. Given that it is often specific hypotheses that motivate empirical research, their absence may in part account for why there has been relatively little empirical work on the developmental connection between sex typing of others and self. Later, and with the hope of encouraging more work in this area, we offer four such specific hypotheses, and present some initial empirical data bearing upon them.

EMPIRICAL LITERATURE IN THE CONSTRUCTIVIST TRADITION

One of the major changes in conceptualizing gender in the past two decades has been the increasing recognition that sex typing is multidimensional rather than monolithic (see Antill, Russell, Goodnow, & Cotton, 1993; Huston, 1983; Ruble & Martin, 1998; Spence, 1993). A particularly important distinction within gender schemata is between, first, gender attitudes about others and, second, sex typing of the self (e.g., Deaux, Kite, & Lewis, 1985; Edwards & Spence, 1987; Katz & Ksansnak, 1994; Serbin et al., 1993; Signorella et al., 1993). The nature of the relation between these two constructs is a crucial issue for gender research because, as noted earlier, many prominent theories of sex-role development posit that individuals' stereotypes about others play an important causal role in shaping sex typing of the self. Even theorists who disagree about the relative role of cognitive versus environmental factors agree that children's assimilation of cultural stereotypes plays a role in guiding and shaping their own gender role behavior.

For example, and as explained earlier, Martin and Halverson (1981) asserted in their gender schema theory that gender stereotypes guide behavior by influencing which objects and activities are avoided or approached. They offered the example of a young girl who encounters a truck. The activation of her gender schema, which includes the stereotypic belief that trucks are for boys, leads the little girl to avoid playing with the truck. In this way, the girl's belief that girls do not play with trucks (a cultural gender stereotype about others that she has already appropriated) shapes her play behavior (and thus the further development of her own sex-typed behavior and identity).

Bussey and Bandura's (1992) social cognitive theory also posited an important role for beliefs about others—that is, for internalized gender norms of the culture. In this theory, mechanisms such as modeling and direct tuition are thought to lead children to develop and internalize a standard (or a stereotype) of how people of each sex ought to behave. In turn, this standard becomes the model children use to evaluate, and hence regulate, their own behavior (in addition to continued external environ-

14

mental controls such as differentiated reinforcement for gender "appropriate" versus "inappropriate" behaviors). Again using toy play as an illustration, Bussey and Bandura (1992) reported that children show evidence by the age of four of regulating their own behavior via internalized gender norms. Consider a young girl who is presented with a truck. Her past learning experiences would have paired trucks with boys, leading her to have developed a self-sanction against truck play. Faced with the truck, she would thus anticipate feeling disappointed with herself were she to play with the truck. The anticipation of this negative self-evaluation leads her to avoid playing with the truck

What evidence has accrued during the past 20 years to suggest that children's and adults' gender attitudes toward others (i.e., stereotypes, beliefs) may further shape sex typing of the self (i.e., personality traits, behaviors)? Approaches to this issue have been different in the social and developmental literatures, but the empirical data concerning the relations between gender attitudes toward others and sex typing of the self are probably best characterized as weak among adults and inconclusive among children.

Research with adults was initially based on unifactorial theoretical models of sex typing, positing that "feminine" and "masculine" qualities (i.e., traits, roles, interests) were polar opposite dimensions (e.g., Bem, 1974). Later work by Spence and her colleagues challenged these models, arguing that sex typing was multifactorial and multidimensional (Spence & Helmreich, 1978). Their empirical work centered primarily on expressive and instrumental personality characteristics (assessed by the Personal Attributes Questionnaire, or PAQ; Spence & Helmreich, 1978) and clearly supported the contention that sex typing of the self consisted of multiple factors, and that instrumentality and expressiveness were unrelated. Although a few researchers reported relations among personality measures such as the Bem Sex Role Inventory (BSRI; Bem, 1974) and gender attitudes (e.g., Bem, 1981; O'Heron & Orlofsky, 1990; Taylor & Falcone, 1982), other investigators failed to replicate these effects. Edwards and Spence (1987) reported, for example, that individuals' responses to measures of trait and occupational stereotyping were unrelated to their self-endorsements of expressive and instrumental personality traits (see also Deaux et al., 1985). Little social psychological work, however, has examined gender-related aspects of the self other than personality traits, or how relations between sex typing of the self and others may change across age.

Research with children has employed multiple measures of particular gender constructs, thereby providing potentially relevant data on the relations among gender attitudes toward others and sex typing of the self. Resulting data do not, however, produce a consistent, systematic set of relations. In a study of children in middle school, Katz and Ksansnak

(1994) reported that children's tolerance of gender-role nonconformity in others and their gender-related attributions for the self were conceptually distinct aspects of gender-role development (as shown by their separate loadings in factor analysis). These two factors were correlated with each other modestly, but were related to different predictor variables.

In a conceptually similar study, Spence and Hall (1996) reported that fourth- through sixth-grade children's gender stereotypes about others were unrelated to their self-ratings of expressive and instrumental personality traits. Using a sample of younger children and different dependent measures, Serbin et al. (1993) reported that children's attitudes toward others were related to several (but not all) measures of sex typing of the self. The magnitude of the relations was quite small, and yet regression analyses were consistent with the notion that gender attitudes were predictive of sex typing of the self. However, given that these data were gathered at the same time, the regression analysis would be equally relevant to (and consistent with) a hypothesis of the reverse direction of effect.

More recently, Signorella (1999) published a meta-analysis that examined the strength of associations between pairs of sex-typing measures in children and adolescents. Of the 26 pairs examined, approximately half concerned relations between sex typing of self and sex typing of others (e.g., between interests in masculine activities for the self and sex typing of culturally stereotyped activities for others). The degree of association was generally weak, with rs ranging from .01 to .17, although several relations were statistically significant. Signorella (1999) argued that additional research is needed to identify the variable and complex relations among these constructs in children and adults, and that these relations should be examined by assessing sex typing of self and others in multiple domains.

Finally, and as explained earlier, past literature has not provided relevant longitudinal data. That is, to our knowledge there have been no studies in which the hypothesized predictor variable was assessed at some time prior to the outcome variable and the resulting data analyzed with regression analyses. Such analyses bear upon the hypothesis implicit in the constructivist theories reviewed earlier that attitudes about others play a causal role in shaping sex typing of the self.

In summary, extant data are incomplete and ambiguous with respect to the question of whether, and to what extent, the stereotypes held by children and adults about others shape the continuing development of self-relevant gender schemata and behaviors. Importantly, and as others have noted earlier (e.g., see Downs & Langlois, 1988; Hort, Leinbach, & Fagot, 1991), interpretation of the empirical inconsistencies is problematic because there have been critical methodological differences in the ways that gender attitudes toward others and sex typing of the self have been measured within and across studies and across ages. In the following section, we focus on these measurement issues directly.

CONCEPTUAL ANALYSIS OF EXTANT MEASURES

Many researchers have argued that the study of sex typing in general has suffered from the lack of careful conceptual treatment of measurement issues (Beere, 1990; Downs & Langlois, 1988; Hort et al., 1991). Our more specific concern is that measurement problems have seriously hampered the investigation of the structural and developmental relations between sex typing of self and sex typing of others. Highly varied scales have been used to assess sex typing of the self and sex typing of others, with little attention to whether variations among the scales affect response patterns. In this section we highlight five major dimensions on which measures used to assess self and other constructs, within and across age populations, often differ. These differences can be problematic because data that appear to imply something about differences between constructs may in actuality reflect something about the differences in the ways that each construct has been measured.

Substantive Domain

The first important dimension relevant to assessing gender concepts is the substantive domain of sex typing—that is, the topic (such as play or work) addressed by the measure. Although some scales tap sex typing within a single domain, many others include—within a single measure—items that tap sex typing within a wide range of domains (e.g., the Attitudes Toward Women Scales for Adolescents [AWSA], Galambos, Petersen, Richards, & Gitelson, 1985; the Gender Attitudes Scale for Children [GASC], Signorella & Liben, 1985; the Attitudes Toward Women Scale [AWS], Spence & Helmreich, 1972). Sampling across domains has some advantages. However, broad scales will be less likely to detect consistencies between attitudes toward others and sex typing of the self in those cases in which links hold only within highly focused domains. For example, gender stereotyping of occupations may predict personal interest in nontraditional occupations but such a relation may not be detectable when using a gender stereotyping assessment that includes many additional domains (e.g., traits, roles, values).

Psychological Processes: Knowledge Versus Attitudes

A second important dimension concerns whether the psychological phenomenon being tapped by a particular measurement method concerns

17

knowledge or attitudes. That is, measures that are aimed at assessing respondents' sex typing of others may, because of variations in question type and response format, inadvertently vary with respect to whether they are measuring individuals' attitudes or instead are measuring individuals' knowledge about cultural gender stereotypes. This issue is particularly (although not exclusively) relevant to the developmental literature. Meta-analyses (Signorella et al., 1993) have suggested that attitudes are assessed when children (a) are asked "Who can ... ?" or "Who should ... ?" perform various occupations or activities or possess various traits, and (b) are given the option of assigning items to both sexes. In contrast, knowledge of societal stereotypes is assessed when children (a) are asked "Who usually ... ?" performs various occupations or activities or possesses various traits, and/or (b) are forced to respond by choosing one or the other sex. Many previous studies of the relation between gender attitudes toward others and sex typing of the self used measures that tap children's knowledge of gender stereotypes, rather than their personal endorsement of gender stereotypes (Hort et al., 1991). However, knowledge of cultural gender stereotypes is unlikely to predict to sex typing of the self, in part because children's knowledge is near ceiling levels in many domains after early childhood (see Ruble & Martin, 1998). A more potent predictor is thus likely to be whether individuals themselves endorse those cultural gender stereotypes.

The Relation Between Masculine and Feminine Items

A third methodological dimension concerns the relation between masculine and feminine items used within a single scale. Embedded within the selection of masculine and feminine items are several more specific concerns. One concern is whether the measure allows or precludes the independent assessment of masculine and feminine constructs. It is important for measures to distinguish responses to the two constructs because to do otherwise is to assume that masculinity and femininity fall along a single, unitary dimension, which is an untenable assumption (Spence, 1993; Spence & Helmreich, 1978). An illustration of this issue may be found in the most commonly used developmental measure of sex typing (see Beere, 1990), the Sex Role Learning Inventory, or SERLI (Edelbrock & Sugawara, 1978). Specifically, the "Sex Role Preference" section of the SERLI asks children to rank order preferences for 10 activities (5 masculine, 5 feminine) by ordering drawings depicting these activities. This method obviates the possibility of independently assessing the child's interest in both own- and other-sex activities. In light of this limitation, it is unfortunate that many previous studies of the relation between sex typing of self and others have employed the SERLI as the measure of sex typing of the self (e.g., Katz & Ksansnak, 1994; Serbin et al., 1993).

18

Another concern is whether or not the masculine and feminine items are comparable *except* on the intended dimension of gender. Two potential confounds appear to be especially important: (a) the degree to which items are stereotypically associated with males or females, and (b) the degree to which items are viewed as desirable. Researchers often compare the degree of sex typing of a particular set of masculine versus feminine items. Such findings are difficult to interpret, however, because it is impossible to determine whether significant differences stem primarily from the selection of items (e.g., on a particular scale, feminine items might be associated with females more strongly than the masculine items are associated with males) or from the attitudes of the participants (e.g., children might view the feminine role as more constrained than the masculine role). Evidence of comparability of items has rarely been discussed in past presentations of sex-typing measures.

Even if, however, masculine and feminine items are selected to yield comparable degrees of cultural stereotyping, they are unfortunately still likely to differ on the dimension of desirability. Again, the commonly used SERLI (Edelbrock & Sugawara, 1978) illustrates this point. As described earlier, the preference section of the SERLI asks children to rank order drawings of 10 (5 masculine, 5 feminine) activities. The masculine activities are baseball, digging, hammering, car play, and fighting; the feminine activities are sewing, ironing, sweeping, washing dishes, and cooking. As many critics have noted (e.g., Aubry, Ruble, & Silverman, 1999; Serbin et al., 1993), the sex type of the activities (i.e., masculine vs. feminine) is confounded with desirability, with the chore-like nature of the feminine items making them less desirable for anyone.

Unfortunately, there is no perfect way to avoid all problems concerning the stereotypicality and desirability of items because cultural stereotypes do, in fact, confound sex type (i.e., masculinity, femininity), stereotypicality, and desirability. A common finding in the developmental gender-role literature is that feminine items are more highly sex typed than are masculine items (e.g., Shepard & Hess, 1975; Smetana, 1986), perhaps reflecting greater societal discomfort with males who exhibit nontraditional gender role behavior than with females who do so. Another problematic confound is that masculine occupations (as a group) are higher in status than feminine occupations, something that even elementary school children appear to know (Liben, Bigler, & Krogh, 2001). Children have been found to rate masculine items as more desirable than feminine items (e.g., Antill, Cotton, Russell, & Goodnow, 1996). Increasing the problem in the occupational domain is the fact that, in U.S. culture, stereotypically masculine occupations far outnumber stereotypically feminine occupations (e.g., see Jacobs, 1989; Jacobs & Powell, 1985; U.S. Department of Labor, 1991).

19

Given these conditions, the population of items from which scale items can be drawn is biased with respect to stereotypicality and desirability. Removing the bias by sampling items differentially from the population of potential masculine and feminine items (e.g., by including all of the small subset of moderately high status feminine occupations and omitting most of the high status masculine occupations) is problematic because it compromises the external and ecological validity of the scale. In addition, this type of sampling rules out the possibility of studying potentially interesting questions that are linked to the confounds in our culture.

Comprehensibility of Measures

The fourth methodological issue is the comprehensibility of the measures given to children and younger adolescents (e.g., see Beere, 1990). One concern is whether children of different ages are able to comprehend the individual items. This issue may be illustrated by measures in the domain of occupational stereotyping which include items that may be unfamiliar to children, such as "secretary" and "stockbroker" (e.g., Biernat, 1991; Martin, Wood, & Little, 1990; Signorella & Liben, 1985). Furthermore, some research suggests that children's understanding of many sex-typed occupational labels is not always comparable to that of adults, and, thus, children may not interpret items as expected for the sex-typing measures (Liben et al., 2002).

An additional concern with respect to comprehensibility is whether children understand the specific question they are being asked. Various question formats have been used across and even within measures. The Attitudes Toward Women Scale for Adolescents (AWSA; Galambos et al., 1985), for example, varies phrasing across items, including items that begin "Boys are better . . . ," "Girls should have . . . ," "It is more important . . . ," and "It would be a good idea. . . ." Although variety may be a strength in certain circumstances, it may also confuse children (and perhaps even adolescents) and may lead to unreliable measurement (see also Beere, 1990).

Age-Appropriate Content

A fifth methodological dimension concerns whether the gender content of the measures is equivalently appropriate for samples of different ages. Some researchers have argued that the same items should be used across all ages, made viable by simplifying language for younger children (e.g., see Biernat, 1991). This strategy does not, however, take into account the deeper issue of whether given items are equally relevant to gender schemata at different ages. It seems likely that some occupations, activities, and traits that are sex typed by adults will—even if familiar to children—be less central to children's gender schemata, and vice versa. For example, children (unlike adults) spend much of their lives in school settings and thus items related to school settings might be particularly good for tapping sex typing in children, but of little use for tapping sex typing in adults.

Some evidence for equivalence of the comprehensibility and relevance of measures may be provided by reliability coefficients. These reliabilities should be calculated separately for different age groups, irrespective of whether the scales used with different groups are identical or different. Unfortunately, however, most researchers who have used the same scale with a wide age-range of participants have not reported the scale reliabilities separately for each age group (e.g., Biernat, 1991; Powlishta, Serbin, Doyle, & White, 1994). Another means of evaluating the relevance of particular items for different age groups is to examine the way that items within scales function for samples of particular ages. Those items that work best to tap children's versus adults' attitudes can then be selected and compared.

Continued Caveats

Before turning to a description of our own attempts to address the various measurement issues discussed above, we acknowledge that there are not always perfect solutions to every problem. As noted already, some problems are the consequence of confounds in the culture under study. We also acknowledge that other researchers before us have developed measures that address a subset of the concerns raised here (e.g., the multidimensional nature of gender attitudes; see Antill et al., 1993, 1996; Spence & Helmreich, 1978). However, and perhaps most importantly with respect to an interest in studying the developmental *relation* between gender attitudes toward others and sex typing of the self, extant measures have not provided scales for self and other sex typing that are equivalent along critical dimensions. That is, past work bearing on the relation between the two constructs has often mixed items in ways that confound domain, psychological phenomena (i.e., knowledge and attitudes), and/or comprehensibility of items. For example, children's sex typing of others is often assessed by asking about household-related activities or occupations (e.g., as in the SERLI), whereas children's sex typing of the self is often assessed by asking about play-related preferences or traits. As a consequence, when researchers fail to find a strong relation between other and self constructs, the explanation might rest either in a lack of relation between the constructs or in the different domains and methodologies used in the measures. We next describe the development of a suite of measures designed to minimize the identified problems, and discuss the patterns that we expected to observe in empirical work using these measures.

III. GENDER CONSTRUCTIVISM RECONSIDERED

DESIGNING MEASURES

Overview of Scales

Having identified important limitations in extant measures for the study of the relation between gender attitudes toward others and sex typing of the self, we sought to improve the situation by designing a suite of sex-typing scales. These scales included parallel forms with the same format and content explicitly designed to assess (a) sex-typed attitudes toward others (attitude measure or AM) and (b) sex typing of the self (personal measure or PM). Our goal was to devise separate subscales for multiple domains. We thus systematically sampled three domains: occupations, activities, and traits (OAT). Having several domains was meant to allow researchers to detect hypothesized relations between sex typing of self and others within focused gender domains, to have scales that might be especially well-suited for particular purposes (e.g., the domain of occupations for research related to career choice), and to provide subscales that—if strong relations were observed among them—could be used interchangeably (e.g., using two subscales in counterbalanced order for pretest and posttest purposes). In addition, our goal was to devise separate, psychometrically sound subscales both for children (COAT-AM and COAT-PM scales) and for adults (OAT-AM and OAT-PM scales). Finally, and as explained in more detail below, we developed all subscales in both long and short forms.

To measure sex typing of others, we asked respondents about whether men and women "should" perform various jobs or activities, or have various personality characteristics. We asked the "should" question rather than the "who usually does" question because, as noted earlier, the former taps individuals' attitudes toward gender stereotypes rather than their knowledge of stereotypes (see Signorella et al., 1993). Our measures provide respondents with the option that items are appropriate for both (or, in some cases, neither) men and women. To measure sex typing of self, we asked respondents about their own interests in jobs, involvement in activities, and identification with various traits.

Masculine and feminine items were selected so that the scales would allow the independent assessment of masculine and feminine sex typing, and so that within both forms of sex typing, items would span a wide range of stereotypicality and desirability. As noted briefly in Chapter II, scales that sample broadly over these dimensions allow for the possibility of detecting patterns of sex typing that are related to the way our culture confounds masculinity and femininity with stereotypicality and desirability. For example, broad scales can be used to determine whether the finding that females show greater interest than males in cross-sex-typed jobs is attributable to females' greater willingness to cross gender stereotypes, or is due to the cultural link between masculinity and more highly desirable jobs. At the same time that broad scales are well suited for exploring a large range of hypotheses, it is likely that such scales will have complex internal factor structures. This possibility, and its implications for the interpretation of scale results, should be explored in future work.

Item Selection

Because of concerns about comprehensibility and the relevance of items for different age groups, we selected items for children's and adults' versions of the scales separately. For the item pool used for the long forms of the scales, we chose items for each of the target age groups on the basis of previous research that had suggested the relevance of particular items for the given age group. That is, items for the COAT scales were selected from a broad range of previous gender-related work on sex typing in children (e.g., Edelbrock & Sugawara, 1978; Hall & Halberstadt, 1980; Signorella & Liben, 1985; Williams, Bennett, & Best, 1975), and items for the OAT scales were selected from studies of adults (e.g., Spence & Helmreich, 1978).

To provide a check on whether the items selected from this earlier research have maintained their stereotypicality in contemporary society, we asked a group of college students ($N = 120$) to rate each item with respect to how each is viewed in U.S. culture. Specifically, respondents were asked to use a 7-point scale to rate each item according to whether most people believe it is appropriate (1) *for males only,* (2) *much more likely for males,* (3) *somewhat more likely for males,* (4) *equally likely for males and females,* (5) *somewhat more likely for females,* (6) *much more likely for females,* or (7) *for females only.*

Means of the ratings of individual scale items are presented in Appendix A. We categorized items receiving a mean score of 3.4 or below as

"Masculine," those receiving a mean score of 4.6 or above as "Feminine," and all others as "Neutral." These rating data provide evidence that the items taken from older research continue to be judged as stereotypically masculine, feminine, and neutral. In addition, the data document that the items included in the OAT and COAT scales cover a considerable range of stereotypicality.[1]

To examine whether masculine and feminine items were equivalent in the degree to which they were rated as culturally stereotyped, ratings were subtracted from 4 (the neutral point of the 7-point scale), and the absolute values taken. With this system, a score of 0 represents the most neutral rating possible and a score of 3 represents the most stereotyped rating possible. The summary data for each category of items within each of the three domains are presented in Appendix B. An analysis of variance revealed no significant differences in the ratings of feminine and masculine items on any of the subscales. Further, there were no significant differences in the ratings given by male and female respondents. However, consistent with the general finding that feminine items have a greater stereotypic valence than masculine items in our culture (discussed earlier), the numerical ratings were higher for feminine than masculine items for each subscale of the long forms. Also evident from the data is the finding that the trait subscale contains items that are less highly stereotyped than those on the occupation and activity subscales. This characteristic affects the interpretation of the trait scale data and is, therefore, discussed in greater detail later in this *Monograph*.

Developing Short Forms of Scales

The full set of items just described appeared on the long forms of the scales. Data from participants' responses to the long scales (i.e., on the COAT-AM, COAT-PM, OAT-AM, and OAT-PM) were used to select the best-performing items for the short versions of the scales. Specifically, we selected those items that had the highest item-total score correlations for each subscale (e.g., sex typing of masculine traits for others) to obtain the 10 best masculine, 10 best feminine, and 5 best neutral items. These item-total correlations were computed separately for child and adult

---

[1]We also administered a similar rating scale to sixth- and seventh-grade children ($N = 22$, tested individually). Children's ratings were very similar to those of adults, especially for occupational and activity items. Children did, however, rate a few trait items as somewhat more sex typed and a few as somewhat less sex typed than did adults. Although the sample size is too small to justify including the details of the rating data in the *Monograph* proper, the data provide additional reassurance that the items selected on the basis of older research literature have generally maintained their stereotypic valences in contemporary culture.

samples. Not surprisingly, given that the items were selected for the short scales on the basis of their empirical performance on the long scales, different items were selected for the adult and child versions of the scales. These differences support our argument that the relevance of particular items can be expected to differ for different age groups. The empirically based selection of items also resulted in having different items for the scales measuring sex typing of self and sex typing of others. The wording format, however, remained constant across parallel scales.

It is important to note that the short and long versions of the scales serve two different purposes. The long forms, because they are broader and have identical items on self and other scales, are particularly well suited for examining relations between sex typing of the self and sex typing of others (a topic to which we will turn in the next section of the *Monograph*). The short forms of the scales are useful as efficient measures of individuals' general leveling of sex typing of self and others within multiple domains and across multiple ages (age 11 years to adulthood).

Summary

To summarize our argument thus far, we suggest that what sometimes has appeared as a lack of coherence between gender attitudes toward others and sex typing of the self may instead be a reflection of differences in the ways the constructs have been measured within and across studies and across age groups. If the field is to advance in its understanding of the etiology, structure, and developmental pathways of sex typing, it is crucial to have valid, reliable, and comparable measures of gender attitudes toward others and sex typing of the self for use with both children and adults. For this reason, we developed the suite of measures presented here, and then used them to examine theoretically based predictions about the relations between sex typing of self and others.

DEVELOPMENTAL PATHWAYS

As just reviewed, a major purpose of our work has been to develop a suite of scales for measuring key gender-differentiation constructs, in turn allowing for more compelling investigations of the relations among those constructs. As detailed in this section, a second purpose of our work is to heighten attention to the possible pathways through which sex typing of self and others may be related, still using gender constructivism as a theoretical base.

As discussed earlier, extant constructivist theories emphasize a developmental pathway in which a child's beliefs about others provide the major impetus for the child's own pursuits and hence identity. To illustrate, the model proposed by Martin and Halverson (1981) is reproduced in Figure 1. As evident in the figure, this model gives primacy to the child's gender schemata or assimilation of cultural norms about what is "for boys" and what is "for girls." The contents of these schemata are then combined with the child's judgment about self (i.e., either "I am a girl" or "I am a boy") to motivate the child's own approach or avoidance of the focal object. Girls' own-sex schemata are thereby more fully elaborated with respect to culturally feminine things; whereas boys' own-sex schemata are more fully elaborated with respect to culturally masculine things.

Although this particular pathway is commonly implicit or explicit in constructivist approaches to gender development, it is not the only possible one. That is, an essential feature of a constructivist approach to gender is not that schemata about *others* have developmental primacy. Instead, what is important is that children construct gender schemata that, in turn, shape further cognitive processing and development. In this light, it is also reasonable to expect that the child's constructions about *self* will shape beliefs about *others*. In the sections that follow, we therefore describe both pathways, and summarize the key dimensions on which our own models extend earlier formulations. It is important to note that—as implied in the prior discussion—our pathway models are not addressed to the *origins* of gender-related concepts and identity, but rather to developmental pathways that are operative after initial gender cognitions have been formed. Consistent with this emphasis, the children included in our empirical work (described later) were drawn from middle schools (roughly 10–13 years of age), long after gender identity has been established. Rich discussions of theoretical and empirical issues related to earlier developmental periods may be found in Martin, Ruble, and Szkrybalo (in press).

Attitudinal Pathway Model

Our first model, labeled an *attitudinal pathway model*, is depicted in Figure 2. In this other-to-self pathway, attitudes about others are depicted as playing a causal role in shaping the individual's own behavior or engagement with a particular object, person, or event (OPE), thus ultimately influencing gender identity. In general terms, this model is much like that proposed by Martin and Halverson (1981). One important difference, however, is that the new model is more explicit in highlighting opportunities for individual differences.

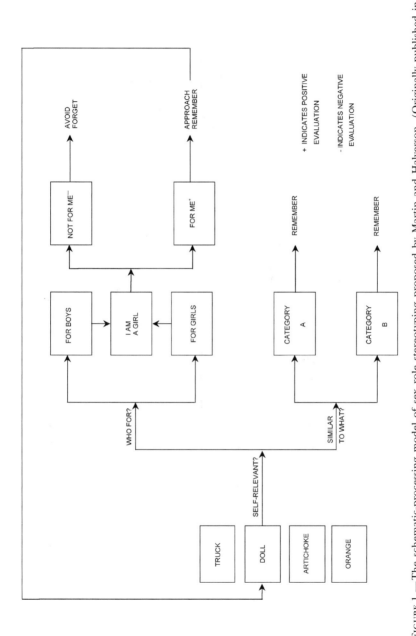

FIGURE 1.—The schematic-processing model of sex role stereotyping proposed by Martin and Halverson. (Originally published in "A Schematic Processing Model of Sex Typing and Stereotyping in Children," by C. L. Martin and C. Halverson, 1981, *Child Development*, **52**, p. 1121.)

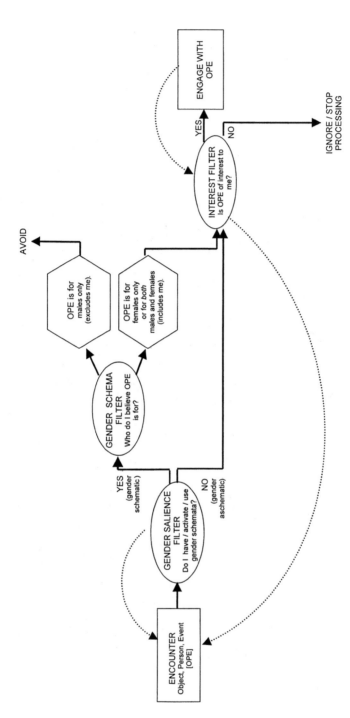

FIGURE 2.—The *attitudinal pathway model* illustrated for a female. Constructs in rectangles represent behaviors, those in ellipses represent decision filters, and those in hexagons represent gender schematic cognitions/beliefs.

More specifically, this model includes a *gender salience filter* that asks "Do I have, activate, or use gender schemata?" This filter is intended to represent the notion that the salience of gender schemata varies among individuals (hereafter assumed to be children), similar to the distinction between "schematic" versus "aschematic" adults offered by Bem (1981). The gender salience filter itself is presumed to be shaped by a host of environmental factors (e.g., exposure to parental, peer, and media messages) and organismic factors (e.g., age, cognitive-developmental level) that, for the sake of graphic clarity, are omitted from the figure itself.

The figure shows different pathways for children who tend to apply gender-related constructs to their experiences (gender schematic) and for those who do not (gender aschematic). In gender schematic children, the gender schema filter leads the child to apply attitudes about whether the particular OPE is or is not appropriate for someone of the child's own sex. Note that in the model presented here these gender schemata refer to attitudes about (or endorsement of) cultural stereotypes rather than knowledge about them. (The latter is presumed to be almost universal at least by middle childhood.) OPEs that are believed by the child to be appropriate only for the other sex will be avoided. For OPEs that are believed to be consistent with the child's own sex, the pathway then leads to an *interest filter*. Children who are gender aschematic reach this interest filter directly.

The interest filter, which provides another important individual difference component in the model, is intended to account for the operation of any particular child's idiosyncratic set of interests in a particular OPE. Again, for graphic clarity, the origins of these interests are not depicted in the figure, but they are presumed to include both environmental factors (e.g., history of exposure to related OPEs; parental, peer, and media influences) and organismic factors (e.g., cognitive level; profile of cognitive abilities; personality traits). We propose that individual qualities like these join with the child's gender-related processing (assuming a gender schematic child) to determine behavioral (and hence identity) outcomes.

It should be noted that just as there are differences among individuals in the strength of their gender schematicity (Bem, 1981; Carter & Levy, 1988), there are differences among the conditions that render gender schematic processing more or less likely (Bigler, 1995; Deaux & Major, 1987). For example, being the only man or woman in a large group might enhance an individual's tendency to activate the gender salience filter. In other words, our current focus on individuals is not meant to imply that we view contextual or situational factors as unimportant. Again, the figures as drawn do not attempt to depict all potentially important factors, nor do they depict all potentially important links.

We comment here on several other aspects of this model as well. The feedback arrow from *engagement* to the interest filter is intended to suggest that the experience of engaging with an object, person, or event may affect future interest, with its valence (positive or negative) depending on the nature of the experience during engagement. The arrows from the gender salience filter and from the interest filter back to the initial *encounter* are intended to suggest that children are not simply passive recipients of the objects, people, and events that just happen to be in their environment. Rather, individuals are presumed to have a powerful impact on which of the many potentially available environmental stimuli they even "encounter." Most importantly, in the attitudinal pathway model, the gender schematic individual's engagement with an OPE is driven primarily by gender-related attitudinal schemata. There is no strong likelihood for revising attitudes on the basis of behavioral engagement. (Of course, exceptions may occur if there is some particularly compelling reason for an individual to engage in an OPE that would normally have been avoided as gender-inappropriate.) For gender aschematic individuals, it is the interest filter that primarily affects engagement and encounters, again with no strong pathway to or from gender schemata.

Personal Pathway Model

Our second model, labeled as a *personal pathway model*, is shown in Figure 3. In this self-to-other pathway, children's own qualities and behaviors are depicted as playing the primary role in shaping the child's gender attitudes about others. Here the child's own interests (again, an outcome of skills, experiences, etc.) motivate the decision about whether or not to approach the object, person, or event offered in the environment. If the child does so engage, and if the child is gender schematic (see the discussion above), the child will use his or her own engagement to construct beliefs about whether that object or event is, in general, for boys or for girls. If the child engages but is not gender schematic, there is no consequence for gender attitudes, although that engagement may be expected to influence the individual's subsequent interest in that OPE.

A notion related to the personal pathway model was proposed by Martin, Eisenbud, and Rose (1995) with respect to children's tendencies to project their own preferences to others on the basis of sex. Their empirical data showed that preschool children used their own preferences for novel, non-sex-typed toys as the basis for predicting other children's preferences (e.g., "what I like, children of my own sex will also like"). As conceptualized here, the personal pathway model has an important temporal aspect. OPEs that are unfamiliar (such as the novel toys used by Martin et al., 1995) will initially establish their sex typing (assuming gender

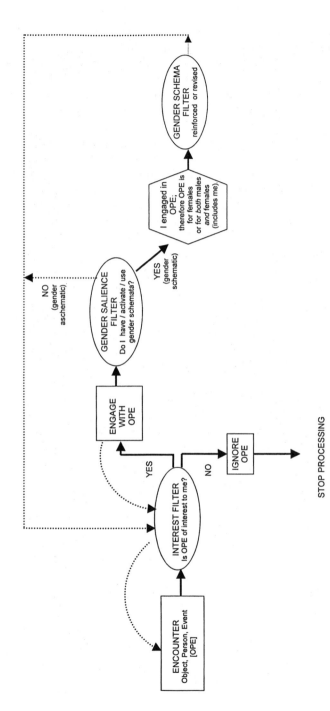

FIGURE 3.—The *personal pathway model* illustrated for a female. Constructs in rectangles represent behaviors, those in ellipses represent decision filters, and those in hexagons represent gender schematic cognitions/beliefs.

schematic children) as a consequence of personal interests. For OPEs that are already familiar (e.g., via past exposure to media), children will be knowledgeable about which sex is associated with the target OPE—and may personally hold (endorse) the cultural stereotype at the time that the opportunity for engagement arises. In this model, gender schemata do *not*, however, guide behavior. Instead, personal interest in the OPE drives the child's engagement, which in turn influences the further development of attitudes. That is, under this proposed model, gender schematic children will come to (or reinforce) personally held cultural stereotypes when they themselves have engaged in the same-sex-typed OPE, and these children will give up (or reduce) their prior cultural stereotypes when they themselves have engaged in a cross-sex-typed OPE. Additional comments about the attitudinal pathway model (e.g., the nonpassive nature of initial encounters) apply to the personal pathway model as well.

To illustrate how the personal pathway might operate, consider a boy who becomes interested in ballet and begins to take ballet classes. If the boy is gender schematic so that he tends to interpret experiences through the lenses of gender, and if he had not already developed attitudes about the gendered nature of ballet (perhaps because he had never before been exposed to ballet), his own involvement would lead him to develop the attitude that ballet is for boys. If instead, prior to his own involvement, he had already developed the attitude that ballet is only for girls (e.g., on the basis of what he had earlier encountered in the culture), his new personal interest and involvement in ballet would drive him to revise his gender attitude about ballet. In essence, this is the plot line of the recent movie, *Billy Elliot*, in which a young boy (and his father) come to revise their sexist attitudes about ballet as a function of Billy's own interest, training, and success in dance.

Pathway Models in Context

The attitudinal and personal pathways just described extend earlier work along a number of dimensions, many of which have already been noted. At the broadest level, however, what is most important is that these models are far more explicit than earlier work about directional effects, and that they articulate the possibility of a pathway that operates in a direction that is the reverse of that implied in earlier constructivist formulations. We caution, however, against a likely tendency to characterize these two models in "either/or" or "splitting" terms (Overton, 1998). That is, although we have described them separately, they need not be mutually exclusive. Indeed, our own expectation is that both pathways operate, perhaps unevenly for different children, at different points in development, and in different contexts.

In closing the description of our models, we should reiterate the point made earlier that these models assume that there has already been considerable development of children's attitudes and of self-related experiences. Thus our models do not focus on the early development of gender schemata that may emerge via embodied, constructive processes such as those proposed almost 40 years ago by Kohlberg (1966), or via social constructive processes such as those proposed more recently by Bussey and Bandura (1999). Nor do our models focus on the factors that influence the degree to which particular children develop into more versus less gender schematic individuals, nor do they depict all potential constructs and interactions either within or between the two models. Although the models are therefore subject to future expansion and refinement, they are offered as heuristics for exploring the developmental connections between sex typing of the self and others.

We consider empirical data in relation to both attitudinal (other-to-self) and personal (self-to-other) pathways in Chapter V. Before turning to these empirical data, however, we discuss several factors that we hypothesize will have significant effects on the strength of the observed association between gender attitudes toward others and sex typing of the self.

THE RELATION BETWEEN SEX TYPING OF OTHERS AND SEX TYPING OF SELF

In an attempt to provide specific hypotheses of the kind we argued earlier were useful for generating empirical work, in this section we propose four factors that we predict will be related to the strength of the observed relation between gender attitudes about others and sex typing of self. These are listed in the first column of Table 1.

Content Match

The first factor concerns the degree to which there is a close content match between the domains and specific items used to measure attitudes toward others and sex typing of self. Based on the substantial social psychological literature on conditions that promote strong attitude-behavior correlations (e.g., Ajzen & Fishbein, 1973, 1977; Fishbein & Azjen, 1974; Wicker, 1971), holding gender stereotyped attitudes about others in one domain is predicted to be more highly related to sex typing of the self in that same domain than it will be to sex typing of self in some different domain. Furthermore, relations between attitudes toward others and sex typing of the self will be enhanced in proportion to the closeness of the specific content within the general domain (see also Aubry et al., 1999).

TABLE 1

FACTORS AFFECTING THE STRENGTH OF THE OBSERVED RELATION BETWEEN
SEX-TYPED ATTITUDES ABOUT OTHERS AND SEX TYPING OF SELF

Factor Type	Conditions Linked to Stronger Self-Other Relation in Attitudinal Pathway Model	Conditions Linked to Stronger Self-Other Relation in Personal Pathway Model
Content match (degree to which content of domains and items match)	Closer domain/item match	Closer domain/item match
Individual's level of sex typing (strength of the individual's sex typing)	Stronger sex typing of others	Weaker sex typing of self
Sex type (whether item is same or cross-sex typed for respondent)	Cross-sex-typed items	Cross-sex-typed items
Social status (whether cross-sex-typed items are high or low in social status)	Cross-sex-typed items that are high in social status (thus relevant primarily for females)	Cross-sex-typed items that are high in social status (thus relevant primarily for females)

At the extreme, the observed relation between attitudes toward others and sex typing of the self should be greatest when items used not only tap the same domain, but also have the identical content.

Martin and Halverson's (1981) original model implicitly illustrates this assumed relation. When describing a child's decision about whether to approach a toy truck, for example, they suggested that it is the child's gender attitude concerning trucks in particular (e.g., "trucks are for boys") that is triggered and that thereby guides the child's behavior. This item match (both items concern trucks) is thus a closer match than a general domain match (as would occur, for example, if the self item focused on toy trucks and the attitude item focused on, say, toy guns). The latter, in turn, would be expected to show a closer relation than when there is not even a domain match (as would occur, for example, if the self item focused on play with toy trucks [activities domain] and the attitude item focused on engineering [occupational domain]). This example is thus illustrative of how the factor of content match would be expected to operate in the attitudinal (other-to-self) pathway model.

A similar relation is predicted for the personal (self-to-other) pathway model. That is, we again predict that the observed self-other relation will be stronger when domains and items are matched. Thus, for example, a girl who is herself interested in trucks will be more likely to develop egalitarian views about trucks in particular than about toys in general, which, in turn, will be more likely than developing egalitarian attitudes about, say, personality traits. Based on this reasoning, we predict that empirical data will reveal only weak relations between gender attitudes toward others and sex typing of self when measures for the two constructs tap different domains, or when measures collapse across multiple domains. In contrast, we predict that empirical data will reveal strong relations between gender attitudes toward others and personal sex typing of self when scales draw items from the same domain. We predict that relations will be even stronger when the same content is tapped within the chosen domain (i.e., when the content of the items is identical).

Individual's Level of Sex Typing

The second factor listed in Table 1 concerns the individual's own level of sex typing. We predict that the relation between gender attitudes toward others and sex typing of the self will differ in individuals who are more versus less sex typed. More specifically, within the attitudinal pathway model, we predict that individuals with highly stereotyped attitudes toward others will necessarily (and consistently) show low levels of self-endorsement of cross-sex-typed items. For example, a girl who holds the belief that only boys should do culturally masculine activities is unlikely to engage in masculine activities herself. In contrast, individuals with less stereotyped attitudes toward others need not follow a consistent pattern with respect to self because in these individuals there are no particular gender-related constraints on self interests and behaviors. That is, having low stereotyping of others sets the stage for the possibility of the adoption of cross-sex interests or behaviors, but it does not necessitate them. Individuals with less stereotyped attitudes toward others are simply free to reach decisions about self on the basis of other factors (e.g., relevant skills). So, for example, a girl who holds the belief that both boys and girls should do culturally masculine activities may or may not engage in those masculine activities herself because she may or may not find them of interest in light of her own idiosyncratic profile of interests, abilities, and history (see Spence, 1985). Based on this model, we predict that the relation observed between sex typing of others and sex typing of the self will be higher in individuals with highly stereotyped attitudes toward others than it will be in individuals with less-stereotyped attitudes toward others. As a corollary, we predict that if data are collapsed across individuals with more and less stereotyped attitudes then, at the group level, only a low to moderate relation between sex typing of self and sex typing of others will be observed.

Within the personal pathway model, we predict that the relation observed between sex typing of self and attitudes toward others will be higher in individuals with low levels of sex typing of the self than it will be in individuals with higher levels of sex typing of the self. That is, individuals who show high levels of endorsement of cross-sex-typed items as self-descriptive will necessarily (and consistently) show low levels of stereotyping of others. For example, a girl who has high levels of personal interest in masculine activities (e.g., trucks) would be likely to form nonsexist beliefs about those activities, or to revise earlier sexist beliefs toward more egalitarian ones because the two cognitions (e.g., "I like trucks" and "trucks are only for boys") are incompatible. In contrast, those individuals with low levels of self-endorsement of cross-sex-typed items will not necessarily show any consistent level of sex typing of others. So, for example, a girl who has little personal interest in masculine activities would have little reason to modify whatever beliefs about others she may have had because her self interests (e.g., "I dislike trucks") are logically compatible with both sex-typed attitudes (e.g., "trucks are only for boys") *and* non-sex-typed attitudes (e.g., "trucks are okay for both boy and girls"). Similarly, a girl with high personal interest in feminine activities (e.g., "I like knitting") would have little motivation to modify her beliefs about others because her personal interests are compatible with sex-typed attitudes toward others (e.g., "knitting is only for girls") as well as with non-sex-typed attitudes toward others (e.g., "knitting is okay for both boys and girls").

It should be noted that, within the depiction of the personal pathway model shown in Figure 3, we have posited that when someone lacks interest in a particular OPE there is no automatic triggering of any particular cognition about how the OPE relates to members of the *other sex*. This is why the arrow in the figure from "ignore OPE" ends with an indication that processing stops without affecting any gender-schematic cognition or belief. Using the example above, a girl who has no interest in trucks simply stops processing—that is, in the depicted model, she has no reason to conclude that trucks are only for boys. An alternative possibility, however, is that gender schematic children (especially at early developmental stages) might use their own lack of interest in some OPE to draw the conclusion that individuals of the other sex *would* be interested in that OPE. In other words, at some stages children might tend to see OPEs in highly gendered terms so that if they, themselves, are not interested in a particular OPE, they would presume that this lack of interest is true for others of their own sex, and, simultaneously, they would presume that those of the other sex *would* be interested in this OPE. This possibility begins to build reciprocal relations with the attitudinal pathway model, and remains as one of a number of open issues that we hope will be explored in future work.

36

Given the current models, we predict that the observed relation between sex typing of others and sex typing of self will be higher in individuals with high levels of cross-sex-typed interests than in individuals with low levels of cross-sex-typed interests, and that, if data from both kinds of individuals are pooled, the overall relation observed between sex typing of self and sex typing of others will be only low to moderate.

Sex Type of Item

The third factor listed in Table 1 concerns whether the focus is on behaviors, interests, and qualities that are considered by the culture to be sex appropriate or inappropriate for an individual. We refer to the former as *same-sex-typed* and the latter as *cross-sex-typed*. To illustrate from the domain of occupations, the items nurse and librarian would be same-sex-typed items for female respondents and cross-sex-typed items for male respondents; the items engineer and astronaut would be same-sex-typed items for male respondents and cross-sex-typed items for female respondents.

Taking the attitudinal pathway model first, we predict that it is for cross-sex items that individuals' gender attitudes toward others will play a particularly strong role in shaping their personal sex typing of self. For example, when a girl encounters an object or potential action that she considers to be for boys, the girl should decide quickly (based on her attitudes and her own sex) that the object or action is "not for me" and hence not pursue it. In contrast, when a girl encounters an object that she considers to be for girls, her decision about whether or not to pursue the object is not constrained by her gender attitudes, and thus whether or not she pursues it will depend on her personal, idiosyncratic interests and history. Data consistent with this interpretation were reported by Signorella (1999). Her meta-analysis revealed that when close relations were found between attitudes toward others and personal endorsements, they almost always occurred under conditions in which the focal item was cross-sex-typed for the respondent.

A comparable prediction about the strength of the self-other relation holds for the personal pathway model, except that the proposed pathway of influence differs. For example, consider a girl who is interested in both toy trucks and dolls. Her interest in trucks will lead her to revise a previously nonegalitarian view so as to hold the view that trucks are appropriate for girls as well as for boys. In the case of the doll, however, her own interests would not have any cause for her to change an existing attitude. That is, her own interest would be in accord with *either* a belief that dolls are only for girls or a belief that dolls are for both boys and girls. For these reasons, we predict that sex typing of self should be related

37

to sex typing of others more strongly for cross-sex than for same-sex items. Thus, for boys, the observed relation between sex typing of others and sex typing of self should be stronger for feminine items than for masculine items, whereas for girls, the observed relation between sex typing of others and sex typing of self should be stronger for masculine items than for feminine items.

Social Status of Items

The fourth factor listed in Table 1 concerns the social status of the cross-sex items. As noted earlier, masculine attributes, activities, and roles are more numerous, diverse, and higher in status than their feminine counterparts. Furthermore, research suggests that children are aware of and endorse the belief that masculine items are higher in status than feminine items. For example, even preschool and elementary-school children rate stereotypically masculine jobs as higher in status than feminine jobs (Levy, Sadovsky, & Troseth, 2000; Liben et al., 2001).

The differential status of traditionally masculine and feminine traits and roles leads us to predict that, under the attitudinal pathway model, boys—*whether or not* they hold egalitarian gender attitudes—will show little interest in cross-sex-typed items (i.e., traditionally feminine jobs and activities). This is because even if they are willing to cross traditional cultural lines, they will not do so because the feminine jobs and activities are inherently unattractive. Girls with egalitarian attitudes, on the other hand, are predicted to have greater interest in cross-sex-typed items (i.e., for them, traditionally masculine items) because these items are inherently attractive. Girls with stereotypic gender attitudes would not, however, allow themselves to pursue these otherwise attractive items. Under the personal pathway model, the differential status of traditionally masculine and feminine traits and roles leads us to predict that girls' interest in cross-sex items will be stronger than boys' interest in cross-sex items, hence leading girls to be more likely than boys to develop egalitarian views about cross-sex items. That is, in general, girls will be more interested in cross-sex-typed items than will boys, and thus girls will be led to develop more egalitarian views about cross-sex items than will boys.

Summary

To summarize the predictions about the four factors discussed above, the second and third columns of Table 1 highlight the predictions under each of the two pathway models. Briefly, under the attitudinal pathway (other-to-self) model, we predict that sex typing of self and others will be more strongly related for (a) matched content, with the relation particularly strong for identical items; (b) children with greater levels of sex typing of others; (c) cross-sex-typed items; and (d) cross-sex-typed items that are high in status (a condition that occurs primarily for female respondents because masculine items have higher status in our culture). Under the personal pathway (self-to-other) model, we propose that sex typing of self and other will be more strongly related for (a) matched content, with the relation particularly strong for identical items; (b) children with lower levels of sex typing of the self; (c) cross-sex-typed items; and (d) cross-sex-typed items that are high in status.

We now turn to our empirical studies. As explained earlier, the major purpose of our first four studies was to develop a suite of sex-typing scales that met the desiderata for sex-typing measures discussed earlier. Our fifth study provides longitudinal data bearing on the proposed developmental pathways of effects. In addition, we use our data to begin exploring our predictions concerning the conditions under which the observed relation between self and other sex typing would be relatively stronger and weaker.

IV. EMPIRICAL DATA RELATED TO SCALE DEVELOPMENT

OVERVIEW OF STUDIES

Drawing from earlier research but attempting to avoid the limitations of existing measures discussed above, we designed a suite of measures to assess gender attitudes toward others and sex typing of self, and explored the relation between these two constructs. Ultimately, the lifespan study of gender differentiation will require the development of measures like these for each major age group from preschool through old age. The work described here begins moving toward this goal by offering measures for children in the middle-school years and for young adults. The middle-school age period (approximately ages 11–13 years) seemed a particularly important period with which to begin developing children's measures because (a) it is a period associated with increased sex typing of others and of the self (termed *gender intensification*; see Galambos, Almeida, & Petersen, 1990; Hill & Lynch, 1983), (b) it is a time that is especially important for educational and vocational choices (e.g., Eccles, Jacobs, & Harold, 1990), and (c) it is a period that is arguably close to childhood on the one hand (late elementary school) and yet nearing the transition to adulthood on the other (early adolescence). The initial focus on middle childhood and young adults thus provides a good base on which to build scales for both older and younger groups.

The four studies described in the current chapter were thus conducted (a) to obtain data bearing on the validity and reliability of a suite of scales for use in middle childhood and adulthood, and (b) to study interrelations between paired measures of sex typing of others and sex typing of the self. In Study 1 we describe the development of measures for children and report results of exploratory factor analyses. The relation between the self and other scales is examined via correlational analyses. In Study 2 we describe the parallel work for adults.

In Studies 3 and 4 the gender schemata structures identified in Studies 1 and 2 were cross-validated, using confirmatory factor analysis.

Importantly, these structures were tested with new data sets (e.g., Breckler, 1990) and were obtained from shortened versions of the adult and child measures, developed on the basis of findings from Studies 1 and 2. Various forms of validity and reliability are reported for shortened versions of the measures, and the relations among factors identified via the factor analyses were examined using regression analyses.

STUDY 1: SCALE DEVELOPMENT FOR CHILDREN

In the first study, sex-typing measures for self and others were developed and exploratory factor analysis was used to fit measurement models to the observed covariance matrices. Study 1 was carried out with sixth-grade children. At this age, children are extremely knowledgeable about gender stereotypes, and yet are likely to show variability in their personal endorsement of, and behavioral conformity to, such stereotypes (see Signorella, 1987).

Method

Participants. Data were collected as part of a larger study of young adolescents (Replication and Extension of the Pennsylvania Early-Adolescent Transitions Study; Lerner, Lerner, & von Eye, 1992). Participants were 154 (68 boys, 86 girls) sixth graders attending school in central Pennsylvania whose parents had signed permission slips, and who themselves had agreed to participate in the larger project. Because the sample was 98% white and drawn virtually entirely from middle-class families, caution must be exercised with respect to generalization.

Description of scale and procedure. Scale items that address occupations, activities, and traits were drawn from a broad range of previous gender-related developmental work (e.g., Edelbrock & Sugawara, 1978; Signorella & Liben, 1985; Williams et al., 1975). As explained earlier, items comprising the long version of the COAT are shown in Appendix A, Tables A1–A3.

To obtain data on children's beliefs about others (COAT-AM), children rated occupations (64), activities (66), and traits (62) as appropriate for "only men [boys]," only women [girls]," or "both men and women [boys and girls]." The occupational scales used "men" and "women" response options because these roles were not relevant to children; the activity and trait scales used "boys" and "girls" response options. For the sake of simplicity, hereafter only the terms "men" and "women" are used

41

in this text. The trait scale, because it included several negative traits, also offered a "neither men nor women" response option. As explained in our prior conceptual review, the "both men and women" option was included based on previous findings showing that this response option is important for tapping participants' *beliefs in* (rather than simply their knowledge of) cultural gender stereotypes (Signorella et al., 1993). In addition, the question was phrased "Who should . . . ?" (e.g., "Who should be a librarian?") rather than "Who usually is . . . ?" because the former taps attitudes rather than knowledge (again, see Signorella et al., 1993).

Responses may be scored in one of two ways. Specifically, the dependent measure may be scored as (1) the proportion of "both men and women" (or "neither") responses so that higher scores indicate greater *flexibility* of gender attitudes, or as (2) the proportion of feminine items assigned to "only women," plus the proportion of masculine items assigned to "only men" so that higher scores indicate greater *stereotyping*. Scores on these two dependent measures are typically equivalent (although the values are the inverse of one another) when respondents are highly knowledgeable about cultural gender stereotypes. In other words, children with knowledge of cultural gender stereotypes very rarely attribute a sex-typed item to the culturally incorrect sex (e.g., they rarely answer that "only males" should be nurses). Thus, the number of "both men and women" responses is equal to the total number of items minus the number of stereotyped responses.

We note that it is possible that in some instances children may select the "both" option simply because they are completely unfamiliar with an item (e.g., they do not know the named occupation) or because they have no knowledge about the cultural sex type of the particular item. According to our models, however, these conditions would also lead to low levels of sex typing for the self. That is, if the child is ignorant about an item or its cultural sex typing, the child would not be affected by the item's gender stereotyping. Thus, we used the flexibility measure (i.e., the number of "both men and women" responses) for all attitude measures reported here. The availability of two coding systems is, however, an important asset for researchers who wish to use this scale with somewhat younger children. That is, a dependent measure of the number of stereotypic responses (rather than the number of "both" responses) would allow these scales to be used with children who have more limited knowledge of cultural gender stereotyping and who, therefore, might produce counter-stereotypic responses (such as "only men should be nurses") as well as egalitarian responses.

To obtain data on children's sex typing of the self, children were asked to rate the same items as a personal measure (COAT-PM). Specifically, children rated their personal interest in occupations, the extent to

42

which they participate in activities, and the degree to which traits are self descriptive.

Occupational items ("How much would you like to be a(n) ___?") were accompanied by a 4-point rating scale (*not at all, not much, some,* and *very much*). Activity items ("How often do you ___?") were accompanied by a 5-point scale (*never, rarely, sometimes, often,* and *very often*). Trait items ("This [trait] is ___") were accompanied by a 4-point scale (*not at all like me, not much like me, somewhat like me,* and *very much like me*). The activity response options were later converted to a four-point scale by collapsing *often* and *very often* for comparability with the other four-point personal measure scales. This conversion was based on analyses indicating that the extreme response option was selected infrequently and that collapsing across the two points did not alter the patterns of findings obtained with the original scale. The dependent measure was the number of points awarded for masculine, feminine, and neutral items, divided by the total number of items of each type.

All children were given the COAT questionnaire in a school classroom by a female experimenter. Because previous research suggests that individuals' behaviors are more likely to comply with their attitudes when the relevant attitudes are made salient (e.g., Fazio, Powell, & Herr, 1983), children completed the COAT-PM prior to the COAT-AM, thus minimizing the extent to which gender role attitudes were made salient prior to self ratings. Within the COAT-AM and COAT-PM scales, the occupation scale was given first, followed by the activity, and then the trait scale. Masculine and feminine items appeared in a single randomized order within subscales.

Data-analytic strategy. Data analysis was a multistep process. First, scale reliability was assessed using Cronbach's alpha and Guttman split-half reliability statistics. Second, means and correlations among the COAT subscales were computed and analyses of variance were used to evaluate effects of sex of participant, substantive domain, and item type (as discussed in our prior conceptual analysis). Third, the multiple subscales of the COAT were submitted to exploratory factor analysis to determine the factor structure of the COAT. Finally, the relations between children's gender attitudes toward others and sex typing of the self were examined via correlational analyses.

Results

COAT reliability and means. Cronbach alphas and Guttman split-half reliabilities for the six COAT-AM subscales and the six COAT-PM subscales are reported in Table 2 and show that the scales are highly reliable.

TABLE 2

RELIABILITY STATISTICS FOR THE COAT SCALE (LONG FORM)

Subscale	Number of Items	Cronbach's Alpha	Guttman Split-Half
Fem COAT-AM	16	.86	.85
Fem COAT-AM	21	.91	.85
Fem COAT-AM	20	.93	.90
Mas COAT-AM	41	.96	.96
Mas COAT-AM	24	.93	.92
Mas COAT-AM	25	.95	.93
COAT-AM	64	.97	.93
COAT-AM	66	.97	.92
COAT-AM	62	.99	.94
Fem COAT-PM	16	.91	.91
Fem COAT-PM	21	.88	.84
Fem COAT-PM	20	.81	.75
Mas COAT-PM	41	.90	.85
Mas COAT-PM	24	.86	.80
Mas COAT-PM	25	.83	.80

Notes.—Overall reliability statistics are not provided for the COAT-PM because they are meaningless given that they would collapse across self-endorsements for masculine and feminine items. C denotes children's scale; underscored O, A, and T indicate occupations, activities, and traits, respectively; AM is attitude measure (attitude toward others); PM is personal measure (sex typing of self).

The means and standard deviations for each of the COAT subscales are presented in Table 3. A $2 \times 3 \times 2$ (Sex of participant × Domain: occupations, activities, traits × Item gender: masculine, feminine) analysis of variance examined variation in the degree of gender attitude flexibility (COAT-AM scores) and sex-typed self-endorsements (COAT-PM scores). Here and throughout the remainder of this *Monograph*, when significant, main effects are described prior to interaction effects because, in most cases, higher order interactions involve differences only in the *degree* to which responding differed by groups (rather than in whether or in which direction effects occurred). All post-hoc comparisons among means reported here and in subsequent studies were conducted using the Duncan Multiple-Range statistic.

COAT-AM. Results indicated significant main effects of domain, $F(92, 304) = 182.70$, $p < .01$, and of item gender, $F(1, 304) = 113.90$, $p < .01$, showing that children gave a greater number of egalitarian responses for traits than for occupations or activities (which did not differ from each other), and for masculine than for feminine items. These effects were qualified by two-way interactions with sex of participant. One was an interaction between sex of participant and domain, $F(2, 304) = 4.66$, $p < .05$,

TABLE 3

MEAN SCORES (STANDARD DEVIATIONS) FOR THE COAT-AM
AND COAT-PM SCALES (LONG FORMS)

	Participants		
	Boys	Girls	Combined
Subscale	M (SD)	M (SD)	M (SD)
Fem COAT-AM	.38 (.27)	.39 (.29)	.38 (.28)
Fem COAT-AM	.38 (.30)	.36 (.27)	.36 (.28)
Fem COAT-AM	.68 (.34)	.80 (.28)	.75 (.31)
Mas COAT-AM	.44 (.30)	.54 (.28)	.50 (.29)
Mas COAT-AM	.47 (.33)	.56 (.26)	.52 (.29)
Mas COAT-AM	.66 (.36)	.82 (.26)	.75 (.32)
COAT-AM	.41 (.27)	.46 (.27)	.44 (.27)
COAT-AM	.42 (.30)	.46 (.25)	.44 (.28)
COAT-AM	.67 (.35)	.81 (.26)	.75 (.31)
Fem COAT-PM	1.3 (.34)	2.3 (.55)	1.9 (.67)
Fem COAT-PM	1.5 (.34)	2.4 (.64)	2.0 (.71)
Fem COAT-PM	2.5 (.45)	2.7 (.41)	2.6 (.43)
Mas COAT-PM	1.8 (.46)	1.6 (.37)	1.7 (.42)
Mas COAT-PM	2.6 (.67)	1.9 (.44)	2.2 (.65)
Mas COAT-PM	2.8 (.44)	2.5 (.41)	2.6 (.44)
COAT-PM	1.6 (.36)	2.0 (.40)	1.8 (.43)
COAT-PM	2.0 (.43)	2.2 (.45)	2.1 (.45)
COAT-PM	2.7 (.41)	2.6 (.37)	2.6 (.39)

Notes.—COAT-AM scores represent the proportion of "both men [boys] and women [girls]" responses. COAT-PM scores represent the average rating for masculine and feminine items on 4-point scales, with higher ratings indicating greater self-endorsement. C denotes children's scale; underscored O, A, and T indicate occupations, activities, and traits, respectively; AM is attitude measure (attitude toward others); PM is personal measure (sex typing of self).

and the other was between sex of participant and item gender, $F(1,304) = 22.59$, $p < .01$. These interactions indicate that although the patterns just described were true for both boys and girls, they were even stronger for girls than for boys. Also significant was the interaction between domain and item gender, $F(2, 304) = 53.14$, $p < .01$, indicating that children held significantly more flexible beliefs about masculine than feminine items in the domains of occupations and activities, but not within the domain of traits.

The above effects were all further qualified by a three-way interaction of domain, item gender, and sex of participant, $F(2, 304) = 3.56$, $p < .05$, indicating that this pattern (i.e., greater flexibility for masculine occupations and activities than feminine occupations and activities) was even stronger among girls than it was among boys.

COAT-PM. Results indicated a significant main effect of domain, $F(2, 238) = 282.37$, $p < .01$, with children showing greater self-endorsement of traits than occupations or activities, and greater self-endorsement of activities than occupations. These effects were qualified by several two-way interactions. First, an interaction of domain and item gender, $F(2, 238) = 19.02$, $p < .01$, indicated that children showed greater self-endorsement of feminine than masculine occupations, but greater self-endorsement of masculine than feminine activities. Second, an interaction of domain and sex of participant, $F(2, 238) = 19.99$, $p < .01$, indicated that girls showed greater self-endorsement of occupations and activities (but not traits) than did boys.

Also significant was the two-way interaction of item gender and sex of participant, $F(1,119) = 288.08$, $p < .01$. As expected, girls showed greater endorsement of feminine items than did boys, whereas boys showed greater endorsement of masculine items than did girls.

These interactions were all subsumed by a significant three-way interaction of domain, item gender, and sex of participant, $F(2,238) = 38.63$, $p < .01$, indicating that this pattern of effects (i.e., greater endorsement of "sex appropriate" items) was stronger in the domains of occupations and activities than in the domain of traits.

Correlations among subscales. Separate correlation matrices were computed for boys and girls and are presented in Table 4. Particularly interesting in these data is the finding that children's stereotyping of occupations, activities, and traits (the AM scores; see the upper left quadrant

TABLE 4

ZERO-ORDER CORRELATIONS AMONG COAT (LONG FORM)
SUBSCALES FOR BOYS AND GIRLS

	1	2	3	4	5	6	7	8	9	10	11	12
1. Fem COAT-AM	—	.81	.47	.85	.75	.52	.04	.12	.24	.07	-.02	.21
2. Fem COAT-AM	.86	—	.66	.85	.90	.71	.06	.15	.24	.08	-.06	.19
3. Fem COAT-AM	.50	.50	—	.63	.71	.97	.05	.04	.35	.27	-.04	.27
4. Mas COAT-AM	.80	.79	.49	—	.90	.67	.14	.16	.33	.22	.09	.25
5. Mas COAT-AM	.72	.80	.54	.84	—	.75	.19	.21	.35	.26	.05	.28
6. Mas COAT-AM	.53	.51	.93	.47	.56	—	.02	.03	.34	.20	-.04	.27
7. Fem COAT-PM	-.23	-.29	-.20	-.16	-.22	-.21	—	.62	.31	.57	.29	.21
8. Fem COAT-PM	.11	.05	.14	.23	.08	.14	.60	—	.15	.53	.43	.20
9. Fem COAT-PM	.18	.23	.06	.26	.19	.11	.24	.46	—	.22	.09	.66
10. Mas COAT-PM	.23	.20	.10	.29	.24	.07	.44	.54	.35	—	.42	.19
11. Mas COAT-PM	.36	.39	.23	.42	.51	.29	.03	.42	.18	.55	—	.23
12. Mas COAT-PM	.40	.36	.18	.39	.33	.22	.12	.46	.64	.42	.41	—

Notes.—Boys' correlations are presented above the diagonal; girls' correlations are presented below the diagonal. C denotes children's scale; underscored O, A, and T indicate occupations, activities, and traits, respectively; AM is attitude measure (attitude toward others); PM is personal measure (sex typing of self). Bold correlations are significant at $p < .05$.

of Table 4) were uniformly highly correlated. That is, children appeared to be consistent in their sex typing of others across domains. Interpretation of the correlational patterns for the self-endorsement scales (the PM scores; see the lower right quadrant of Table 4) is more difficult because children's endorsement of masculine and feminine items was always moderately correlated within a particular domain. That is, children were generally open to endorsing relatively many, or relatively few, items as self-descriptive. The patterns suggest, however, that self-endorsements of masculine items, as well as feminine items, were moderately correlated *across* content domains for both boys and girls.

Examination of the correlations of gender attitudes toward others and self-endorsement measures (see the upper right and lower left quadrants of Table 4) shows a pattern that, overall, provides some evidence that sex typing of others and sex typing of self are related in ways that would be predicted from constructivist models. Among girls (see the lower left quadrant), egalitarian gender attitudes toward masculine items are associated with increased endorsement of masculine items for the self. Among boys (see the upper right quadrant), egalitarian gender attitudes across domains are associated with increased endorsement of feminine traits. At the same item, egalitarian gender attitudes (among both boys and girls) are sometimes related to increased endorsement of same-sex-typed items for the self.

Exploratory factor analyses. The six subscales of the COAT were factor analyzed using a principal-components analysis with Varimax rotation. The results revealed three meaningful factors with eigenvalues greater than 1.00 (see Table 5). This three-factor solution accounted for 73% of the variance. Inspection of the factor loadings indicates that the COAT taps three gender-related constructs: gender-related attitudes, feminine self-endorsements, and masculine self-endorsements.

We performed two additional types of analyses designed to examine the robustness of the three-factor model. First, we examined the factor structure derived from an oblique rotation, allowing for possible correlations among factors. Second, we examined the factor structures derived from single sex samples (for both types of rotations). Although the factor loadings varied slightly, the pattern of findings (i.e., a three-factor model consisting of COAT-AM scales, feminine PM scales, and masculine PM scales), was identical for each type of analysis.

Discussion

The data from Study 1 suggest that the COAT scales are reliable measures of children's stereotyping of others and sex typing of the self. The

TABLE 5

FACTOR MATRIX FOR COAT SCALE (LONG FORM)

| | Factor-Derived Constructs | | |
Subscale	Factor 1: Gender Attitudes	Factor 2: Feminine Self	Factor 3: Masculine Self
Fem COAT-AM	.796	.258	−.101
Fem COAT-AM	.864	.227	−.159
Fem COAT-AM	.797	−.111	.182
Mas COAT-AM	.850	.231	.127
Mas COAT-AM	.877	.216	.098
Mas COAT-AM	.827	−.112	.201
Fem COAT-PM	−.052	.935	−.065
Fem COAT-PM	.124	.902	.026
Fem COAT-PM	.288	.507	.447
Mas COAT-PM	.071	.292	.737
Mas COAT-PM	−.018	−.256	.786
Mas COAT-PM	.235	.005	.755

Notes.—C denotes children's scale; underscored O, A, and T indicate occupations, activities, and traits, respectively; AM is attitude measure (attitude toward others); PM is personal measure (sex typing of self).

means obtained on the COAT-AM indicate that children hold gender stereotypes, particularly in the domains of occupations and activities. Fewer than half of the items in these domains were believed to be appropriate for both men and women. The findings that children hold more flexible beliefs about masculine than about feminine items and about items in the domain of traits than items in other domains are consistent with previous work (Serbin et al., 1993; Signorella et al., 1993). The means on the COAT-PM indicate that, as expected, boys showed greater self-endorsement of masculine items than feminine items whereas the reverse was true for girls.

With respect to the issue raised in Chapter I concerning whether gender differentiation is monolithic or fragmented, the correlational data suggest that sex typing of others forms a cohesive construct that operates across domains. Thus, the correlational data from the attitudinal subscales lend partial support to Bem's (1979, 1981) argument that gender schemata are composed of well-integrated beliefs about the importance of gender across multiple domains. That is, correlations indicate that children's stereotypic beliefs about the domains of occupations, activities, and traits are very highly related: Children who held stereotypic beliefs in one domain also tended to hold stereotypic beliefs in other domains, and children who held stereotypic beliefs about masculine items also tended to hold stereotypic beliefs about feminine items. In addition, children who endorsed cross-sex items as self-descriptive tended to do so across domains, though the correlations among self scales (i.e., COAT-PM, COAT-PM, and COAT-PM) were substantially lower than the correlations among attitude scales (i.e., COAT-AM, COAT-AM, and COAT-AM).

The notion that gender attitudes about others and the self are separate components of gender schemata is also supported by the factor analysis of the COAT subscales. The factor loadings indicated that one component of gender schemata is comprised of beliefs about others and that these beliefs are consistent across domains. Importantly, both masculine and feminine items loaded on the attitude measure. This was not true of the personal measure and further supports the notion that beliefs about others are conceptually distinct from beliefs about one's own personal attributes.

Based on our reasoning about the conditions under which sex typing of others should be observed to be related to sex typing of the self (see the discussion of Table 1 in Chapter III), we did not expect to find overall strong correlations between the way individuals respond to scales tapping sex typing of self and sex typing of others. Consistent with our expectations, correlations among the subscales indicate that endorsement of same-sex-typed and cross-sex-typed items as self descriptive was only sometimes related to the expression of gender stereotypic beliefs about others (i.e., 50% of such correlations were significant among girls; 33% were significant among boys), and significant relations, when they appear, were generally modest in magnitude. Further, and again as expected, the pattern of relations among attitudes and self-endorsements was different for boys and girls. Because we were interested in conducting more detailed analyses of the relations between sex typing of others and the self, we later collected longitudinal data on these children (see Study 5 in Chapter V). As discussed in more detail in the description of Study 5, these longitudinal data allowed us to examine responses to individual scale items over time, to conduct concurrent and predictive regression analyses examining the predictors of sex typing of the self and of others, and to test our specific hypotheses concerning the factors that influence the strength of observed relations between individuals' sex typing of self and sex typing of others. Before addressing these longitudinal and structural relations, however, we conducted additional research explicitly directed to the development of scales.

STUDY 2: SCALE DEVELOPMENT FOR ADULTS

Because one important goal was to develop parallel scales for children and adults, Study 2 was designed to develop scales for adults like those just described for children. It was also designed to explore whether the data from adults would show similar patterns with respect to the relation between sex typing of the self and sex typing of others. Validity and reliability data for the scale are presented and exploratory factor analysis was used to assess the structure of adults' gender schemata.

Method

Participants. The participants were 248 undergraduates (49 males, 199 females) enrolled in a psychology class at a large public university. Participation earned extra course credit. Although formal demographic data were not collected, samples drawn from the psychology subject pool generally reflect the larger student body which is heterogenous with respect to socioeconomic background, but is predominately white. Thus, caution is needed with respect to generalizing across racial, ethnic, and cultural groups.

Description of scale and procedure. As in the COAT, scale items addressed occupations, activities, and traits, and were drawn from a variety of sources. As explained earlier, items comprising the long version of the OAT are shown in Appendix A, Tables A4–A6.

To obtain data on adults' beliefs about others (OAT-AM), respondents were asked to rate occupations (80), activities (71), and traits (62) as appropriate for "only men," "mostly men, some women," "both men and women," "mostly women, some men," or "only women." The dependent measure was the proportion of "both men and women" responses, and thus higher scores indicate greater flexibility of gender attitudes.

To obtain data on adults' sex typing of the self (OAT-PM), respondents were asked to rate the same items as a personal measure. Specifically, respondents were asked to rate their personal interest in occupations, the extent to which they participate in activities, and the degree to which traits are self descriptive. As in the COAT, occupational items ("How much would you like to be a[n] ___?") were accompanied by a 4-point rating scale (*not at all, not much, some,* and *very much*). Activity items ("How often do you ___?") were accompanied by a 5-point scale (*never, rarely, sometimes, often,* and *very often,* later converted to a four-point scale as explained in the description of the method used in Study 1). Trait items ("This [trait] is ___") were accompanied by a 4-point scale (*not at all like me, not much like me, somewhat like me,* and *very much like me*). The dependent measure was the number of points awarded for masculine, feminine, and neutral items, divided by the total number of items of each type.

Adults were given the OAT questionnaire in large groups by a female experimenter. Ordering of measures was as described in Study 1.

Data-analytic strategy. The data analytic strategy was identical to that used for the COAT. First, scale reliability was assessed using Cronbach's alpha and Guttman split-half reliability statistics. Second, means and correlations among the OAT subscales were computed, and analyses of variance were used to evaluate the effects of sex of participant, substantive domain, and item type. Third, the multiple subscales of the OAT were submitted to exploratory factor analysis to determine the factor structure of the OAT.

Results

OAT reliability and means. Cronbach's alphas and Guttman split-half reliabilities for the six OAT-AM and six OAT-PM subscales are presented in Table 6. All of the scales show high reliability, with the exception of the feminine trait scale for the self, which shows only adequate reliability, on a par with other trait sex-typing measures (see Beere, 1990). The means and standard deviations for each of the OAT subscales are presented in

TABLE 6

RELIABILITY STATISTICS FOR THE OAT SCALE (LONG FORM)

Subscale	Number of Items	Cronbach's Alpha	Guttman Split-Half
Fem OAT-AM	20	.89	.85
Fem OAT-AM	22	.91	.87
Fem OAT-AM	20	.75	.71
Mas OAT-AM	52	.96	.95
Mas OAT-AM	27	.93	.92
Mas OAT-AM	25	.89	.88
OAT-AM	80	.96	.94
OAT-AM	71	.95	.94
OAT-AM	62	.94	.90
Fem OAT-PM	20	.87	.78
Fem OAT-PM	22	.81	.74
Fem OAT-PM	20	.63	.41
Mas OAT-PM	52	.94	.76
Mas OAT-PM	27	.93	.92
Mas OAT-PM	25	.89	.88

Notes.—Overall reliability statistics are not provided for the OAT-PM because they are meaningless given that they would collapse across self-endorsements for masculine and feminine items. Underscored O, A, and T indicate occupations, activities, and traits, respectively; AM is attitude measure (attitude toward others); PM is personal measure (sex typing of self).

Table 7. A 2 × 3 × 2 (Sex of participant × Domain: occupations, activities, traits × Item gender: masculine, feminine) analysis of variance examined variation in the degree of gender attitude flexibility (OAT-AM scores) and sex-typed self-endorsements (OAT-PM scores).

OAT-AM. Results from the OAT-AM indicated a significant main effect of sex of participant, $F(1, 246) = 25.67$, $p < .01$, with women giving significantly more egalitarian responses than men. Also significant was the main effect of domain, $F(2, 492) = 109.62$, $p < .01$, indicating that adults gave significantly more egalitarian responses for traits than for occupations or activities, and more egalitarian responses for activities than for occupations. The main effect for item gender was also significant, $F(1, 246) = 34.23$, $p < .01$, indicating that adults gave more egalitarian responses for masculine than for feminine items.

These effects were qualified by two-way interactions. The interaction of sex of participant and domain, $F(2, 492) = 3.62$, $p < .05$, indicated that

TABLE 7

Mean Scores (Standard Deviation) for the OAT-AM and OAT-PM (Long Form)

	Participants		
	Men	Women	Combined
Subscales	M (SD)	M (SD)	M (SD)
Fem OAT-AM	.59 (.26)	.75 (.20)	.72 (.22)
Fem OAT-AM	.67 (.25)	.80 (.19)	.78 (.21)
Fem OAT-AM	.80 (.20)	.90 (.12)	.88 (.14)
Mas OAT-AM	.64 (.22)	.78 (.18)	.76 (.20)
Mas OAT-AM	.73 (.25)	.90 (.18)	.83 (.20)
Mas OAT-AM	.81 (.21)	.90 (.14)	.89 (.16)
OAT-AM	.62 (.23)	.77 (.19)	.74 (.20)
OAT-AM	.70 (.24)	.83 (.18)	.80 (.20)
OAT-AM	.81 (.19)	.90 (.12)	.88 (.14)
Fem OAT-PM	1.6 (.37)	2.0 (.43)	1.9 (.45)
Fem OAT-PM	2.1 (.34)	2.6 (.39)	2.5 (.43)
Fem OAT-PM	2.9 (.27)	3.2 (.27)	3.1 (.30)
Mas OAT-PM	2.1 (.44)	1.6 (.34)	1.7 (.41)
Mas OAT-PM	2.1 (.39)	1.5 (.25)	1.7 (.36)
Mas OAT-PM	2.9 (.36)	2.6 (.34)	2.7 (.35)
OAT-PM	1.9 (.37)	1.9 (.35)	1.8 (.35)
OAT-PM	2.1 (.27)	2.1 (.27)	2.1 (.27)
OAT-PM	2.9 (.22)	2.9 (.23)	2.9 (.23)

Notes.—OAT-AM scores represent the proportion of "both men and women" responses. OAT-PM scores represent the average rating for masculine and feminine items on 4-point scales, with higher ratings indicating greater self-endorsement. Underscored O, A, and T indicate occupations, activities, and traits, respectively; AM is attitude measure (attitude toward others); PM is personal measure (sex typing of self).

women gave significantly more flexible responses for occupations and activities (but not traits) than men. Also significant was the interaction of domain and item gender, $F(2, 492) = 10.61$, $p < .01$, indicating that adults held significantly more flexible beliefs about masculine than feminine items in the domains of occupations and activities, but not within the domain of traits.

OAT-PM. Results indicated a significant main effect of domain, $F(2, 448) = 757.46$, $p < .01$, with adults showing greater self-endorsement of traits than occupations or activities, and greater self-endorsement of activities than occupations. The main effect of item gender was also significant, $F(1, 224) = 99.23$, $p < .01$, indicating that adults showed greater endorsement of feminine than masculine items. These main effects were qualified by two-way interactions. The significant interaction of domain and item gender, $F(2, 448) = 115.81$, $p < .01$, indicated that this pattern of effects (greater endorsement of feminine than masculine items) was stronger in the domain of activities than in the domains of occupations and traits. As expected, there was also a significant interaction of item gender and sex of participant, $F(1, 224) = 284.70$, $p < .01$, with women showing greater self-endorsement of feminine items than men, and men showing greater self-endorsement of masculine items than women.

These effects were further subsumed within a significant three-way interaction of domain, item gender, and sex of participant, $F(2, 448) = 38.63$, $p < .01$, indicating that this pattern of effects (i.e., greater endorsement of "sex appropriate" items) was stronger in the domain of occupations than in the domains of activities and traits.

Correlations among subscales. Separate correlation matrices were computed for men and women and are presented in Table 8. As was true of children, what is particularly interesting in the matrix is the finding that adults' stereotypes of occupations, activities, and traits were highly correlated (see the upper left quadrant of Table 8). Thus, individuals tend to hold either sex-typed or non-sex-typed attitudes across a wide array of domains.

As was true of children, adult males and females showed numerous correlations (8 of 15 possible for each sex) among subscales of personal measures (see the lower right quadrant of Table 8). All of the correlations are positive, and, overall, indicate that individuals had either a higher or lower willingness to consider a broad range of occupations, activities, and traits as appropriate for themselves.

As predicted, flexibility of adults' gender attitudes toward others was related only very infrequently to the tendency to endorse sex-typed

TABLE 8

Zero-Order Correlations Among OAT (Long Form)
Subscales for Men and Women

	1	2	3	4	5	6	7	8	9	10	11	12
1. Fem OAT-AM	—	**.87**	**.48**	**.82**	**.82**	**.63**	-.25	-.13	-.09	**-.34**	-.21	.08
2. Fem OAT-AM	**.81**	—	**.56**	**.77**	**.85**	**.67**	-.16	-.02	-.09	-.24	-.11	.07
3. Fem OAT-AM	**.54**	**.58**	—	**.42**	**.55**	**.73**	-.12	-.24	-.13	-.02	-.01	.05
4. Mas OAT-AM	**.85**	**.76**	**.50**	—	**.77**	**.62**	-.21	-.05	.01	-.23	-.18	.18
5. Mas OAT-AM	**.78**	**.81**	**.52**	**.83**	—	**.69**	-.25	**-.29**	-.17	**-.27**	-.13	.17
6. Mas OAT-AM	**.51**	**.54**	**.73**	**.53**	**.57**	—	-.24	-.22	-.09	-.13	-.02	.17
7. Fem OAT-PM	-.06	-.04	-.06	-.09	-.09	-.07	—	**.42**		**.61**	.10	-.03
8. Fem OAT-PM	.09	.03	-.01	.02	.02	-.02	**.38**	—	**.35**	.17	.19	.03
9. Fem OAT-PM	-.14	-.17	-.11	-.13	**-.21**	-.15	**.26**	**.32**	—	**.38**	.03	-.04
10. Mas OAT-PM	.09	.05	.06	.07	.09	.05	**.58**	.12	-.02	—	**.49**	**.35**
11. Mas OAT-PM	.16	.15	.07	.09	**.21**	.06	**.24**	**.40**	.05	**.41**	—	**.38**
12. Mas OAT-PM	.08	.05	.07	.02	.08	.14	-.04	.06	.09	.20	**.35**	—

Notes.—Men's correlations are presented above the diagonal; women's correlations are presented below the diagonal. Underscored O, A, and T indicate occupations, activities, and traits, respectively; AM is attitude measure (attitude toward others); PM is personal measure (sex typing of self). Bold correlations are significant at $p < .05$.

occupations, activities, or traits for the self. Among women (see the lower left quadrant of Table 8), it was only attitudes toward masculine activities that showed any significant relation to self-endorsements. Specifically, more egalitarian attitudes toward masculine activities were associated with greater self-endorsement of masculine activities and lower self-endorsement of feminine traits. Among men (see the upper right quadrant of Table 8), egalitarian attitudes toward masculine activities were also related to self-endorsements. Specifically, more egalitarian attitudes toward masculine activities were associated with lower self-endorsement of masculine occupations and of feminine activities. In addition, more egalitarian attitudes toward feminine occupations were associated with lower self-endorsement of masculine occupations.

Exploratory factor analyses. The six subscales of the OAT were factor analyzed using a principal-components analysis with Varimax rotation. The results, shown in Table 9, revealed three meaningful factors with eigenvalues greater than 1.00. This three-factor solution accounted for 70% of the variance. Inspection of the factor loadings indicates that the OAT taps three gender-related constructs: gender-related attitudes, feminine self-endorsements, and masculine self-endorsements. Again, we performed two additional types of analyses designed to examine the robustness of the three factors. We examined the factor structures derived from, first,

TABLE 9

FACTOR MATRIX FOR OAT SCALE (LONG FORM)

| Subscale | Factor-Derived Constructs | | |
	Factor 1: Gender Attitudes	Factor 2: Feminine Self	Factor 3: Masculine Self
Fem OAT-AM	.907	.035	−.086
Fem OAT-AM	.909	.041	−.075
Fem OAT-AM	.754	.071	.098
Mas OAT-AM	.899	.028	−.095
Mas OAT-AM	.914	−.013	−.023
Mas OAT-AM	.787	.017	.008
Fem OAT-PM	.006	.832	.160
Fem OAT-PM	.139	.789	−.117
Fem OAT-PM	−.030	.755	−.175
Mas OAT-PM	−.123	.130	.854
Mas OAT-PM	−.147	−.136	.825
Mas OAT-PM	.092	−.113	.664

Notes.—Underscored O, A, and T indicate occupations, activities, and traits, respectively; AM is attitude measure (attitude toward others); PM is personal measure (sex typing of self).

an oblique rotation, allowing for possible correlations among factors and, second, from single sex samples (for both types of rotations). Although the factor loadings varied slightly, the pattern of findings (i.e., a three-factor model consisting of COAT-AM scales, feminine PM scales, and masculine PM scales) was identical for each analysis.

Discussion

The data from Study 2 suggest that the OAT scales are reliable measures of adults' stereotyping of others and sex typing of the self. The means from the OAT-AM indicate that although adults are less stereotyped in their gender attitudes than are children, adults nevertheless stereotype many items as more appropriate for one or the other sex. Men were particularly likely to indicate that feminine occupations and activities were not equally appropriate for both men and women. Attitudes toward traits were considerably more egalitarian than were attitudes toward occupations and activities. As expected, men endorsed greater numbers of masculine items than feminine items as self-descriptive, whereas the reverse was true among women. Again, masculine and feminine trait items were the least likely to be endorsed differentially by males and females.

As was found to be true among children in Study 1, the correlational data suggest that adults' sex typing of *others* forms a monolithic construct that is applied across domains. Correlations indicate that adults' stereo-typic beliefs about the domains of occupations, activities, and traits are very highly related. In other words, adults who held stereotypic beliefs in one domain also tended to hold stereotypic beliefs in other domains, and across masculine and feminine items.

The notion that gender attitudes about others and the self are separate components of gender schemata is further supported by the factor analysis of the OAT subscales. Eigenvalues indicated that the six OAT subscales tapped three major constructs: gender attitudes, self-endorsement of feminine items, and self-endorsement of masculine items, indicating that self-perceived adherence to culturally stereotypic notions of gender is not embedded within the same construct as is belief in the validity of cultural stereotypes about males and females.

Overall, the adult correlational data are consistent with the child data indicating that expression of gender stereotyping about *others* is not consistently related to the endorsement of sex-typed items as *self* descriptive in ways predicted by most constructivist theories of sex typing (e.g., Bem, 1981; Bussey & Bandura, 1999; Martin & Halverson, 1981). As was true of the child data, however, some relations were found, suggesting the utility of exploring such relations using more sophisticated conceptual models (e.g., analyses based on the four factors described earlier) and statistical methods. (e.g., regression analyses).

Given that a major goal of our work was to develop sex-typing scales that would be not only methodologically strong but also well-suited to diverse research questions (see the *Designing Measures* section in Chapter III), we conducted Studies 3 and 4 to develop shortened versions of the COAT and OAT scales, respectively, and to provide data on the reliability and validity for these short scales. Studies 3 and 4 were also designed to examine, via confirmatory factor analyses, whether findings concerning the structure of gender schemata in children and adults would be replicated using the shortened scales, and whether similar patterns of findings would be evident in a racially and ethnically diverse sample of children. In addition, relations among the scale factors were examined using regression analyses.

STUDY 3: SCALE REFINEMENT FOR CHILDREN

In Study 3, the factor model of children's gender schemata developed in Study 1 was cross-validated using confirmatory factor analyses, and the relations among factors were examined via regression analyses. Confirmatory factor analysis is a more powerful statistical technique than exploratory factor analysis because it allows for more precise tests of the derived hypotheses concerning the structure of a set of variables (see Jöreskog & Sörbom, 1984). A second and more ethnically diverse sample was used for these analyses and a shortened version of the COAT scale was used to assess schema structure. The inclusion of children from diverse ethnic and racial backgrounds (including African American, Native American, and Latino children) allowed us to test whether the gender schema structure identified in Study 1 which had involved primarily a white, middle-class sample would also be found in more diverse samples.

In addition, several forms of reliability for the short form of the COAT, including inter-item and test-retest reliability, were examined. Test-retest reliability is critical for establishing that a particular measure taps a stable construct, and is often lacking for measures of gender attitudes. Test-retest reliability is particularly crucial in work with children because researchers frequently use measures to examine change resulting from natural developmental processes or from attitudinal or behavioral interventions. To use measures for these purposes, one must first be reasonably confident that responses on such measures are relatively impervious to repeated testing effects or random fluctuations across administrations.

Evidence concerning the convergent validity of the COAT measure is also presented. As discussed earlier, the COAT measure is especially useful because it uses similar methods and items to assess gender-related beliefs across domains (i.e., occupations, activities, and traits) and across targets (self and others). Importantly, included among the individual constructs tapped by the COAT are some that are conceptually related to constructs tapped by existing measures. There should, therefore, be close relations between certain COAT subscales and the existing scales that tap the corresponding construct. We tested these relations here. Because the majority of scales with well-documented reliability and validity for both adults and children concern self-endorsements of traits (e.g., Bem Sex Role Inventory, see Bem, 1974; Personality Attributes Questionnaire, see Spence, Helmreich, & Stapp, 1974; Children's Sex Role Inventory, see Boldizar, 1991; and Children's Personality Attributes Questionnaire, see Hall & Halberstadt, 1980), the particular relations examined here were between the relevant subscales of the COAT and existing trait scales.

Method

Participants. Participants were drawn from two different samples. The first sample consisted of 165 (98 boys, 67 girls) sixth-graders in an urban city in the Midwest. Included were 46 Euro-American (29 males, 17 females), 90 African American (54 males, 36 females), 22 Native American

(10 males, 12 females), and 7 Latino (5 males, 2 females) children. The second sample consisted of 33 (19 boys, 14 girls) sixth-graders in a mid-sized urban city in the Southwest. All of these participants were white. Data on socioeconomic status were not available for either sample.

COAT scales. A shortened version of the COAT was created by computing item-total correlations from the sample reported in Study 1. As explained earlier, the 10 masculine, 10 feminine, and 5 neutral items with the highest item-total correlations on each of the six subscales were selected for inclusion. Item-total correlations for those items selected ranged from .89 to .97. Appendix A (Tables A1–A3) provides data on cultural sex typing of the selected items as explained earlier, Appendix C (Figures C1–C6) provides the scales in administration format, and Appendix D provides information on procedures and scoring.

Test-retest reliability and external validity. The second sample of participants completed the COAT twice to enable us to assess the test-retest reliability of the scale. Data from the second administration were used to calculate test-retest reliability. Data from the initial testing were used for all other analyses described below. Those children who participated in the COAT retest also completed the Children's Sex Role Inventory (CSRI; Boldizar, 1991) and the Children's Personal Attributes Questionnaire (CPAQ; Hall & Halberstadt, 1980) to assess the external validity of the scale. Based on the finding from Study 1 that ratings of personal traits do not relate systematically to attitudes, external validity of the COAT measures would be demonstrated by findings that CSRI and CPAQ scales were, first, strongly correlated with the trait subscale of the COAT-PM, and, second, moderately correlated with the occupation and activity subscales of the COAT-PM.

Procedure. All children were tested in small groups (10–15 children) by a female experimenter. In both samples, children completed the short form of the COAT questionnaire. Approximately two weeks later, children in the second sample returned for an additional session. These children were first asked to complete the COAT questionnaire again, and then given the CSRI and the CPAQ (in counterbalanced order).

Data-analytic strategy. Data analysis was again a multistep process. First, reliability and validity of the COAT-short form were assessed using Cronbach's alpha and Guttman split-half reliability statistics. Test-retest correlation coefficients were also computed. Second, the correlations among the COAT subscales, and among the COAT subscales and the CSRI and CPAQ, were computed. Third, the COAT subscales were submitted to confirmatory factor analysis to test the viability of the factor structure derived from the exploratory factor analysis in Study 1. The relations among these factors were examined using regression analyses.

Results

COAT (short form) reliability and means. Cronbach's alphas and Guttman split-half reliabilities for each of the subscales of the shortened version of the COAT are reported in Table 10. These data indicate that, despite the smaller number of items, the subscales continued to have high internal consistency. Only one subscale, the masculine traits scores for the self, showed a coefficient in the adequate (rather than high) range. The test-retest reliability for the subscales also showed the COAT to be highly stable over a short period of time (see Table 10).

As described earlier, these data were collected from a racially and ethnically diverse sample to help ensure that our scales were appropriate (e.g., reliable and valid) when used with a diverse range of participants. This work was not, however, directed at comparing patterns of sex typing among *specific* racial and ethnic groups (indeed, our sample size for some groups was too small to permit such analyses). We did, however, examine the effect of race on response patterns on the COAT via preliminary analyses of variance, using a $4 \times 3 \times 2$ design (Race of participant: African American, Euro-American, Latino, Native American × Domain: occupations, activities, traits × Item gender: masculine, feminine). Results indicated

TABLE 10

RELIABILITY STATISTICS FOR THE COAT (SHORT FORM)

Subscale	Cronbach's Alpha	Guttman Split-Half	Test-Retest
Fem COAT-AM	.81	.79	.76
Fem COAT-AM	.83	.79	.79
Fem COAT-AM	.84	.79	.75
Mas COAT-AM	.83	.85	.78
Mas COAT-AM	.87	.85	.79
Mas COAT-AM	.85	.81	.73
Fem COAT-PM	.82	.81	.82
Fem COAT-PM	.83	.78	.77
Fem COAT-PM	.82	.77	.71
Mas COAT-PM	.78	.78	.73
Mas COAT-PM	.80	.80	.77
Mas COAT-PM	.67	.63	.72

Notes:—All subscales consist of 10 items. Test-retest reliabilities are correlations between scores at time 1 and time 2. C denotes children's scale; underscored O, A, and T indicate occupations, activities, and traits, respectively; AM is attitude measure (attitude toward others); PM is personal measure (sex typing of self).

a significant main effect of race on children's COAT-AM responses but no other main effects or interactions involving race for either the COAT-AM or COAT-PM. The data indicate that Native American and Hispanic children gave a greater proportion of egalitarian responses across all the AM scales than did Euro-American and African American children. Means (and standard deviations) for these four groups were, respectively, 63 (23), 72 (19), 56 (26), and 50 (26). These data must be interpreted cautiously, however, due to the small samples of some of these groups. Additional work on the effects of race and ethnicity on sex typing is clearly needed.

We next performed a 2 × 3 × 2 (Sex of participant × Domain: occupations, activities, traits × Item gender: masculine, feminine) analysis of variance to examine variation in the degree of gender attitude flexibility (COAT-AM scores) and sex-typed self-endorsements (COAT-PM scores). The means and standard deviations for each of the COAT subscales are presented in Table 11.

COAT-AM. Results indicated a significant main effect of domain, $F(2, 326) = 35.28$, $p < .01$, showing that children gave a greater number of egalitarian responses for traits than for occupations or activities, and a greater number of egalitarian responses for occupations than for activities. The main effect for item gender was also significant, $F(2, 326) = 10.56$, $p < .01$, indicating that children gave a greater number of egalitarian responses for masculine than for feminine items. The effect of item gender was qualified by a two-way interaction with sex of participant, $F(1, 326) = 4.25$, $p < .05$, indicating that this pattern was stronger among girls than boys (i.e., girls were even more likely to differentiate between masculine and feminine items than were boys). Also significant was the interaction between domain and item gender, $F(2, 326) = 15.28$, $p < .01$, indicating that children held significantly more flexible beliefs about masculine than feminine items in the domain of occupations, but not within the domains of activities or traits.

The above effects were all further qualified by a three-way interaction of domain, item gender, and sex of participant, $F(2, 326) = 3.42$, $p < .05$, indicating that the pattern of responding to masculine versus feminine items differed between boys and girls only with respect to activities. That is, both boys and girls showed more flexible beliefs about masculine than feminine occupations, and neither sex differentiated between masculine and feminine traits. However, boys gave more egalitarian responses to feminine activities than to masculine activities, whereas girls showed the reverse pattern.

COAT-PM. Results indicated a significant main effect of sex of participant, $F(1,86) = 6.35$, $p < .05$, with girls showing greater self-endorsement

TABLE 11

Mean Scores (Standard Deviations) for the COAT-AM
and COAT-PM (Short Forms)

| | Participants | | |
| | Boys | Girls | Combined |
Subscale	M (SD)	M (SD)	M (SD)
Fem COAT-AM	.47 (.31)	.50 (.27)	.48 (.30)
Fem COAT-AM	.46 (.31)	.44 (.29)	.45 (.31)
Fem COAT-AM	.63 (.33)	.66 (.30)	.65 (.32)
Mas COAT-AM	.58 (.32)	.59 (.28)	.58 (.30)
Mas COAT-AM	.42 (.33)	.48 (.28)	.44 (.31)
Mas COAT-AM	.61 (.32)	.69 (.28)	.64 (.30)
COAT-AM	.52 (.30)	.54 (.26)	.53 (.29)
COAT-AM	.44 (.31)	.46 (.26)	.45 (.29)
COAT-AM	.62 (.31)	.68 (.28)	.64 (.30)
Fem COAT-PM	1.5 (.52)	2.4 (.52)	1.9 (.67)
Fem COAT-PM	2.3 (.75)	3.3 (.86)	2.7 (.94)
Fem COAT-PM	2.9 (.65)	3.2 (.49)	3.0 (.60)
Mas COAT-PM	2.2 (.74)	2.0 (.57)	2.2 (.68)
Mas COAT-PM	3.0 (.82)	2.2 (.74)	2.6 (.88)
Mas COAT-PM	3.0 (.51)	2.9 (.49)	2.9 (.50)
COAT-PM	1.9 (.56)	2.2 (.48)	2.0 (.55)
COAT-PM	2.6 (.62)	2.7 (.64)	2.6 (.63)
COAT-PM	2.9 (.52)	3.0 (.44)	3.0 (.49)

Notes.—COAT-AM scores represent the proportion of "both men [boys] and women [women]" responses. COAT-PM responses represent the average rating of masculine and feminine items on 4-point scales, with higher scores indicating greater self-endorsement. C denotes children's scale; underscored O, A, and T indicate occupations, activities, and traits, respectively; AM is attitude measure (attitude toward others); PM is personal measure (sex typing of self).

of COAT-PM items than did boys. Also significant was the main effect of domain, $F(2, 172) = 126.05$, $p < .01$, with children showing greater endorsement of traits than occupations or activities, and greater endorsement of activities than occupations. This main effect of domain was qualified by a two-way interaction with item gender, $F(2,172) = 11.31$, $p < .01$. Children showed greater self-endorsement of feminine than masculine occupations, but showed equivalent levels of self-endorsements of masculine and feminine items within the domain of activities and traits.

Also significant was the two-way interaction of item gender and sex of participant, $F(1,86) = 104.19$, $p < .01$. As expected, girls showed greater self-endorsement of feminine items than did boys, whereas boys showed greater self-endorsement of masculine items than did girls.

These interactions were all subsumed by a three-way interaction of domain, item gender, and sex of participant, $F(2,172) = 33.64$, $p < .01$, indicating that this pattern of effects (i.e., greater endorsement of "sex appropriate" items) was particularly true for occupations and activities.

Correlations among subscales. Separate correlation matrices were computed for boys and girls and are presented in Table 12. The pattern of correlations was very similar to that found in Study 1 using the long form of the COAT. As in Study 1 (see Table 4), children's gender attitudes in the domains of occupations, activities, and traits were highly correlated (see the upper left quadrant of Table 12). Within each domain, attitudes toward masculine and feminine items were also very highly correlated. Across domains, attitudes toward occupations and activities were most strongly related. Two notable differences appeared with the use of the short form. The first difference was an increase in the number of significant correlations for boys' self-endorsement of items across domains (all but one correlation was significant; see above the diagonal, lower right quadrant). The second difference was a decrease in the number of significant correlations between responses to the self and other measures. Gender attitudes toward others were significantly related only to a small subset of the personal measures. Among boys, more flexible attitudes toward feminine traits were related to higher levels of self-endorsements for feminine traits, and more flexible attitudes toward masculine activities and traits were related to higher levels of self-endorsement of masculine traits (see the upper right quadrant). Among girls, more flexible attitudes toward masculine occupations were correlated with lower self-endorsement of feminine occupations, and with greater self-endorsement of masculine traits (see the lower left quadrant).

TABLE 12

ZERO-ORDER CORRELATIONS AMONG COAT (SHORT FORM)
SUBSCALES FOR BOYS AND GIRLS

	1	2	3	4	5	6	7	8	9	10	11	12
1. Fem COAT-AM	—	.53	.27	.82	.54	.35	.03	.04	.06	−.12	−.06	.07
2. Fem COAT-AM	.54	—	.46	.56	.81	.45	.11	−.01	.13	.19	−.14	.13
3. Fem COAT-AM	.28	.42	—	.28	.45	.83	.09	.01	.26	.14	−.12	.21
4. Mas COAT-AM	.80	.43	.26	—	.60	.35	.04	.05	.07	−.09	−.10	.09
5. Mas COAT-AM	.49	.64	.34	.51	—	.48	.05	−.07	.20	.14	−.16	.23
6. Mas COAT-AM	.18	.35	.81	.24	.32	—	.15	−.12	.18	.13	−.11	.22
7. Fem COAT-PM	−.22	−.06	−.09	−.28	−.17	−.17	—	.54	.27	.60	.20	.23
8. Fem COAT-PM	−.08	−.04	−.16	−.07	.01	−.18	.53	—	.45	.32	.23	.28
9. Fem COAT-PM	−.03	.01	.01	−.08	−.04	−.02	.29	.37	—	.39	.23	.53
10. Mas COAT-PM	−.07	.01	.01	−.01	.01	−.15	.53	.36	.22	—	.39	.52
11. Mas COAT-PM	.09	−.08	.05	.01	−.05	.01	.20	.34	.27	.41	—	.23
12. Mas COAT-PM	.22	.10	.13	.26	.20	.06	.16	.35	.49	.48	.43	—

Notes.—Boys' correlations are presented above the diagonal; girls' correlations are presented below the diagonal. C denotes children's scale; underscored O, A, and T indicate occupations, activities, and traits, respectively; AM is attitude measure (attitude toward others); PM is personal measure (sex typing of self). Bold correlations are significant at $p < .05$.

External validity. Correlations among the subscales of the COAT-PM and corresponding scales of the CSRI and CPAQ are presented in Table 13. In support of the validity of the COAT, responses to the feminine trait items of the personal measure of the COAT (i.e., Fem COAT-PM) were significantly correlated with the F scales of the CSRI and CPAQ, and responses to the masculine trait items on the personal measure (i.e., Mas COAT-PM) were significantly correlated with the M scales of the CSRI and CPAQ. The patterns of associations accorded generally (although not perfectly) with expectations insofar as it was the trait scales of the personal measure of the COAT that were particularly strongly associated with the CPAQ and CSRI measures. As explained earlier, this finding is consistent with the prediction that there would be a close relation between the self trait COAT scales and the CPAQ and CSRI measures. Also consistent with our expectations was the finding that responses on the feminine *activity* subscale of the COAT were associated with responses on the feminine subscale of the CRSI. The relatively large size of the correlation (.49) probably reflects the fact that the CSRI includes several items related to activities (e.g., "I like to do things that girls and women do").

Confirmatory factor analysis. Confirmatory factor analysis was used to test whether the three-factor model derived from Study 1 would fit the data obtained using the short form of the COAT. Importantly, the confirmatory analyses were conducted using a new sample. Based on the results of the exploratory factor analysis described in Study 1, a three-factor model of gender schemata was specified. This model included gender attitudes, feminine self-endorsements, and masculine self-endorsements. This model

TABLE 13

CORRELATIONS AMONG COAT (SHORT FORM) PERSONAL MEASURE SUBSCALES
AND CSRI AND CPAQ SCALES

	CSRIF	CSRIM	CPAQF	CPAQM	CPAQMF
Fem COAT-PM	.25	−.23	.03	−.14	−.17
Fem COAT-PM	**.49**	−.11	.14	.03	−.10
Fem COAT-PM	**.53**	**.27**	.40	.23	.16
Mas COAT-PM	**.28**	.24	**−.26**	−.17	−.24
Mas COAT-PM	−.05	−.12	−.08	−.08	.02
Mas COAT-PM	.22	**.58**	.23	**.61**	.11

Notes.—CSRI is the Children's Sex Role Inventory and CPAQ is the Children's Personal Attributes Questionnaire (with F and M specifying feminine and masculine traits, respectively). C denotes children's scale; underscored O, A, and T indicate occupations, activities, and traits, respectively; AM is attitude measure (attitude toward others); PM is personal measure (sex typing of self). Bold correlations are significant at $p < .05$.

was compared to a null model that specified no relations among the observed measures.

A variety of goodness-of-fit indexes are available to assess how well a model fits the data (see Marsh, Balla, & McDonald, 1988). Three commonly used indexes are reported here as measures of fit: (a) the chi-square statistic divided by the degrees of freedom (e.g., Carmines & McIver, 1981), with scores of 2.0 or less indicating a very good fit; (b) the Jöreskog and Sörbom (1984) goodness-of-fit index (GFI), with scores greater than .90 indicating a very good fit; and (c) the Bentler and Bonett Fit Index (1980) comparing the prescribed model to a null model that specifies no relations among the observed measures, with scores greater than .90 indicating a very good fit. According to these three indexes, the three-factor model derived in Study 1 fit the data moderately well. The chi-square divided by degrees of freedom was 2.40, the GFI was .88, and the Bentler and Bonett Fit Index was .86. The factor loadings for the model are presented in Table 14.

Relations among factors. In order to examine the relation of children's gender attitudes to their self-endorsement of same-sex-typed and cross-sex-typed items, a composite gender attitude score was formed by calculating the mean proportion of "both men and women" responses across

TABLE 14

FACTOR LOADINGS FOR THE THREE-FACTOR MODEL OF CHILDREN'S GENDER SCHEMATA

| | Factor-Derived Constructs | | |
Subscale	Factor 1: Gender Attitudes	Factor 2: Feminine Self	Factor 3: Masculine Self
Fem COAT-AM	.831		
Fem COAT-AM	.830		
Fem COAT-AM	.693		
Mas COAT-AM	.841		
Mas COAT-AM	.813		
Mas COAT-AM	.691		
Fem COAT-PM		.894	
Fem COAT-PM		.833	
Fem COAT-PM		.678	
Mas COAT-PM			.754
Mas COAT-PM			.788
Mas COAT-PM			.743

Notes.—Standardized factor loadings for the entire sample are presented. C denotes children's scale; underscored O, A, and T indicate occupations, activities, and traits, respectively; AM is attitude measure (attitude toward others); PM is personal measure (sex typing of self).

64

TABLE 15

RESULTS OF REGRESSION ANALYSES EXAMINING THE EFFECT OF GENDER ATTITUDES
ON SELF-ENDORSEMENTS IN BOYS AND GIRLS

Participants	Standardized Regression Coefficient	F	p
Boys $(N = 98)$			
feminine self-endorsements	.18	.58	.45
masculine self-endorsements	−.06	.05	.83
Girls $(N = 67)$			
feminine self-endorsements	−.48	1.89	.17
masculine self-endorsements	.23	.39	.54

the occupation, activity, and trait (masculine and feminine) subscales of the COAT-AM (i.e., six COAT-AM subscales). Next, composite scores for children's masculine and feminine self-endorsements were created by calculating the average rating across the masculine, and then feminine, items of the occupation, activity, and trait subscales of the COAT-PM.

As a preliminary means of assessing the viability of the attitudinal pathway, the composite attitude score was regressed onto separate composite scores of children's masculine and feminine self-endorsements. That is, we examined whether sex typing of others, generally, would relate to the degree to which masculine and feminine items were endorsed for the self. (We note, though, that evidence of a significant relation would also be compatible with the personal pathway model, as well as with other possible models.) Because the predictors of self-endorsements have been found to differ for boys and girls (e.g., Katz & Ksansnak, 1994), separate models were tested for males and females. Results, shown in Table 15, indicate that gender attitudes did not significantly predict self-endorsements of masculine or feminine items among either boys or girls (or, in the language of the personal pathway, self-endorsements did not predict to gender attitudes). Because longitudinal data are better suited to testing the attitudinal versus personal pathways of influence between sex-typing constructs, additional tests of relations (e.g., using subscale rather than composite scores) were conducted in Study 5, and are reported in Chapter V.

Discussion

The results suggest that the short form of the COAT is a reliable measure of children's gender-related attitudes and gender self characterizations.

The very high similarity between the patterns of reliabilities, means, and correlations found using the long and short forms of the COAT suggests that the short form can be used when a brief measure of sex typing within one or multiple domains is desired, and the specific content (e.g., items) that individuals endorse as sex typed is not the focus of the research.

Importantly, the pattern of effects found with a more diverse sample of participants closely resembled that found with the Euro-American sample in Study 1. Although the racially and ethnically diverse sample showed overall lower rates of gender stereotyping (see our earlier discussion), the patterns of stereotype attitudes (e.g., stronger gender stereotypes for occupations than for traits and activities) were highly similar in the two samples.

The confirmatory factor analyses indicate that the three-factor model of children's gender schemata derived from Study 1—consisting of gender attitudes, feminine self-endorsements, and masculine self-endorsements—accounts reasonably well (although not exceptionally well) for correlations among measures in this second, more racially and ethnically diverse, sample. This finding suggests that alternative models may be better able to account for the relations among these measures.

Finally, the regression analyses indicate that children's overall gender attitudes toward others were unrelated to self-endorsement of masculine and feminine items (collapsed across domains). This finding is consistent with earlier reports (e.g., Spence & Hall, 1996) that children's responses to measures of gender stereotyping are unrelated to their endorsements of sex-typed items for the self. One possible explanation is that the lack of a relation truly indicates that gender attitudes do not guide the development of self interests and behaviors (or the reverse—that personal interests do not guide the formation or revision of gender attitudes). However, it is also possible that the lack of an observed relation is instead the consequence of the breadth of earlier measures. That is, as argued initially, measures that draw items from a variety of domains and that use very different formats may obscure relations that are actually there. Earlier in this *Monograph*, we predicted that sex typing of the self and sex typing of others would, in fact, show strong relations under some circumstances, including conditions in which the two sets of assessments employed matched content. We could not, however, examine this possibility using the data set of Study 3 because the items included in the short versions of the scales were selected on the basis of item-total correlations, rather than for the purpose of including identical items in both measures. Thus, we postpone examining the relations between children's sex typing of others and of self until our discussion of Study 5 in which identical items were used in the self and other measures.

STUDY 4: SCALE REFINEMENT FOR ADULTS

In Study 4, the structural model of adults' gender schemata developed in Study 2 was cross-validated using confirmatory factor analysis (Breckler, 1990) and the relations among factors were examined via regression analyses. In parallel to the work presented in Study 3, a shortened version of the scale was developed, scale validity and reliability (including test-retest reliability) were tested, and the data were used to assess the model of gender schemata derived from Study 2.

Method

Participants. Participants were 167 (82 males, 85 females) undergraduates, recruited as in Study 2. A subsample of the participants (N = 75; 35 males, 40 females) returned two weeks later to complete additional measures, following the logic presented in Study 3.

OAT scales. A shortened version of the OAT (OAT short form) was created by computing item-total correlations from the sample reported in Study 2. As explained earlier, the 10 masculine, 10 feminine, and 5 neutral items with the highest item-total correlations on each of the six subscales were selected for inclusion. Item-total correlations for the selected items ranged from .91 to .97. Appendix A (Tables A4–A6) provides data on cultural sex typing of the selected items as explained earlier, Appendix C (Figures C7–C12) provides the scales in administration format, and Appendix D provides information on procedures and scoring.

Test-retest reliability and external validity. The subsample of participants who completed the OAT for a second time to assess test-retest reliability of the scale also completed the BSRI (Bem, 1974) and PAQ (Spence et al., 1974) to assess the external validity of the scale. Based on the finding from Study 2 that ratings of personal traits (i.e., with self as target) do not relate to gender attitudes toward others, external validity would be demonstrated by findings that BSRI and PAQ scales were, first, strongly correlated with the trait subscale of the OAT-PM, and, second, moderately correlated with the occupation and activity subscales of the OAT-PM.

Procedure. Adults were tested in a large group by a female experimenter. In the first session, respondents completed the short form of the OAT questionnaire. Two weeks later, a subsample of participants returned for a second session. These participants were first asked to complete the OAT questionnaire again, and then given the BSRI and the PAQ (in counterbalanced order). Data from the initial administration of the OAT were used in all subsequent analyses (with the obvious exception of analyses on test-retest reliability).

Data-analytic strategy. Data analysis was again a multistep process. First, reliability of the OAT short form was assessed using Cronbach's alpha and the Guttman split-half reliability statistic. Test-retest reliability correlations were also computed. Second, the means and the correlations among the OAT subscales, and correlations among the OAT, BSRI, and PAQ subscales were computed. Third, the OAT subscales were submitted to confirmatory factor analysis to test the viability of the factor structure derived from the exploratory factor analysis in Study 2, with the relations among factors examined via regression analyses.

Results

OAT (short scale) reliability and means. Cronbach's alphas and Guttman split-half reliabilities for each of the subscales of the shortened version of the OAT are reported in Table 16. These data indicate that the subscales had high internal consistency. The one exception to this characterization was the feminine trait scale for the self, which had only adequate reliability. The test-retest reliability (i.e., correlation coefficients) for the scales indicated that adults' responses on the OAT scales were very stable across a short period of time (see Table 16).

TABLE 16

RELIABILITY STATISTICS FOR THE OAT (SHORT FORM)

Subscale	Cronbach's Alpha	Guttman Split-Half	Test-Retest
Fem OAT-AM	.89	.92	.77
Fem OAT-AM	.87	.82	.72
Fem OAT-AM	.75	.61	.74
Mas OAT-AM	.91	.89	.74
Mas OAT-AM	.89	.89	.75
Mas OAT-AM	.79	.69	.73
Fem OAT-PM	.76	.78	.72
Fem OAT-PM	.81	.75	.78
Fem OAT-PM	.65	.68	.82
Mas OAT-PM	.73	.71	.76
Mas OAT-PM	.75	.77	.79
Mas OAT-PM	.71	.68	.88

Notes.—All subscales consist of 10 items. Test-retest reliabilities are correlations between scores at time 1 and time 2. Underscored O, A, and T indicate occupations, activities, and traits, respectively; AM is attitude measure (attitude toward others); PM is personal measure (sex typing of self).

The means and standard deviations for each of the OAT subscales are presented in Table 17. A $2 \times 3 \times 2$ (Sex of participant × Domain: occupations, activities, traits × Item gender: masculine, feminine) analysis of variance examined variation in the degree of gender attitude flexibility (OAT-AM scores) and sex-typed self-endorsements (OAT-PM scores).

OAT-AM. Results indicated a significant main effect of sex of participant, $F(1, 165) = 9.62$, $p < .01$, indicating that women gave more egalitarian responses to OAT-AM items than did men. The main effect of domain was also significant, $F(2, 330) = 69.08$, $p < .01$, indicating that adults gave a greater number of egalitarian responses for traits than for occupations or activities, and a greater number of egalitarian responses for occupations than for activities. Also significant was the main effect of item gender, $F(1, 165) = 9.54$, $p < .01$, indicating that adults gave a greater number of egalitarian responses for feminine than for masculine items.

TABLE 17

MEAN SCORES (STANDARD DEVIATIONS) FOR THE OAT-AM AND OAT-PM (SHORT FORMS)

	Participants		
	Men	Women	Combined
Subscale	M (SD)	M (SD)	M (SD)
Fem OAT-AM	.59 (.34)	.74 (.30)	.67 (.32)
Fem OAT-AM	.64 (.29)	.77 (.25)	.71 (.28)
Fem OAT-AM	.78 (.26)	.90 (.16)	.84 (.22)
Mas OAT-AM	.55 (.35)	.65 (.34)	.60 (.35)
Mas OAT-AM	.67 (.33)	.76 (.30)	.72 (.32)
Mas OAT-AM	.76 (.29)	.88 (.18)	.82 (.25)
OAT-AM	.57 (.33)	.70 (.31)	.64 (.32)
OAT-AM	.66 (.30)	.77 (.26)	.71 (.28)
OAT-AM	.77 (.26)	.89 (.16)	.83 (.22)
Fem OAT-PM	1.3 (.31)	1.7 (.43)	1.5 (.41)
Fem OAT-PM	2.8 (.61)	3.3 (.57)	3.1 (.63)
Fem OAT-PM	2.8 (.36)	3.0 (.37)	2.9 (.39)
Mas OAT-PM	2.1 (.49)	1.8 (.49)	1.9 (.52)
Mas OAT-PM	2.3 (.64)	1.8 (.41)	2.0 (.60)
Mas OAT-PM	2.9 (.39)	2.6 (.47)	2.7 (.47)
OAT-PM	1.7 (.33)	1.7 (.36)	1.7 (.34)
OAT-PM	2.6 (.49)	2.6 (.35)	2.6 (.42)
OAT-PM	2.8 (.27)	2.8 (.27)	2.8 (.27)

Notes.—OAT-AM scores represent the proportion of "both men and women" responses. COAT-PM responses represent the average rating of masculine and feminine items on 4-point scales, with higher scores indicating greater self-endorsement. Underscored O, A, and T indicate occupations, activities, and traits, respectively; AM is attitude measure (attitude toward others); PM is personal measure (sex typing of self).

The main effect of item gender was qualified by two interactions. An interaction of item gender and sex of participant, $F(1, 165) = 3.89$, $p < .05$, indicated that this pattern (more egalitarian responses for feminine than for masculine items) was true for women but not for men (for whom there was no significant difference between responses to masculine and feminine items). Also significant was the interaction of domain and item gender, $F(2, 330) = 9.15$, $p < .01$, indicating that adults held significantly more flexible beliefs about feminine than masculine items within the domains of occupations and traits, but not within the domain of activities.

OAT-PM. Results indicated a significant main effect of domain, $F(2, 310) = 875.45$, $p < .01$, with adults showing greater self-endorsement of traits than occupations or activities, and greater self-endorsement of activities than occupations. The main effect of item gender was also significant, $F(1, 155) = 55.18$, $p < .01$, with adults showing greater self-endorsement of feminine than masculine OAT-PM items.

These main effects were qualified by two interactions. An interaction of item gender and sex of participant, $F(1, 155) = 96.93$, $p < .01$, showed that, as expected, women responded with greater self-endorsement of feminine than masculine items, whereas men showed the reverse pattern (i.e., greater self-endorsement of masculine than feminine items). An interaction of domain and item gender, $F(2, 310) = 99.34$, $p < .01$, indicated that adults showed greater self-endorsement of masculine than feminine occupations, but greater self-endorsement of feminine than masculine activities and traits.

Correlations among subscales. Separate correlation matrices were computed for women and men and are presented in Table 18. Consistent with each of the previous studies, adults' stereotypes of occupations, activities, and traits were highly correlated (see the upper left quadrant). Gender attitudes toward others were significantly related to a few of the self-endorsement measures, although again the pattern differed for men and women. Among men (see the upper right quadrant), more egalitarian gender attitudes were generally correlated with fewer self-endorsements of masculine occupations, activities, and traits, with the most consistent association of more egalitarian responding being to low rates of self-endorsement of masculine activities. Only one correlation ran counter to the general notion that more egalitarian responding would be associated with greater self-endorsement of cross-sex-typed items. Specifically, more egalitarian attitudes toward masculine traits were associated with *lower* self-endorsements of feminine activities. Among women (see the lower left quadrant), more egalitarian gender attitudes were generally (although not always) correlated with greater self-endorsement of masculine traits. In

TABLE 18

ZERO-ORDER CORRELATIONS AMONG OAT (SHORT FORM)
SUBSCALES FOR MEN AND WOMEN

	1	2	3	4	5	6	7	8	9	10	11	12
1. Fem OAT-AM	—	.87	.60	.81	.82	.54	.07	−.02	−.04	−.11	−.36	−.07
2. Fem OAT-AM	.81	—	.68	.77	.86	.65	.06	.05	.11	−.12	−.36	−.10
3. Fem OAT-AM	.38	.49	—	.62	.68	.88	.05	.23	.04	−.30	−.44	−.14
4. Mas OAT-AM	.84	.74	.43	—	.78	.61	.04	.07	−.03	−.06	−.35	−.02
5. Mas OAT-AM	.77	.79	.43	.80	—	.64	.01	−.01	.12	−.13	−.36	.01
6. Mas OAT-AM	.43	.52	.81	.43	.47	—	−.02	−.25	.06	−.28	−.42	−.22
7. Fem OAT-PM	.01	−.06	−.10	.06	−.01	−.14	—	.14	.05	.34	−.09	−.07
8. Fem OAT-PM	.06	−.01	−.03	−.03	−.08	.10	.38	—	.25	−.10	.20	−.09
9. Fem OAT-PM	−.07	−.08	−.10	−.09	−.19	−.06	.26	.32	—	−.06	.11	−.02
10. Mas OAT-PM	.06	.04	.13	.15	.13	.11	.58	.12	−.02	—	.35	.19
11. Mas OAT-PM	.04	.08	.18	.03	.13	.22	.24	.40	.05	.41	—	.09
12. Mas OAT-PM	.20	.23	.14	.26	.31	.18	−.04	.06	.09	.20	.35	—

Notes.—Men's correlations are presented above the diagonal; women's correlations are presented below the diagonal. Underscored O, A, and T indicate occupations, activities, and traits, respectively; AM is attitude measure (attitude toward others); PM is personal measure (sex typing of self). Bold correlations are significant at $p < .05$.

addition, egalitarian attitudes about masculine traits were associated with self-endorsement of masculine activities.

External validity. Correlations among the subscales of the OAT-PM and corresponding scales of the PAQ and BSRI are presented in Table 19. In support of the validity of the OAT, responding to the feminine items of the OAT-PM was significantly positively correlated with the F scales of the

TABLE 19

CORRELATIONS AMONG OAT (SHORT FORM) PERSONAL MEASURE SUBSCALES
AND BSRI AND PAQ SCALES

	BSRIF	BSRIM	PAQF	PAQM	PAQMF
Fem OAT-PM	.39	−.38	.19	−.19	−.39
Fem OAT-PM	.45	−.40	.24	−.28	−.52
Fem OAT-PM	.56	−.24	.52	−.35	−.67
Mas OAT-PM	−.22	.23	−.24	−.16	.39
Mas OAT-PM	−.19	.05	−.14	−.07	.05
Mas OAT-PM	−.23	.68	−.05	.57	.45

Notes.—BSRI is the Bem Sex Role Inventory and PAQ is the Personal Attributes Questionnaire (with F and M specifying feminine and masculine traits, respectively). Underscored O, A, and T indicate occupations, activities, and traits, respectively; AM is attitude measure (attitude toward others); PM is personal measure (sex typing of self). Bold correlations are significant at $p < .05$.

PAQ and BSRI, whereas responding to the masculine items on the OAT-PM was significantly positively correlated with the M scales of the PAQ and BSRI. Interestingly, high levels of endorsement of feminine traits on the OAT-PM were also *negatively* associated with scores on the masculine sub-scales of the BSRI and PAQ—and with scores on the PAQMF, a scale that includes many masculine traits. Given adults' tendency to self-endorse sex-typed items across domains (see Study 2), it is not surprising to find that the activity and occupation subscales of the OAT-PM also showed some significant correlations with the BSRI and PAQ scales.

Confirmatory factor analysis. Confirmatory factor analysis was used to test whether the three-factor model of adults' gender schemata derived from Study 2 would fit the data from the short form of the OAT. Importantly, the confirmatory analyses were conducted using a new sample. Based on the results of the exploratory factor analysis described in Study 2, a three-factor model of gender schemata was specified. This model included gender attitudes, feminine self-endorsements, and masculine self-endorsements and was compared to a null model that specified no relations among the observed measures.

As in Study 3, three goodness-of-fit indexes were used to determine whether the model derived from Study 2 would fit the data from the short form of the OAT, including (a) the chi-square statistics divided by the degrees of freedom (e.g., Carmines & McIver, 1981), (b) the Jöreskog and Sörbom (1984) goodness-of-fit index, and (c) the Bentler and Bonett Fit Index. The chi-square divided by the degrees of freedom was 2.3, indicating a good fit to the data; the GFI was .90; and the Bentler-Bonett statistic was .90, indicating that the model was significantly better than a null model. The factor loadings for the model are presented in Table 20.

Relations among factors. In order to examine the relation of adults' gender attitudes to their endorsement of same-sex-typed and cross-sex-typed items, a composite gender attitude score was formed by calculating the mean proportion of "both men and women" responses across the occupation, activity, and traits subscales of the OAT-AM. Next, composite scores for adults' masculine and feminine self-endorsements were created by calculating the average rating across the masculine, and then feminine, items of the occupation, activity, and trait subscales of the OAT-PM.

As a preliminary means of assessing the viability of the attitudinal pathway, the composite attitude score was regressed onto separate composite scores of adults' masculine and feminine self-endorsements. That is, we examined whether sex typing of others, generally, would relate to the degree to which masculine and feminine items were endorsed for the self. (Again, we note that evidence of a significant relation would also be

TABLE 20

FACTOR LOADINGS FOR THE THREE-FACTOR MODEL OF ADULTS' GENDER SCHEMATA

| | Factor-Derived Constructs | | |
Subscale	Factor 1: Gender Attitudes	Factor 2: Feminine Self	Factor 3: Masculine Self
Fem OAT-AM	.819		
Fem OAT-AM	.880		
Fem OAT-AM	.774		
Mas OAT-AM	.744		
Mas OAT-AM	.785		
Mas OAT-AM	.770		
Fem OAT-PM		.359	
Fem OAT-PM		.502	
Fem OAT-PM		.317	
Mas OAT-PM			.596
Mas OAT-PM			.565
Mas OAT-PM			.402

Notes.—Standardized factor loadings for the entire sample are presented. Underscored O, A, and T indicate occupations, activities, and traits, respectively; AM is attitude measure (attitude toward others); PM is personal measure (sex typing of self).

compatible with the personal pathway model.) As in Study 3, separate models were tested for males and females. Results are shown in Table 21. Among men, gender attitudes predicted self-endorsement of masculine (but not feminine) items. Males with more egalitarian gender attitudes showed lower self-endorsement of masculine items than those males with less egalitarian

TABLE 21

RESULTS OF REGRESSION ANALYSES EXAMINING THE EFFECT OF GENDER ATTITUDES ON SELF-ENDORSEMENTS AMONG MEN AND WOMEN

Participants	Standardized Regression Coefficient	F	p
Men ($N = 82$)			
feminine self-endorsements	.34	.87	.35
masculine self-endorsements	**−1.54**	**13.90**	**<.01**
Women ($N = 85$)			
feminine self-endorsements	−.28	.37	.54
masculine self-endorsements	**1.27**	**5.62**	**<.05**

Note.—Bold scores are significant at $p < .05$.

attitudes. Among women, gender attitudes also predicted self-endorsements of masculine (but not feminine) items. Women with more egalitarian attitudes showed greater self-endorsement of masculine items than women with less egalitarian attitudes. Again, both of these findings could be phrased in the language of the personal pathway model, suggesting the utility of self-endorsements for predicting sex typing of others.

Discussion

The results suggest that the short form of the OAT is a reliable measure of adults' self-reports of gender-related attitudes, attributes, and behaviors. The very high similarity between the patterns of means and correlations found using the long and short forms of the OAT suggests that the short form can reliably be used when a shorter measure is desired and the specific content (e.g., items) that individuals endorse as sex typed is not the focus of the research. Importantly, the patterns of means and correlations among the OAT subscales are very similar to those found in Study 2, using the long form of the OAT scale.

The confirmatory factor analyses indicate that adults' gender schemata are composed of three distinct components: gender attitudes, feminine self-endorsements, and masculine self-endorsements. The various fit indices all indicate that the three-factor model provides a good fit to the observed correlations among the subscales.

Finally, the regression analyses indicate that adults' gender attitudes were related to their self-endorsements of gender-related items. Interestingly, more egalitarian attitudes were related to masculine (but not feminine) self-endorsements among both men and women. Women with more egalitarian attitudes showed greater self-endorsement of masculine items, whereas men with more egalitarian attitudes showed lower self-endorsement of masculine items. This particular pattern of findings provides partial support for our hypotheses concerning the conditions under which sex typing of self and sex typing of others would show strong relations. As predicted, women's sex typing of others was related to sex typing of the self for cross-sex-typed (but not for same-sex-typed) items. Although men's sex typing of self and sex typing of others was related for same-sex-typed (rather than cross-sex-typed) items, this relation is likely to be caused by the low status (and hence low attractiveness) of feminine items. That is, we found support for our prediction that men with egalitarian attitudes will not be more interested in feminine items than will men with less egalitarian gender attitudes. Again, however, direct evaluation of each of the factors hypothesized to affect the observed relation between sex typing of self and sex typing of others, and discussion of the causal direction of influence, are postponed until Study 5.

The pattern of findings from the adult data in Study 4 is very different from that reported for children in Study 3. That is, as reported earlier, children's gender attitudes did not predict to self-endorsement for masculine or feminine items. The finding that adults' gender attitudes did predict to their self constructs suggests that adults' gender schemata may be less fragmented and more integrated than children's gender schemata. The possibility that stronger relations emerge over time is examined with longitudinal data in Study 5.

V. EMPIRICAL DATA RELATED TO
DEVELOPMENTAL PATHWAYS

As discussed earlier, conclusions from previous research on the structure of, and developmental changes within, gender schemata are problematic because of limitations in the measures that have been used to assess the key constructs. More specifically, we have argued that there have been confounds—along the dimensions of target person, substantive domain, and target processes—both within and across studies of different age groups. In addition, previous research has not examined whether patterns of relations across time are consistent with the hypothesis implicit in earlier constructivist theories that sex typing of others plays a causal role in the sex typing of the self. The research discussed in the prior chapter was designed to begin to address these lacunae in earlier work. The major goal of these four studies was to design a suite of psychometrically sound measures that could be used to examine relations among core gender constructs. A secondary goal was to examine concurrent relations among these constructs that are derived from cognitive theories of gender differentiation.

Although the data on concurrent relations among constructs are useful, more telling developmental data require the examination of how the relation between children's sex typing of others and sex typing of the self may change over time. For example, many (but not all) children show declining levels of sex typing of others beginning in middle and late elementary school (e.g., Ruble & Martin, 1998; Signorella et al., 1993). According to existing constructivist models, these attitudinal changes should produce subsequent changes in behavior. That is, sex typing of others at one point in time should predict sex typing of the self at some later point in time. A fifth study was thus conducted to begin to examine, longitudinally, the relation between children's sex typing of others and of the self.

STUDY 5: LONGITUDINAL STUDY OF DEVELOPMENTAL PATHWAYS

To examine the longitudinal relations between sex typing of self and others, children from our original sample of sixth-grade children (tested in Study 1) were given the long form of the COAT measures four times across a two-year period. Data from these administrations of the COAT allowed us to examine whether relations among sex typing constructs over time are consistent with the attitudinal or the personal pathway models of gender differentiation presented earlier. We also used the data from Study 5 to examine whether the strength of the observed relation between sex typing of others and of self was moderated by the four factors outlined in Chapter III (and summarized in Table 1).

Method

Participants. Participants were children who had participated in Study 1. We were able to obtain complete data across four waves of testing for about half of the original sample of 154 children. The final sample for this study thus consisted of 78 children, divided evenly by sex, whose parents had signed permission slips, who themselves agreed to participate, and who were tested in both the fall and spring of the sixth and seventh grades. Preliminary analyses of the COAT means for time 1 (i.e., the Study 1 sample) indicated no significant differences between children for whom complete data across the two years were later available versus children who were later dropped from the longitudinal sample because of incomplete data. Thus, although the sample was reduced in size for Study 5, it did not appear to have been systematically distorted in ways relevant to the central questions addressed in this research.

Results

The means and standard deviations for each of the COAT subscales are presented in Tables 22 and 23 for boys and girls, respectively. A $2 \times 3 \times 2 \times 4$ (Sex of participant $\times$ Domain: occupations, activities, traits $\times$ Item gender: masculine, feminine $\times$ Time: [1] fall of grade 6, [2] spring of grade 6, [3] fall of grade 7, and [4] spring of grade 7) analysis of variance, with the last three factors as repeated measures, examined variation in the degree of gender attitude flexibility (COAT-AM scores) and sex-typed self-endorsements (COAT-PM scores).

COAT-AM. Results indicated significant main effects of domain, $F(2, 152) = 37.10$, $p < .01$, and of item gender, $F(1, 76) = 141.60$, $p < .01$. Specifically, children gave a greater number of egalitarian responses for

TABLE 22

MEANS (STANDARD DEVIATIONS) OF BOYS' SCORES ON COAT (LONG FORM)
ACROSS SIXTH AND SEVENTH GRADES

Subscale	Time 1 (Fall, 6th)	Time 2 (Spring, 6th)	Time 3 (Fall, 7th)	Time 4 (Spring, 7th)
Fem COAT-AM	.42 (.28)	.44 (.37)	.54 (.32)	.59 (.33)
Fem COAT-AM	.44 (.30)	.40 (.37)	.50 (.35)	.54 (.36)
Fem COAT-AM	.69 (.26)	.65 (.32)	.69 (.29)	.74 (.31)
Mas COAT-AM	.51 (.31)	.51 (.36)	.65 (.33)	.68 (.32)
Mas COAT-AM	.55 (.30)	.51 (.36)	.64 (.33)	.67 (.34)
Mas COAT-AM	.66 (.28)	.63 (.34)	.70 (.29)	.70 (.26)
Fem COAT-PM	1.4 (.25)	1.4 (.36)	1.2 (.21)	1.2 (.31)
Fem COAT-PM	1.5 (.33)	1.6 (.52)	1.4 (.29)	1.4 (.28)
Fem COAT-PM	2.6 (.40)	2.6 (.36)	2.6 (.49)	2.5 (.53)
Mas COAT-PM	1.9 (.42)	1.8 (.39)	1.8 (.40)	1.8 (.41)
Mas COAT-PM	2.7 (.79)	2.6 (.85)	2.6 (.75)	2.5 (.66)
Mas COAT-PM	2.8 (.40)	2.9 (.42)	2.8 (.47)	2.8 (.41)

Notes.—COAT-AM scores represent the proportion of "both men [boys] and women [girls]" responses. COAT-PM responses represent the average rating of masculine and feminine items on 4-point scales, with higher scores indicating greater self-endorsement. C denotes children's scale; underscored O, A, and T indicate occupations, activities, and traits, respectively; AM is attitude measure (attitude toward others); PM is personal measure (sex typing of self).

traits than for occupations or activities (which did not differ from each other), and for masculine than for feminine items. The effect of item gender was, however, qualified by an interaction with sex of participant, $F(1, 76) = 15.20$, $p < .01$, indicating that on feminine items, boys gave a greater number of egalitarian responses than did girls, whereas for masculine items, there was no significant difference in relation to participant sex. Also significant was the interaction between domain and item gender, $F(2, 152) = 78.50$, $p < .01$, indicating that in the domains of occupations and activities, children held significantly more flexible beliefs about masculine than feminine items, whereas in the domain of traits there was no effect of item gender.

These findings, in which data were collapsed across two years, are consistent with those from the original sample (Study 1) and from data collected using the short form of the COAT (Study 3). More importantly, these data also indicated significant change over time. Overall, the main effect for time of testing was significant, $F(3, 228) = 10.89$, $p < .01$. Post hoc analyses indicated that children's attitudes became significantly more egalitarian between the spring testing of sixth grade (time 2) and the fall testing of seventh grade (time 3). The effect of time of testing was subsumed by an interaction of time of testing and domain, $F(6, 456) = 2.64$, $p < .05$, indicating that change during this time (i.e., sixth to seventh grade) was greatest within the domains of occupations and activities.

TABLE 23

MEANS (STANDARD DEVIATIONS) OF GIRLS' SCORES ON COAT (LONG FORM)
ACROSS SIXTH AND SEVENTH GRADES

Subscales	Time 1 (Fall, 6th)	Time 2 (Spring, 6th)	Time 3 (Fall, 7th)	Time 4 (Spring, 7th)
Fem COAT-AM	.33 (.26)	.40 (.38)	.48 (.34)	.50 (.35)
Fem COAT-AM	.31 (.23)	.34 (.32)	.49 (.33)	.49 (.34)
Fem COAT-AM	.61 (.26)	.57 (.34)	.67 (.27)	.72 (.25)
Mas COAT-AM	.52 (.25)	.52 (.38)	.67 (.27)	.66 (.30)
Mas COAT-AM	.53 (.26)	.49 (.35)	.66 (.29)	.66 (.32)
Mas COAT-AM	.65 (.25)	.60 (.34)	.71 (.26)	.71 (.21)
Fem COAT-PM	2.3 (.53)	2.0 (.50)	1.9 (.51)	1.9 (.46)
Fem COAT-PM	2.3 (.66)	2.2 (.59)	2.2 (.53)	2.2 (.60)
Fem COAT-PM	2.8 (.31)	2.7 (.42)	2.8 (.41)	2.7 (.49)
Mas COAT-PM	1.6 (.32)	1.5 (.40)	1.5 (.34)	1.4 (.38)
Mas COAT-PM	1.9 (.46)	1.8 (.58)	1.8 (.50)	1.8 (.61)
Mas COAT-PM	2.6 (.36)	2.6 (.42)	2.7 (.45)	2.6 (.53)

Notes.—COAT-AM scores represent the proportion of "both men [boys] and women [girls]" responses. COAT-PM responses represent the average rating of masculine and feminine items on 4-point scales, with higher ratings indicating greater personal interest. C denotes children's scale; underscored O, A, and T indicate occupations, activities, and traits, respectively; AM is attitude measure (attitude toward others); PM is personal measure (sex typing of self).

COAT-PM. Results indicated a significant main effect of domain, $F(2, 62) = 209.50$, $p < .01$, with children showing greater self-endorsement of traits than occupations or activities, and greater self-endorsement of activities than occupations. This effect was qualified, however, by several two-way interactions. First, an interaction between domain and item gender, $F(2, 62) = 9.30$, $p < .01$, indicated that children showed greater self-endorsement of feminine than masculine occupations, but greater self-endorsement of masculine than feminine activities. Second, an interaction between domain and sex of participant, $F(2, 62) = 6.30$, $p < .01$, indicated that girls showed greater self-endorsement of occupations and activities (but not traits) than boys.

The main effect of item gender was also significant, $F(1, 31) = 5.30$, $p < .05$, indicating that children endorsed greater numbers of masculine than feminine items. This effect was subsumed, however, by a two-way interaction of item gender and sex of participant, $F(1,31) = 76.21$, $p < .01$. As expected, girls showed greater endorsement of feminine items than did boys, whereas boys showed greater endorsement of masculine items than did girls.

These interactions were all subsumed by a significant three-way interaction of domain, item gender, and sex of participant, $F(2, 62) = 36.13$, $p < .01$, indicating that the pattern of effects just described (i.e., greater endorsement of "sex appropriate" items) was stronger in the domains of occupations and activities than in the domain of traits.

As was true for the COAT-AM data, the findings on the COAT-PM measure were all highly consistent with those from Studies 1 and 3. Importantly, these data also indicated significant change over time. Overall, the main effect for time of testing was significant, $F(3, 93) = 5.30$, $p < .01$. Post hoc analyses indicated that children endorsed fewer items as self-descriptive at the end of seventh grade (time 4) than they had at the beginning of sixth grade (time 1). The effect of time of testing was subsumed by an interaction of time of testing and domain, $F(6, 186) = 2.80$, $p < .05$, indicating that children endorsed significantly fewer items in the domain of occupations (but not activities or traits) over time. Finally, there was a significant three-way interaction of time of testing, item gender, and sex of participant, $F(3, 93) = 2.67$, $p < .05$. Post hoc analyses indicated that the greatest drop in self-endorsements came from girls' lower rates of self-endorsement of feminine items between the fall of sixth grade (time 1) and spring of seventh grade (time 4).

Attitudinal pathway regression analyses. As in the previous studies, we used regression analyses to examine the relations among the subscales. Because we had longitudinal data, we were able to conduct both concurrent and prospective analyses of relations among subscales. These analyses are useful because they can indicate whether a pattern of findings is consistent with (albeit cannot prove) a causal model of influence among the variables.

Using separate models for girls and boys, we examined first whether children's scores on the attitude measure (entered separately—COAT-AM, COAT-AM, and COAT-AM—or entered as a single composite score) were predictive of sex typing of the self in each of the three domains. Dependent measures were thus occupation, activity, and trait self-endorsements.

Consistent with the findings from Study 3, models using the composite scores of stereotyping were not significant for either boys or girls. Some of the models using individual subscales (rather than a single composite score) as predictors did produce significant results among girls. (None of the models was significant for boys, however.) Significant findings were limited to masculine (rather than feminine) COAT subscales. Thus, Table 24 reports summaries of the concurrent (time 4 attitudes and time 4 self-endorsements) and prospective (time 1 attitudes and time 4 self-endorsements) models only for girls, and only for the data on masculine subscales.

As shown in the top half of Table 24, results indicated that, for girls, holding egalitarian attitudes toward masculine activities in the spring of seventh grade (time 4) was associated with higher concurrent levels of

TABLE 24

REGRESSION MODELS (CONCURRENT AND PROSPECTIVE) EXAMINING ATTITUDINAL
PREDICTORS OF SEX TYPING OF THE SELF AMONG GIRLS

	Predictors: Concurrent (Time 4)				
	$\beta_{\text{MasCOAT-AM}}$	$\beta_{\text{MasCOAT-AM}}$	$\beta_{\text{MasCOAT-AM}}$	Total R^2	F
Dependent variable (Time 4)					
Mas COAT-PM	.34	**.84**	.23	.31	**5.03**
Mas COAT-PM	.35	**.72**	−.12	.25	**3.65**
Mas COAT-PM	.11	.12	−.01	.04	.50
	Predictors: Prospective (Time 1)				
	$\beta_{\text{MasCOAT-AM}}$	$\beta_{\text{MasCOAT-AM}}$	$\beta_{\text{MasCOAT-AM}}$	Total R^2	F
Dependent variable (Time 4)					
Mas COAT-PM	.28	−.15	.25	.06	.52
Mas COAT-PM	−.06	.10	.08	.02	.17
Mas COAT-PM	.19	−.22	.23	.05	.61

Notes.—C denotes children's scale; underscored O, A, and T indicate occupations, activities, and traits, respectively; AM is attitude measure (attitude toward others); PM is personal measure (sex typing of self). Bold entries indicate significance at $p < .05$.

endorsement of masculine occupations and activities for the self. As evident in the data presented in the bottom half of Table 24, girls' sex typing of masculine occupations, activities, and traits in the beginning of sixth grade (time 1), was not, however, associated with the level of self-endorsement of masculine occupation, activities, or traits in the spring of seventh grade (time 4).

Personal pathway regression analyses. Although previous theorizing has focused on the role of attitudes toward others in shaping sex typing of the self, our longitudinal data also made it possible to test the inverse proposition represented by the personal pathway model discussed earlier. That is, we addressed the question of whether changes in children's responses over time were consistent with (albeit could not prove) the hypothesis that sex typing of the self is causally related to sex typing of others. To do so, we examined whether children's scores on the personal measure (entered separately—COAT-PM, COAT-PM, and COAT-PM—or entered as a single composite score) were predictive of sex typing of others in each of the three domains. For these analyses, dependent measures were occupation, activity, and trait attitude scores.

As was true of the attitudinal pathway analyses, models using the composite scores of sex typing were not significant for either boys or girls.

For girls, models using individual subscales (rather than a single composite score) as predictors also failed to produce significant results. However, for boys, models using individual subscales did show significant effects. These significant findings, which involved both feminine and masculine subscales of the COAT, are thus detailed next.

We begin by describing findings involving the feminine subscales. Summaries for the feminine subscales are reported in Table 25. As may be seen in the top half of Table 25, models that examined the ability of sex typing of the self to predict concurrent (rather than prospective) levels of sex typing of others were not significant. As seen in the bottom half of Table 25, boys' endorsement of feminine traits for self at the beginning of sixth grade (time 1) was, however, associated with lower levels of sex typing of others (i.e., with less gender stereotyping or greater flexibility) in all three domains (occupations, activities, and traits) in the spring of seventh grade (time 4). The patterns observed on the masculine subscales, shown in Table 26, were identical to those for the feminine subscales just described. Again, data support the same conclusions. None of the concurrent relations was significant. Prospective models, however, showed that early higher endorsement of feminine traits for the self (PM scores) was significantly associated with later lower levels of attitudinal

TABLE 25

REGRESSION MODELS (CONCURRENT AND PROSPECTIVE) EXAMINING SELF-ENDORSEMENTS
AS PREDICTORS OF FEMININE SEX TYPING OF OTHERS AMONG BOYS

| | Predictors: Concurrent (Time 4) | | | | |
	$\beta_{\text{FemC}\underline{\text{O}}\text{AT-PM}}$	$\beta_{\text{FemCO}\underline{\text{A}}\text{T-PM}}$	$\beta_{\text{FemCOA}\underline{\text{T}}\text{-PM}}$	Total R^2	F
Dependent variable (Time 4)					
Fem C$\underline{\text{O}}$AT-AM	.08	.07	.12	.04	.46
Fem CO$\underline{\text{A}}$T-AM	.05	.23	.13	.11	1.42
Fem COA$\underline{\text{T}}$-AM	.21	−.12	.22	.06	.78
	Predictors: Prospective (Time 1)				
	$\beta_{\text{FemC}\underline{\text{O}}\text{AT-PM}}$	$\beta_{\text{FemCO}\underline{\text{A}}\text{T-PM}}$	$\beta_{\text{FemCOA}\underline{\text{T}}\text{-PM}}$	Total R^2	F
Dependent variable (Time 4)					
Fem C$\underline{\text{O}}$AT-AM	.13	.19	**.46**	.30	**4.63**
Fem CO$\underline{\text{A}}$T-AM	.20	.17	**.33**	.21	**3.03**
Fem COA$\underline{\text{T}}$-AM	.29	−.02	**.38**	.25	**3.62**

Notes.—C denotes children's scale; underscored O, A, and T indicate occupations, activities, and traits, respectively; AM is attitude measure (attitude toward others); PM is personal measure (sex typing of self). Bold entries indicate significance at $p < .05$.

82

TABLE 26

REGRESSION MODELS (CONCURRENT AND PROSPECTIVE) EXAMINING SELF-ENDORSEMENTS
AS PREDICTORS OF MASCULINE SEX TYPING OF OTHERS AMONG BOYS

	Predictors: Concurrent (Time 4)				
	$\beta_{\text{FemC\underline{O}AT-PM}}$	$\beta_{\text{FemCO\underline{A}T-PM}}$	$\beta_{\text{FemCOA\underline{T}-PM}}$	Total R^2	F
Dependent variable (Time 4)					
Mas C\underline{O}AT-AM	.10	.03	.16	.05	.55
Mas CO\underline{A}T-AM	.01	.16	.16	.07	.82
Mas COA\underline{T}-AM	.17	−.12	.17	.04	.46
	Predictors: Prospective (Time 1)				
	$\beta_{\text{FemC\underline{O}AT-PM}}$	$\beta_{\text{FemCO\underline{A}T-PM}}$	$\beta_{\text{FemCOA\underline{T}-PM}}$	Total R^2	F
Dependent variable (Time 4)					
Mas C\underline{O}AT-AM	.15	.15	**.49**	.32	**5.10**
Mas CO\underline{A}T-AM	.18	.08	**.42**	.24	**3.39**
Mas COA\underline{T}-AM	.30	.02	**.40**	.27	**4.08**

Notes.—C denotes children's scale; underscored O, A, and T indicate occupations, activities, and traits, respectively; AM is attitude measure (attitude toward others); PM is personal measure (sex typing of self). Bold entries indicate significance at $p < .05$

sex typing of the masculine items for all three subscale attitude measures (i.e., C\underline{O}AT-AM, CO\underline{A}T-AM, and COA\underline{T}-AM).

Moderators of relations: Overview. Overall, the relations between sex typing of others and sex typing of the self that we observed via correlations in Studies 1–4, and concurrent regression analyses in Study 5 were relatively weak ones. As explained earlier, however, we had in fact hypothesized that weak relations would be observed under conditions in which data are collapsed across participants and subscales. Importantly, we had also argued that observed relations between sex typing of self and sex typing of others would not vary randomly, but would instead differ systematically as a function of (a) the degree to which the items used to measure attitudes toward others and sex typing of the self were matched with respect to general domain and specific item content, (b) the individual's own level of sex typing; (c) whether items were sex "appropriate" or "inappropriate" for the respondent, and (d) the societal status of the cross-sex-typed items. These hypotheses are difficult to test in a sequential manner, however, because specifying only one type of comparison (e.g., relations among sex typing of self and others for matched vs. unmatched items) necessitates collapsing across other dimensions (e.g., "sex appropriate" vs. "inappropriate" items), thereby obscuring relations.

Thus, to study whether the strengths of the observed relations would vary under the conditions as hypothesized (see Table 1), we examined the contingent relations between children's responses to the two different kinds of questions asked about the identical items. For example, we examined the child's response to the question "Who should be a doctor?" (an item on the COAT-AM) in relation to the child's self-reported interest in being a doctor (an item on the COAT-PM). First, for each individual item, we tested whether or not there was an association between responses on the attitude and personal measures by chi-square analyses. To do so, we dichotomized children's responses on the COAT-AM as either sex-typed or non-sex-typed by differentiating the "both" responses from all others (i.e., collapsing "only men" and "only women" responses). We dichotomized children's responses on the COAT-PM as either self-endorsements or not by differentiating all responses that accepted the item for self (e.g., collapsing "some" and "very much") from those that rejected the item for self (e.g., collapsing "not much" and "not at all").

For any item on which the chi-square test of association was significant, we then examined the data descriptively to consider two contingent relations. One contingency was derived from the attitudinal pathway model and asked: "Given that the child expresses a sex-typed belief about others for this particular item, does the child endorse this same item for self?" The second was derived from the personal pathway model and asked: "Given that the child endorses this particular item for self, does the child give a flexible (non-sex-typed) response when judging the suitability of that same item for others?" These data are then discussed in relation to the hypotheses offered earlier (see Chapter III and Table 1) concerning the conditions under which relations between sex typing of self and sex typing of others would be evident.

Chi-square analyses. Overall, the findings from the analytic approach just described indicated that when children were asked to make judgments for the self and others using the *identical items*, their responses were sometimes, but by no means always, highly related. Of the total number of 147 sex-typed COAT items, 26 showed significant chi-squares. What is initially most striking is that sex typing of self and sex typing of others was not related for the majority of COAT items, despite the fact that the content (each individual item) was identical. It is important to remember, however, that we predicted nonsignificant relations in many instances (e.g., for boys' responses to *all* feminine items). Results pertaining to our predictions about moderators of the strength of association are discussed below. In addition, the opportunity to observe significant associations was reduced because in many cases the low number of children self-endorsing cross-sex items precluded finding significant chi squares.

In many other cases, however, there were adequate numbers of self-endorsements to set the stage for finding relations to attitudes toward others, and yet children's sex typing of others was *not* related in strong, systematic ways to sex typing of self.

Contingency tables. For the 26 items for which the chi-square analyses were significant, descriptive data relevant to the contingency questions outlined above are given in Tables 27–32, organized as follows: (a) occupational items, with data shown from the perspective of the attitudinal pathway model (Table 27) and then from the perspective of the personal pathway model (Table 28); (b) activity items, first attitudinal (Table 29) and then personal (Table 30); and finally (c) trait items, first attitudinal (Table 31) and then personal (Table 32). Parallel data for all remaining items (i.e., items for which chi square results were not significant) are provided in Appendix E, Tables E1–E6. For all tables, the first three columns present data from boys and the second three present data from girls.

For each individual item in each table, what is of primary interest are the entries in data columns 2 and 5 which show the relevant contingency data. The entries in data columns 1 and 4 are included to provide information about the proportion of participants for whom the contingency data (provided in columns 2 and 5) were relevant. The entries in columns 3 and 6 are included to provide a baseline against which to judge the values of the contingency data provided in columns 2 and 5. Thus, to take a single example, consider the attitudinal pathway contingency data shown in Table 27 for the job airline pilot, considered by our culture to be masculine. Among boys, 59% (column 1) responded that "only men" should be airline pilots. Of those boys who answered with this stereotyped response to this particular item, 65% (column 2) said that they, themselves, were interested in being a pilot. However, this percentage is not noticeably different from the percentage of boys who expressed interest in being a pilot but who held flexible beliefs about this occupation. Specifically, of boys who said that "both men and women" should be pilots, 56% expressed a personal interest in the job (column 3). Among girls, however, the pattern of data was very different. The data show that 44% of girls (column 4) responded that "only men" should be airline pilots. Of those girls who answered with this stereotyped response, 0% (column 5) said that they, themselves, were interested in being a pilot. Importantly, this percentage is noticeably different from the percentage of girls holding flexible beliefs about pilots who expressed interest in the occupation. Specifically, of girls who said that "both men and women" should be pilots, 45% (column 6) expressed a personal interest in the job. In the following sections, we comment briefly about the patterns of contingency findings in relation to the factors discussed in Table 1.

TABLE 27
ATTITUDINAL PATHWAY: SIGNIFICANT RELATIONS BETWEEN GENDER ATTITUDES AND PERSONAL INTEREST FOR FEMININE AND MASCULINE OCCUPATIONS

Feminine Jobs	Percentages for Boys			Percentages for Girls		
	Sex-Typed Boys ("only women" should do job)	Sex-Typed Boys Interested in Job	Non-Sex-Typed Boys Interested in Job	Sex-Typed Girls ("only women" should do job)	Sex-Typed Girls Interested in Job	Non-Sex-Typed Girls Interested in Job
babysitter*	51	10	21	80	87	50
elementary school teacher*	31	17	30	38	93	58
hair stylist+	56	0	29	77	67	44
Masculine Jobs	Sex-Typed Boys ("only men" should do job)	Sex-Typed Boys Interested in Job	Non-Sex-Typed Boys Interested in Job	Sex-Typed Girls ("only men" should do job)	Sex-Typed Girls Interested in Job	Non-Sex-Typed Girls Interested in Job
airplane pilot*	59	65	56	44	0	45
architect*	46	44	52	38	7	50
construction worker*	77	33	0	77	3	33
football game broadcaster*	67	50	38	74	3	30
scientist*	41	62	61	28	0	43
soldier*	69	26	33	69	0	50

Notes.—*significant chi-square for girls ($p < .05$). + significant chi-square for boys ($p < .05$).

TABLE 28

PERSONAL PATHWAY: SIGNIFICANT RELATIONS BETWEEN PERSONAL INTEREST AND GENDER ATTITUDES FOR FEMININE AND MASCULINE OCCUPATIONS

Feminine Jobs	Percentages for Boys			Percentages for Girls		
	Boys Interested in Job	Boys Interested in Job Who Have "Both" Attitude	Boys Not Interested in Job Who Have "Both" Attitude	Girls Interested in Job	Girls Interested in Job Who Have "Both" Attitude	Girls Not Interested in Job Who Have "Both" Attitude
babysitter*	15	67	45	80	13	50
elementary school teacher*	26	80	66	72	50	91
hair stylist+	13	100	35	62	17	33

Masculine Jobs	Boys Interested in Job	Boys Interested in Job Who Have "Both" Attitude	Boys Not Interested in Job Who Have "Both" Attitude	Girls Interested in Job	Girls Interested in Job Who Have "Both" Attitude	Girls Not Interested in Job Who Have "Both" Attitude
airplane pilot*	62	38	47	26	100	41
architect*	49	58	50	33	92	46
construction worker*	26	0	31	10	75	17
football game broadcaster*	46	28	38	10	75	20
scientist*	62	58	60	31	100	59
soldier*	28	36	29	10	100	0

Notes.—*significant chi-square for girls ($p < .05$). + significant chi-square for boys ($p < .05$).

TABLE 29

ATTITUDINAL PATHWAY: SIGNIFICANT RELATIONS BETWEEN GENDER ATTITUDES AND PERSONAL INTEREST FOR FEMININE AND MASCULINE ACTIVITIES

Feminine Activities	Percentages for Boys			Percentages for Girls		
	Sex-Typed Boys ("only girls" should do activity)	Sex-Typed Boys Who Engage in Activity	Non-Sex-Typed Boys Who Engage in Activity	Sex-Typed Girls ("only girls" should do activity)	Sex-Typed Girls Who Engage in Activity	Non-Sex-Typed Girls Who Engage in Activity
do gymnastics+	49	5	30	69	26	58
grocery shop+	46	11	43	72	50	64

Masculine Activities	Sex-Typed Boys ("only boys" should do activity)	Sex-Typed Boys Who Engage in Activity	Non-Sex-Typed Boys Who Engage in Activity	Sex-Typed Girls ("only boys" should do activity)	Sex-Typed Girls Who Engage in Activity	Non-Sex-Typed Girls Who Engage in Activity
build forts*	77	67	67	64	4	43
build model planes*	54	48	67	74	3	40
build with tools*	69	59	58	72	18	73
go fishing*	56	45	59	38	13	54
play dodgeball*	26	20	50	24	11	52
play video games+	31	58	93	33	46	62
watch televised sports*	38	67	71	44	6	45
shoot bow & arrow*	59	43	50	69	4	33
watch crime/detective shows*	31	75	67	33	15	62

Notes.—*significant chi-square for girls ($p < .05$). + significant chi-square for boys ($p < .05$).

TABLE 30

PERSONAL PATHWAY: SIGNIFICANT RELATIONS BETWEEN PERSONAL INTEREST AND GENDER ATTITUDES FOR FEMININE AND MASCULINE ACTIVITIES

Feminine Activities	Percentages for Boys			Percentages for Girls		
	Boys Who Engage in Activity	Boys Who Engage in Activity With "Both" Attitude	Boys Who Do Not Engage in Activity With "Both" Attitude	Girls Who Engage in Activity	Girls Who Engage in Activity With "Both" Attitude	Girls Who Do Not Engage in Activity With "Both" Attitude
do gymnastics+	18	86	44	36	50	20
grocery shop+	28	82	43	54	33	22

Masculine Activities	Boys Who Engage in Activity	Boys Who Engage in Activity With "Both" Attitude	Boys Who Do Not Engage in Activity With "Both" Attitude	Girls Who Engage in Activity	Girls Who Engage in Activity With "Both" Attitude	Girls Who Do Not Engage in Activity With "Both" Attitude
build forts*	67	23	23	18	86	25
build model planes*	56	54	35	13	80	18
build with tools*	59	30	31	33	62	12
go fishing*	51	50	37	38	87	46
play dodgeball*	42	88	64	42	94	64
play video games+	82	78	29	56	73	59
watch televised sports*	69	63	58	28	91	43
shoot bow & arrow*	46	44	38	13	80	24
watch crime/detective shows*	69	67	75	46	89	48

Notes.—*significant chi-square for girls ($p < .05$). + significant chi-square for boys ($p < .05$).

TABLE 31

ATTITUDINAL PATHWAY: SIGNIFICANT RELATIONS BETWEEN GENDER ATTITUDES AND PERSONAL INTEREST FOR FEMININE AND MASCULINE TRAITS

Feminine Traits	Percentages for Boys			Percentages for Girls		
	Sex-Typed Boys ("only girls" should have trait)	Sex-Typed Boys Who Endorse Trait	Non-Sex-Typed Boys Who Endorse Trait	Sex-Typed Girls ("only girls" should have trait)	Sex-Typed Girls Who Endorse Trait	Non-Sex-Typed Girls Who Endorse Trait
emotional+	15	14	59	21	38	52
follows directions+	21	38	94	26	70	89
good at English+	21	12	71	31	67	63
have good manners+*	21	25	74	33	62	92
helpful+	15	50	94	21	100	87
sentimental+	34	8	60	41	69	65

Masculine Traits	Sex-Typed Boys ("only boys" should have trait)	Sex-Typed Boys Who Endorse Trait	Non-Sex-Typed Boys Who Endorse Trait	Sex-Typed Girls ("only boys" should have trait)	Sex-Typed Girls Who Endorse Trait	Non-Sex-Typed Girls Who Endorse Trait
confident+	15	33	82	21	75	84
enjoy math+	28	27	71	26	50	66
good at geography+	31	17	56	23	44	23
good at math+	26	40	90	28	82	75
good at sports*	38	93	83	26	30	72

Notes.—*significant chi-square for girls ($p < .05$). + significant chi-square for boys ($p < .05$).

TABLE 32

PERSONAL PATHWAY: SIGNIFICANT RELATIONS BETWEEN PERSONAL INTEREST AND GENDER ATTITUDES
FOR FEMININE AND MASCULINE TRAITS

Feminine Traits	Percentages for Boys			Percentages for Girls		
	Boys Who Endorse Trait for Self	Boys Who Endorse Trait With "Both" Attitude	Boys Who Do Not Endorse Trait With "Both" Attitude	Girls Who Endorse Trait for Self	Girls Who Endorse Trait With "Both" Attitude	Girls Who Do Not Endorse Trait With "Both" Attitude
emotional+	51	95	68	49	84	75
follows directions+	82	91	29	84	78	50
good at English+	59	96	56	64	68	71
have good manners +*	64	92	57	82	75	29
helpful+	87	91	40	90	77	100
sentimental+	42	94	45	67	58	61

Masculine Traits	Boys Who Endorse Trait for Self	Boys Who Endorse Trait With "Both" Attitude	Boys Who Do Not Endorse Trait With "Both" Attitude	Girls Who Endorse Trait for Self	Girls Who Endorse Trait With "Both" Attitude	Girls Who Do Not Endorse Trait With "Both" Attitude
confident+	74	93	60	82	81	71
enjoy math+	59	87	50	62	79	78
good at geography+	44	88	54	28	64	82
good at math+	77	87	33	77	70	67
good at sports*	87	59	80	62	88	53

Note.—*significant chi-square for girls ($p < .05$), + significant chi-square for boys ($p < .05$)

Evidence for moderating factors. As outlined earlier, we expected that sex typing of self and sex typing of others would be related only under certain circumstances. With respect to level of sex typing, we predicted that, within the attitudinal pathway model, stronger relations between sex typing of self and sex typing of others would be found among individuals who endorse a sex-typed belief about a particular item than among individuals who endorse a *non*-sex-typed belief about this same item. As noted in the discussion above on the chi-square analyses, significant associations were found on only a small proportion of the total number of items, but the patterns of associations were consistent with the directions of the relations that we proposed under the attitudinal pathway. Specifically, results indicated that those children holding a gender-stereotyped view about a particular item were indeed more likely than those children holding a flexible view about that item to respond similarly on the attitudinal and self versions of the item. So, for example, as illustrated by the airplane pilot example detailed above and shown by the data in Table 27, girls who endorsed stereotypes of particular masculine occupations were consistently less likely to endorse these same occupations for themselves than were girls who did not endorse stereotypes of these jobs (compare columns 5 and 6 in the bottom half of Table 27).

Within the personal pathway model, we expected to see a close relation between responses to self and other items when individuals showed interest in cross-sex jobs. As predicted, results shown in Table 28 indicated that when individuals endorsed cross-sex gender-stereotypic items for themselves, they were likely to express a flexible attitude about the job for others. In contrast, those who did not express self-interest in a cross-sex job were far less likely to express a flexible attitude about the job for others. Again, the data from the airline pilot example are illustrative. Although only 26% of girls expressed a self-interest in this job, fully 100% of these girls showed a flexible attitude about this job for others. Of girls who did not themselves express an interest in the job, only 41% showed a flexible attitude.

As implied by the previous example, the pattern of results was also consistent with our expectation that the strong relations between sex typing of self and sex typing of others would occur when items are defined by the culture as "inappropriate" for someone of the respondent's sex (what we have labeled as cross-sex-typed items; see Table 1). In the airplane pilot case, for example, the striking difference observed for girls was *not* apparent for boys. As seen in Table 28, 62% of all boys were themselves interested in being a pilot. Of these, only 38% gave a flexible attitudinal response about others (i.e., said that "both men and women" should be pilots). But, similarly, of boys who themselves were *not* interested in being a pilot, 47% gave a flexible attitudinal response. The comparison of 38% and 47% for boys stands in sharp contrast to the comparison of 100% to 41% for girls. In general, the data concerning cross-sex-typed items are more compelling with respect to our initial predictions for girls than for boys (in part because so few boys expressed interest in feminine items; see the discussion below). Nevertheless, among both sexes there was reasonable support for the general hypotheses: There were more than twice as many significant chi-squares for cross-sex-typed items (26) than for same-sex-typed items (11).

Finally, we predicted that the higher status of masculine items would produce stronger relations between sex typing of self and sex typing of others for girls than for boys. Overall, the data presented in the contingency table appear to be consistent with this hypothesis. First, as expected, the level of interest in cross-sex-typed items was higher among girls than among boys. More importantly, the personal pathway tables indicated that girls' level of personal interest in cross-sex-typed items was generally related to their attitudinal sex typing, whereas this was less true for boys. That is, girls who expressed an interest in masculine occupations were much more likely to express an egalitarian than a sex-typed attitude about the particular item. This pattern suggested that a girl's personal interest in pursuing inherently attractive occupations and activities increased the likelihood that she would have flexible beliefs about the propriety of females engaging in this item more generally. As expected, this pattern was less true for boys. In fact, there were 17 significant associations (chi-squares) between self and other response patterns on cross-sex-typed items for girls and only 9 for boys. Although the data suggested weaker relations among boys, these data must be interpreted cautiously because so few boys expressed personal interest in feminine items, and thus there was a far smaller baseline from which to examine the hypothesized relations.

Discussion

The longitudinal data are important in several respects. First, the data provide a bridge between the cross-sectional samples of adults and sixth graders. These data indicate that children do appear to hold increasingly more egalitarian attitudes over time, at least through early adolescence, and help to reduce the possibility that cohort effects are responsible for the greater egalitarianism that had been evident in the adult samples. Interestingly, the period between sixth and seventh grade stood out as a particularly important time for attitude change. Although past investigators (e.g., Alfieri, Ruble, & Higgins, 1996) have suggested that increases in gender flexibility occurring during this period of the life span are linked to school transition rather than to age, the sample of children involved in our current work did *not* change schools between sixth and seventh grades. Thus, the changes we observed cannot be attributed to a change in school context. Additional longitudinal studies that employ parallel scales (such as the COAT and OAT) are needed to disentangle the effects of age versus school transitions on children's gender attitudes.

In contrast to children's beliefs about others, we found that children's sex-typed endorsements for themselves showed relatively little change over time, particularly among boys. Girls self-endorsed slightly fewer feminine items over time during middle childhood. This pattern of findings is similar to that reported by Antill et al. (1996). In their longitudinal study of middle-school age Australian children, boys and girls became more egalitarian in their gender attitudes (over approximately a year and a half), but changed little in their self-endorsement of sex-typed traits and interests. Interestingly, they also reported that girls showed declining interest in feminine occupations over time. This shift may result from middle-school age girls coming to recognize the greater tolerance for females engaged in masculine roles as well as the higher status of masculine roles, a developmental change also suggested in data reported by Liben et al. (2001).

The use of concurrent and prospective regression models reveals interesting differences for girls' and boys' patterns of sex typing. For girls, analyses of concurrent relations indicate that girls who held more egalitarian attitudes toward masculine activities also showed greater interest in masculine occupations, and engaged in more masculine activities. These concurrent relations are compatible with either pathway model. However, prospective analyses provide no evidence for directional effects. Among boys, however, although there was no evidence for concurrent other-self relations, the prospective analyses indicate that boys who self-endorsed greater numbers of feminine traits early in grade 6 went on to develop more egalitarian gender attitudes toward others by the end of grade 7. Little previous research has examined the possibility that gender-related personality traits and interests might play a role in shaping attitudes, but the current findings suggest that this possibility is worthy of additional attention in future research.

The chi-square tests of the association between endorsement of specific items on the other and self scales provide mixed support for our hypotheses concerning factors that moderate the strength of self-other associations discussed in Chapter III (Table 1). It is apparent that the two forms of responding are often—but not always—related. As predicted, the relation between attitudes toward others and sex typing of the self was stronger for cross-sex-typed items than for same-sex-typed items. That is, children who gave egalitarian responses to cross-sex typed items were more likely to endorse those items as self-descriptive than were children who did not give egalitarian responses to cross-sex-typed items. Also consistent with expectations, we found that responses to identical scale items tapping sex typing of self and others were more often related among girls, for whom cross-sex-typed items are high in status, than for boys, for whom cross-sex-typed items are low in status.

In summary, the data from Study 5 converge on the findings from Studies 1 and 3 with respect to the structure of constructs and the relations among them. Further, the findings from Study 5 are useful in examining the factors hypothesized to affect the strength of observed relations between endorsement of items for self and attitudes about items for others. In addition, the longitudinal data offer a number of interesting findings that bear on the attitudinal and personal pathway models proposed earlier.

VI. GENERAL DISCUSSION

LOOKING BACK

The present *Monograph* makes four major kinds of contributions to the study of gender. First, the conceptual analysis of gender measures highlights important methodological issues in the study of gender schemata. Particularly important is the recognition that to study gender schemata developmentally, it is crucial that any observed changes be attributable to changes in psychological constructs rather than to differences in the techniques used to measure them. Our analysis points to several specific qualities of measurement devices that may play an important role: the substantive domain addressed, the target psychological process assessed, the stereotypicality and desirability of masculine and feminine items, the comprehensibility of measures, and the degree to which individual items are appropriate for participants of different ages.

Second, our presentation of the attitudinal and personal pathway models draws attention to alternative routes by which gender attitudes may affect, and be affected by, individuals' self schemata and behaviors. Particularly important is the explicit suggestion that individuals' idiosyncratic interests may lead to certain experiences that, in turn, lead to the establishment or revision of gender-related cognitions. Although additional work is needed to develop and test these models in more detail, they have already proven useful here for exploring the developmental course of gender differentiation.

Third, our empirical findings are relevant to evaluating and extending theoretical positions concerning the structure of gender schemata in children and adults (e.g., Bem, 1981; Spence, 1993), and the development of relations between sex typing of others and sex typing of the self (Bem, 1981; Bussey & Bandura, 1992; Martin & Halverson, 1981).

Fourth, the current series of studies contributes to the study of the development of gender schemata by providing a suite of measures that serve purposes not already served by other scales. In addition to their value for future theoretical work, these scales and associated data are valuable for designing and evaluating interventions to reduce gender stereotyping of others, and to increase the options (e.g., career choices) considered by individuals for themselves.

SELECTED HIGHLIGHTS

With respect to the structure of gender schemata, the present studies provide further support for the position that gender schemata are not unitary constructs, but are instead multifactorial and multidimensional. Specifically, the present studies found support for the conceptual distinction among individuals' (a) sex typing of others, or gender attitudes; (b) self-endorsement of traditionally feminine items (i.e., occupations, activities, and traits); and (c) self-endorsement of traditionally masculine items. Importantly, this distinction appeared in both children and adults, and across ethnically and racially diverse samples. This three-factor model of gender schemata is highly consistent with Spence's (1993) model of gender schemata. The finding that there is a major differentiation in gender schemata between attitudes toward others and endorsements for the self is also consistent with previous developmental research on gender (e.g., Antill et al., 1993; Bigler & Liben, 1990; Katz & Ksansnak, 1994; Katz & Walsh, 1991; Serbin et al., 1993). The current data are important in demonstrating that the independence observed in prior work is not due to differences in the methods used to assess attitudes about others across domains and across targets.

Importantly, masculine and feminine items emerged as separate components of gender schemata, but they were distinct only in relation to self-endorsements. This suggests that attitudes toward gender encompass beliefs about both males and females, but that masculinity and femininity retain important differences with respect to the self. Spence (1984, 1993) has argued that individuals' sense of masculinity versus femininity originates in childhood and that this core sense of self identity gradually becomes blended with certain characteristics that are deemed "sex appropriate." She argued, however, that although the core sense of gender identity remains stable and unchanged, individuals' sex-typed and non-sex-typed traits and interests can vary over time in a manner orthogonal to gender identity. The finding here that self-endorsements of "sex appropriate" items were occasionally positively correlated with the endorsements of "sex inappropriate" items is consistent with Spence's argument that gender-incongruent characteristics do not necessarily detract from individuals' sense of "traditional" masculinity or femininity or their tendency to adopt gender-congruent characteristics (Spence, 1984, 1993).

97

Although gender role attitudes about others, in general, do seem to be distinct from personal characteristics and roles, our studies showed very high consistency among children's and adults' *attitudes* across domains and across masculine and feminine items. Of the total of 120 possible correlations among the attitude subscales (15 each for males and females, across the four studies), 118 were statistically significant. This consistent pattern is supportive of Bem's argument that individuals hold generally conventional or generally nonconventional attitudes about the relation of gender to traits and roles in society. Overall, individuals tend to believe either that gender should be a criterion for limiting individuals' attributes and behaviors or that men and women should adopt similar roles and attributes in society. Correlations were particularly high between attitudes toward occupations and attitudes toward activities. Together with the data on absolute values (i.e., means), these correlational data suggest that individuals today are less likely to differentiate between the sexes with respect to personality traits than they are with respect to occupations and activities.

In contrast to the high consistency across responding to the attitude scales (i.e., within the OAT-AM and COAT-AM), considerable variation was evident in responses to the personal measure scales (i.e., within the OAT-PM and COAT-PM). That is, there was considerable variation within individuals' self-endorsements of gender-related items from different domains and across masculine and feminine items. Correlations among the subscales of the personal measure indicate that self-endorsement of masculine items in one domain were frequently positively correlated with self-endorsement of feminine items in that same and other domains. At the same time, there were many significant correlations among the same-sex-typed subscales across domains (e.g., masculine OAT-PM and masculine OAT-PM). Antill et al. (1996) reported a highly similar pattern of findings among middle-school age Australian children.

In a finding parallel to that just discussed for the attitude scale, both children and adults were less likely to differentiate between masculine and feminine traits than they were to discriminate between masculine and feminine occupations and activities. Specifically, both men and women showed very high rates of endorsing masculine and feminine trait items. There are several possible explanations for this finding. It is possible, for example, that the selected trait items are less strongly associated with gender than are the occupation and activity items, a possibility that should be explored in future work using alternative traits. A second possibility is that cultural stereotypes of traits have weakened in recent years more than have cultural stereotypes of roles, and that males and females have converged in their personal characteristics. It is also possible that instrumental and expressive personality traits are increasingly in demand for both males and females, causing the gender stereotyping of traits to decline. Consistent with these possibilities, Spence and Buckner (2000) recently reported that sex differences in the self-endorsement of instrumental personality traits have declined since the 1970s and are now quite modest.

With respect to theoretical questions about the role of sex typing of others in shaping sex typing of the self, the current data suggest several interesting findings. Most prominent constructivist theories suggest that sex typing of others shapes the development of sex-typed interests for the self. If such is the case, children's and adults' attitudes should be predictive of their self-endorsements. Interestingly, the patterns of our empirical data differed for females and males.

Among girls and women, concurrent measures of sex typing showed that girls who held fewer stereotypes of masculine activities and women who held fewer stereotypes overall showed greater self-endorsement of masculine items. Although these findings are consistent with the attitudinal pathway model, they are equally consistent with the personal pathway model. Prospective analyses, however, provided no evidence that preadolescents' gender attitudes were predictive of self-endorsements at subsequent times (nor for the reverse pathway). Additional longitudinal research is clearly necessary in order to establish the pathway through which the association between sex typing of the self and others in girls and women comes about.

Data for the boys showed a strikingly different pattern. Of particular importance is the finding that prospective analyses indicated that preadolescent boys who endorsed greater numbers of feminine traits as self-descriptive in sixth grade went on to develop increasingly egalitarian gender attitudes by the end of seventh grade. To our knowledge, this is the first study that has looked longitudinally at whether sex-typed personality traits are linked to later gender attitudes, and thus the current data must be interpreted cautiously. A search of the literature did, however, reveal one study that reported a related finding. Lobel (1994) examined fifth- and sixth-grade children's judgments about peers who engaged in gender stereotypic versus counterstereotypic behavior. Respondents' judgments of the peer's likeability varied as a function of the gender "appropriateness" of the target's behavior, but also as a function of the children's personality characteristics, as assessed by the Bem Sex Role Inventory (Bem, 1974). Boys who endorsed high numbers of feminine traits (and low numbers of masculine traits) were significantly more positive toward the counterstereotypic target than were all other groups of participants (including masculine boys, masculine girls, undifferentiated girls, and so on).

The finding that self-endorsement of cross sex-typed traits predicts gender attitudes only among boys is extremely interesting. The available data generally support the contention that sex-typed beliefs about others are held more strongly by males than females, and that males receive more negative feedback when they themselves violate gender-stereotypic expectations (see Maccoby, 1998). This combination of rigid beliefs and more severe consequences for cross-sex-typed behavior suggests that an individual's tendency to violate gender-stereotypic expectations may be a more salient—and troubling—characteristic for males than for females. It seems likely that psychological conflict (or cognitive dissonance) is produced when males endorse cross-sex-typed items as self-descriptive. For example, a boy who endorses an item such as "sentimental" as characteristic of himself, and yet holds the view that "only girls should be sentimental" would be expected to experience discomfort when this contradiction is made salient. Importantly, this cognitive dissonance could be reduced by changing one's own personality traits, or by revising one's belief that such traits are only appropriate for females. It seems likely that the latter is more easily achieved, and may account for the pattern of findings in Study 5.

The finding that it is boys' self-endorsement of feminine traits that is *uniquely* predictive of gender attitudes is also interesting. As discussed earlier, the trait domain was the least likely of the three domains that we tested to show differential patterns of endorsement of males and females, and to tap sex-typed attitudes. If used alone, the trait scale is, therefore, likely to underestimate levels of sex typing of self and sex typing of others. At the same time, the trait subscale of the personal measure was unique in its ability to predict boys' development of more egalitarian gender attitudes over time. Again, this finding may be related to the greater constraints placed on boys' expression of counterstereotypic characteristics and roles. Given that adults and peers are only moderately likely to stereotype traits (relative to activities and occupations) as appropriate for only one sex, this may be the domain in which counterstereotypic self-endorsements can most easily appear. The recognition that such traits characterize oneself might, therefore, lead boys to develop egalitarian beliefs, or to revise previously held sex-typed beliefs, over time.

In addition to providing longitudinal data bearing on attitudinal and personal pathway models, we tested four specific hypotheses about the conditions under which the relation between sex typing of the self and sex typing of others would be differentially strong. Specifically, we predicted that those individuals with higher versus lower sex typing should show differing strengths of self-other relations, with links strongest when content is identical, and when items are both cross-sex-typed and high in status. The data on responses to identical items on the two scales suggest that relations are often consistent with predictions. For example, girls who endorsed stereotypes about particular masculine occupations were less likely to be personally interested in these same occupations than girls who did not endorse stereotypes. As predicted, significant relations were found more often for cross-sex-typed than same-sex-typed domains, and among girls, for whom cross-sex-typed items are generally higher in status.

At the same time, many COAT items show a lack of relation between self and other scales. For example, eight girls in the longitudinal sample reported that "only men" should be doctors, but six of these same girls reported that they themselves were interested in becoming a doctor. In a parallel example drawn from the personal pathway contingent analysis, 22 girls reported themselves to be strong, but nearly a third of these same girls (7) stated that "only boys" should be strong. Several explanations for such discrepancies seem possible. For example, it is possible that the development of gender-related beliefs about self and others occurs without the constraints of fully logical reasoning—at least for much of childhood. In other words, most researchers have assumed that the child is logical in applying gender-related beliefs to the self, as, for example, in reasoning: "Trucks are for boys. I am a girl. Therefore, I will not play with this truck." It is possible, however, that age-related limitations in logical reasoning may allow children to simultaneously believe that some behaviors are appropriate only for children of the other sex and yet engage in these seemingly inappropriate behaviors themselves without noticing the logical contradiction. Consistent with this notion, Martin et al. (1995) reported that preschool children showed relatively high levels of interest in toys that were explicitly labeled as appropriate for the other sex (although, overall, their interest levels were lower than when toys were labeled for the child's own sex). The data presented here extend earlier findings by showing that self interest in a cross-sex-typed item sometimes characterizes children who personally endorse the belief that the same item is appropriate only for children of the other gender.

The recognition, and elimination, of such discrepancies should increase with age. This notion is consistent with the finding that boys of middle-school age showed longitudinal change in the direction of increasing consistency of self and other beliefs. That is, boys' endorsement of cross-sex-typed traits for self at the beginning of sixth grade was associated with increasingly egalitarian gender attitudes toward others late in the seventh grade. Discrepancies between gender attitudes toward others and endorsements for the self may, however, remain common across childhood and even adulthood, especially when individuals are strongly motivated to endorse some belief or behavior (e.g., because it is highly valued), and when the discrepancy is not necessarily made salient by the environment. Obviously, this finding is novel to the field and future research is needed to determine its reliability. It is our hope that this preliminary work on conditions associated with self and others will lead researchers to

101

address the question of when and why—not simply whether—sex typing of self and sex typing of others are related.

At the applied level, the studies reported here are useful in contributing reliable and valid measures of sex typing that have parallel forms for both children and adults. Evidence from the analyses of variance and from the factor analyses presented in the empirical studies indicates that the OAT and COAT scales have both discriminant and predictive validity. Discriminant validity is suggested by the finding of consistent, interpretable factors reflecting individuals' differentiation among gender attitudes concerning others, masculine roles and qualities, and feminine roles and qualities. Predictive validity is suggested by the consistency of the sex of participant and item gender effects with those predicted by theories of gender schemata structure and the extant literature on sex typing.

LOOKING FORWARD

Our ongoing work is directed to assessing the validity and reliability of the COAT scales for younger elementary-school children, and to developing valid and reliable versions of the scales for preschool children and for children with limited English skills. To date, the COAT-AM has been used successfully with children in elementary-school grades (Krogh, 1997), and pictorial versions of both attitude and self measures (POAT-AM and POAT-PM) have been used successfully with young deaf children (Lewkowicz, 1995) and with preschool children (Johnston, 1997).

The availability of the OAT-AM/PM and COAT-AM/PM scales should enhance the methodologies available for the study of gender. Understanding the relations among components of gender schemata and external predictors of these components has been severely hindered by the lack of measures tapping sex typing across domains and targets using a consistent format, and one that is suitable for both adults and children. The very high correlations among the subscales of the OAT-AM and COAT-AM (attitude measures) now allow researchers to make use of just one short subscale as a reliable means of tapping individuals' general sex typing of others (i.e., the belief that gender should constrain individuals' traits, activities, and occupational roles). The strong correlations across subscales will also make the OAT-AM and COAT-AM scales particularly useful in certain types of research. For example, separate subscales could be used to test whether an intervention that successfully changes attitudes in one domain (e.g., occupations) has generalized effects on another domain (e.g., activities).

The current studies also have important implications for designing interventions to reduce gender stereotypic beliefs and behavior. Previous

102

researchers have often attempted to change children's gender attitudes with the hope of affecting their gender-related behaviors (e.g., see Liben & Bigler, 1987), peer preferences (e.g., Serbin, Tonick, & Sternglanz, 1977), and occupational goals (e.g., Bigler & Liben, 1990). Although some investigators have successfully effected change with respect to children's gender attitudes toward others, most have failed to effect change with respect to children's beliefs, interests, or behaviors about themselves. For example, an intervention program designed by Bigler and Liben (1990) had a significant impact on young children's responses to a gender attitude measure about the occupations that men and women should have, but had no discernable effect on their reported interests in occupations for themselves.

The current data help to explain this pattern of effects by suggesting that attitudinal schemata are distinct from sex-typed self characteristics and, thus, changes in an individual's attitudes concerning others should not be expected to affect an individual's sex-typed beliefs or behaviors concerning the self. These data suggest, however, that interventions motivated by the inverse (personal) pathway might be effective, at least among boys. For example, given the pattern of findings with respect to boys' self-endorsement of feminine traits, it may be that encouraging young boys to incorporate traditionally feminine traits such as being affectionate and gentle would have the long-term consequence of increasing their later tolerance for nontraditional behaviors in others (e.g., expanding the range of occupations that they believe *should* be done by both men and women). In turn, such beliefs could be expected to increase boys' later ability to process and remember counterstereotypic encounters (e.g., understanding and remembering that a boy's female dentist is, indeed, a dentist rather than a dental assistant). Although it might be at odds with society's general tendency to discourage boys from taking on feminine attributes, evaluation of the impact of interventions aimed at increasing cross-sex-typed traits and behaviors could serve as a much needed experimental test of the hypothesized role of self-endorsements in shaping gender attitudes.

Before closing, we believe that it is important to draw attention to the absence of direct assessments of cognitive variables in the studies reported here. This was a practical rather than a conceptual oversight. We have argued elsewhere (e.g., see Bigler & Liben, 1990, 1992; Liben & Bigler, 1987; Liben & Signorella, 1980; Signorella & Liben, 1984) for the importance of direct assessments of those characteristics thought to be relevant for the target construct. Although chronological age at the group level often serves successfully as a marker for differences in relevant characteristics (e.g., classification reasoning; see Bigler & Liben, 1992), it does so only imperfectly at the individual level. Furthermore, many other characteristics

103

co-vary with chronological age, and thus there may be multiple reasons for an age-related change in some target outcome. Our hope is that future investigators will be able to make use of the COAT sex-typing measures in conjunction with individual cognitive-developmental measures to learn more about the mechanisms by which the observed developmental changes occur.

A similar point must be made with respect to the absence of a direct measure of sex-typed behavior. We began this *Monograph* with a discussion of gender differentiation and the many sex differences that can be observed in the behaviors of males and females. Despite this, the scales that we have developed rely entirely on self-report measures of interests and behaviors, rather than on observations of behaviors by disinterested observers. Ultimately it will be important to study the links between attitudes and actual behaviors, but as a first step it is important to study links even between the two kinds of self reports. Furthermore, when working from a constructivist position, self-perceptions can be important even when they are not perfectly linked to observable behaviors.

In summary, although there is still much work to be done, our research documents a number of compelling relations that bear on current gender theories of gender differentiation, and suggests routes that may be useful for planning and evaluating interventions. Most immediately and most importantly, our data demonstrate the effectiveness of the COAT and OAT scales for investigating gender issues from childhood through adulthood. Work in progress using similar scales with younger and older age groups suggests that we may soon have an integrated set of measures that can be used effectively to study the development of gender attitudes and behaviors across the entire life course. Measures of this kind should prove invaluable as we join the authors of best-selling books in trying to understand "how we are different," "why we are different," and "what we can do about it."

REFERENCES

AAUW Report. (1992). *How schools shortchange girls: A study of major findings on girls and education.* Washington, DC: American Association of University Women Educational Foundation.

AAUW Report. (1998). *Separated by sex: A critical look at single-sex education for girls.* Washington, DC: American Association of University Women Educational Foundation.

Ajzen, I., & Fishbein, M. (1973). Attitudinal and normative variables as predictors of specific behaviors. *Journal of Personality and Social Psychology, 27,* 41–57.

Ajzen, I., & Fishbein, M. (1977). Attitude-behavior relations: A theoretical analysis and review of empirical research. *Psychological Bulletin, 84,* 888–918.

Alfieri, T., Ruble, D. N., & Higgins, E. T. (1996). Gender stereotypes during adolescence: Developmental changes and the transition to junior high school. *Developmental Psychology, 32,* 1129–1137.

American Medical Association. (2001, April 11). *Women in medicine data source.* Retrieved December 11, 2001, from http//www.ama-assn.org/ama/pub/article/171-195.html

Antill, J. K., Cotton, S., Russell, G., & Goodnow, J. J. (1996). Measures of children's sex-typing in middle childhood II. *Australian Journal of Psychology, 48,* 35–44.

Antill, J. K., Russell, G., Goodnow, J. J., & Cotton, S. (1993). Measures of children's sex typing in middle childhood. *Australian Journal of Psychology, 45,* 25–33.

Aubry, S., Ruble, D. N., & Silverman, L. B. (1999). The role of gender knowledge in children's gender-typed preferences. In L. Balter & C. Tamis-LeMonda (Eds.), *Child psychology: A handbook of contemporary issues* (pp. 363–390). Philadelphia: Psychology Press.

Bandura, A. (1977). *Social learning theory.* Englewood Cliffs, NJ: Prentice-Hall.

Bandura, A., Ross, D., & Ross, S. A. (1961). Transmission of aggression through imitation of aggressive models. *Journal of Abnormal and Social Psychology, 63,* 575–582.

Barkley, R. A., Ullman, D. G., Otto, L., & Brecht, J. M. (1977). The effects of sex typing and sex appropriateness of modeled behavior on children's imitation. *Child Development, 48,* 721–725.

Beere, C. A. (1990). *Gender roles: A handbook of tests and measures.* New York: Greenwood.

Bem, S. L. (1974). The measurement of psychological androgyny. *Journal of Consulting and Clinical Psychology, 42,* 155–162.

Bem, S. L. (1979). Theory and measurement of androgyny: A reply to the Pedhazur-Tetenbaum and Locksley-Colten critiques. *Journal of Personality and Social Psychology, 37,* 1047–1054.

Bem, S. L. (1981). Gender schema theory: A cognitive account of sex typing. *Psychological Review, 88,* 354–364.

Bem, S. L., & Bem, D. J. (1973). Does sex-biased advertising "aid and abet" sex discrimination? *Journal of Applied Social Psychology, 3,* 6–18.

Bentler, P. G., & Bonett, D. G. (1980). Significance test and goodness of fit in the analysis of covariance structures. *Psychological Bulletin*, **88**, 588–606.

Berenbaum, S. A., & Hines, M. (1992). Early androgens are related to childhood sex-typed toy preferences. *Psychological Science*, **3**, 203–206.

Biernat, M. (1991). A multicomponent, developmental analysis of sex typing. *Sex Roles*, **24**, 567–586.

Bigler, R. S. (1995). The role of classification skill in moderating environmental influences on children's gender stereotyping: A study of the functional use of gender in the classroom. *Child Development*, **66**, 1072–1087.

Bigler, R. S., & Liben, L. S. (1990). The role of attitudes and interventions in gender-schematic processing. *Child Development*, **61**, 1440–1452.

Bigler, R. S., & Liben, L. S. (1992). Cognitive mechanisms in children's gender stereotyping: Theoretical and educational implications of a cognitive-based intervention. *Child Development*, **63**, 1351–1363.

Boldizar, J. P. (1991). Assessing sex typing and androgyny in children: The Children's Sex Role Inventory. *Developmental Psychology*, **27**, 505–515.

Breckler, S. J. (1990). Applications of covariance structure modeling in psychology: Cause for concern? *Psychological Bulletin*, **107**, 260–273.

Bussey, K., & Bandura, A. (1992). Self-regulatory mechanisms governing gender development. *Child Development*, **63**, 1236–1250.

Bussey, K., & Bandura, A. (1999). Social cognitive theory of gender development and differentiation. *Psychological Review*, **106**, 676–713.

Bussey, K., & Perry, D. G. (1982). Same-sex imitation: The avoidance of cross-sex models or the acceptance of same-sex models? *Sex Roles*, **8**, 773–784.

Calvert, S. L., & Huston, A. C. (1987). Television and children's gender schemata. In L. S. Liben & M. L. Signorella (Eds.), *New directions for child development: Vol. 38. Children's gender schemata* (pp. 75–88). San Francisco: Jossey-Bass.

Carmines, E. G., & McIver, J. P. (1981). Analyzing models with unobserved variables: Analysis of covariance structures. In G. W. Bohrnstedt & E. F. Borgatta (Eds.), *Social measurement: Current issues*. Beverly Hills, CA: Sage.

Carter, D. B., & Levy, G. D. (1988). Cognitive aspects of early sex-role development: The influence of gender schemas on preschoolers' memories and preferences for sex-typed toys and activities. *Child Development*, **59**, 782–793.

Casey, M. B. (1996). Understanding individual differences in spatial ability within females: A nature/nurture interactionist framework. *Developmental Review*, **16**, 241–260.

Collaer, M. L., & Hines, M. (1995). Human behavioral sex differences: A role for gonadal hormones during early development? *Psychological Bulletin*, **118**, 55–107.

Cordua, G. D., McGraw, K. O., & Drabman, R. S. (1979). Doctor or nurse: Children's perceptions of sex typed occupations. *Child Development*, **50**, 590–593.

Cosmides, L., & Tooby, J. (1994). Origins of domain specificity: The evolution of functional organization. In L. A. Hirschfeld & S. A. Gelman (Eds.), *Mapping the mind: Domain specificity in cognition and culture* (pp. 85–116). New York: Cambridge University Press.

Deaux, K., Kite, M. E., & Lewis, L. (1985). Clustering and gender schema: An uncertain link. *Personality and Social Psychology Bulletin*, **11**, 387–397.

Deaux, K., & Major, B. (1987). Putting gender into context: An interactive model of gender-related behavior. *Psychological Review*, **94**, 369–389.

DeVries, R. (1974). Relationship among Piagetian, IQ, and achievement assessments. *Child Development*, **45**, 746–756.

Downs, A. C., & Langlois, J. H. (1988). Sex-typing: Construct and measurement issues. *Sex Roles*, **18**, 87–100.

Eccles, J. S., Jacobs, J. E., & Harold, R. D. (1990). Gender role stereotypes, expectancy effects, and parents' socialization of gender differences. *Journal of Social Issues, 46,* 183–201.

Edelbrock, C., & Sugawara, A. I. (1978). Acquisition of sex-typed preferences in preschool-aged children. *Developmental Psychology, 14,* 614–623.

Edwards, V. J., & Spence, J. T. (1987). Gender-related traits, stereotypes, and schemata. *Journal of Personality and Social Psychology, 53,* 146–154.

Evatt, C. (1993). *Opposite sides of the bed: A lively guide to the differences between women and men.* Berkeley, CA: Conan Press.

Fagot, B. I., & Hagan, R. (1991). Observations of parent reactions to sex-stereotyped behaviors: Age and sex effects. *Child Development, 62,* 617–628.

Fagot, B. I., & Leinbach, M. D. (1989). The young child's gender schema: Environmental input, internal organization. *Child Development, 60,* 663–672.

Fazio, H. R., Powell, M. C., & Herr, P. M. (1983). Toward a process model of the attitude-behavior relation: Assessing one's attitude upon mere observation of the attitude object. *Journal of Personality and Social Psychology, 44,* 723–735.

Fishbein, M., & Ajzen, I. (1974). Attitudes towards objects as predictors of single and multiple behavioral criteria, *Psychological Review, 81,* 59–74.

Fitch, R. H., & Bimonte, H. A. (2002). Hormones, brain, and behavior: Putative biological contributions to cognitive sex differences. In A. McGillicuddy-De Lisi & R. De Lisi (Eds.), *Biology, society, and behavior* (pp. 55–91). Westport, CT: Ablex.

Galambos, N. L., Almeida, D. M., & Petersen, A. C. (1990). Masculinity, femininity and sex role attitudes in early adolescence: Exploring gender intensification. *Child Development, 61,* 1905–1914.

Galambos, N. L., Petersen, A. C., Richards, M., & Gitelson, I. B. (1985). The Attitudes Toward Women Scale for Adolescents (AWSA): A study of reliability and validity. *Sex Roles, 13,* 343–356.

Gaulin, S. J. C. (1993). How and why sex differences evolve, with spatial ability as a paradigm example. In M. Haug, R. E. Whalen, C. Aron, & K. L. Olsen (Eds.), *The development of sex differences and similarities in behavior* (pp. 111–130). Dordrecht: Kluwer Academic Publishers.

Geary, D. C. (2002). Sexual selection and sex differences in social cognition. In A. McGillicuddy-De Lisi & R. De Lisi (Eds.), *Biology, society, and behavior* (pp. 23–53). Westport, CT: Ablex.

Golombok, S., & Fivush, R. (1994). *Gender development.* New York: Cambridge University Press.

Gottlieb, G. (1997). *Synthesizing nature-nurture.* Mahwah, NJ: Lawrence Erlbaum Associates.

Gottlieb, G., Wahlsten, D., & Lickliter, R. (1998). The significance of biology for human development: A developmental psychobiological systems view. In W. Damon (Series Ed.) & R. M. Lerner (Vol. Ed.), *Handbook of child psychology, Vol. 1. Theoretical models of human development* (5th ed., pp. 233–273). New York: Wiley.

Gray, J. (1992). *Men are from Mars, women are from Venus: A practical guide for improving communication and getting what you want in your relationships.* New York: HarperCollins.

Hall, J. A., & Halberstadt, A. G. (1980). Masculinity and femininity in children: Development of the Children's Personal Attributes Questionnaire. *Developmental Psychology, 16,* 270–280.

Halpern, D. F. (2000). *Sex differences in cognitive abilities* (3rd ed.). Hillsdale, NJ: Erlbaum.

Halpern, D. F. (in press). Sex differences in achievement scores: Can we design assessments that are fair, meaningful, and valid for girls and boys? *Issues in Education.*

Hewlett, B. S. (1991). *Intimate fathers: The nature and context of Aka Pygmy paternal infant care.* Ann Arbor: University of Michigan Press.

Hill, J. P., & Lynch, M. E. (1983). The intensification of gender-related role expectations during early adolescence. In J. Brooks-Gunn & A. C. Petersen (Eds.), *Girls at puberty: Biological and social perspectives.* (pp. 201–228). New York: Plenum.

Hines, M. (2000). Gonadal hormones and sexual differentiation of human behavior: Effects on psychosexual and cognitive development. In A. Matsumoto (Ed.), *Sexual differentiation of the brain* (pp. 257–278). Boca Raton, FL: CRC Press.

Hochschild, A. (1989). *The second shift: Working parents and the revolution at home.* New York: Viking/Penguin.

Hort, B. E., Leinbach, M. D., & Fagot, B. I. (1991). Is there coherence among the cognitive components of gender acquisition? *Sex Roles,* **24,** 195–207.

Huston, A. C. (1983). Sex-typing. In P. H. Mussen (Series Ed.) & E. M. Hetherington (Vol. Ed.), *Handbook of child psychology: Vol. 4. Socialization, personality, and social development* (3rd ed., pp. 387–467). New York: Wiley.

Hyde, J. S. (1984). Children's understanding of sexist language. *Developmental Psychology,* **20,** 697–706.

Jacobs, J. A. (1989). *Revolving doors: Sex segregation and women's careers.* Palo Alto, CA: Stanford University Press.

Jacobs, J. A., & Powell, B. (1985). Occupational prestige: A sex-neutral concept. *Sex Roles,* **12,** 1061–1071.

Johnston, K. (1997). *Influences on preschoolers' toy preferences for the self and others: Evidence for a multifactorial gender schema model.* Unpublished master's thesis, Pennsylvania State University.

Jöreskog, K. C., & Sörbom, D. (1984). *LISREL VI: Analysis of linear structural relationships by the method of maximum likelihood.* Chicago: National Educational Resources.

Katz, P. A. (1986). Modification of children's gender-stereotyped behavior: General issues and research considerations. *Sex Roles,* **14,** 591–601.

Katz, P. A., & Ksansnak, K. R. (1994). Developmental aspects of gender role flexibility and traditionality in middle childhood and adolescence. *Developmental Psychology,* **30,** 272–282.

Katz, P. A., & Walsh, P. V. (1991). Modification of children's gender-stereotyped behavior. *Child Development,* **62,** 338–351.

Kimura, D. (1999). *Sex and cognition.* Cambridge, MA: MIT Press.

Kohlberg, L. A. (1966). A cognitive-developmental analysis of children's sex role concepts and attitudes. In E. E. Maccoby (Ed.), *The development of sex differences* (pp. 82–173). Stanford, CA: Stanford University Press.

Krogh, H. R. (1997). *The role of gender-stereotyped attitudes in children's reward allocations.* Unpublished master's thesis, Pennsylvania State University.

Langlois, J. H., & Downs, A. C. (1980). Mothers, fathers, and peers as socialization agents of sex-typed play behavior in young children. *Child Development,* **51,** 1237–1247.

Leaper, C. (2000). Gender, affiliation, assertion, and the interactive context of parent-child play. *Developmental Psychology,* **36,** 381–393.

Leaper, C., Anderson, K. J., & Sanders, P. (1998). Moderators of gender effects on parents' talk to their children: A meta-analysis. *Developmental Psychology,* **34,** 3–27.

Lerner, R. M. (1998). Theories of human development: Contemporary perspectives. In W. Damon (Series Ed.) & R. M. Lerner (Vol. Ed.), *Handbook of child psychology, Vol. 1. Theoretical models of human development* (5th ed., pp. 1–24). New York: Wiley.

Lerner, R. M., Lerner, J. V., & von Eye, A. (1992). *Replication and extension of the Pennsylvania Early Adolescent Transitions Study* (HD23229). Washington, DC: National Institute of Child Health and Human Development.

Levy, G. D. (1989). Developmental and individual differences in preschoolers' recognition memories: The influence of gender schematization and verbal labeling of information. *Sex Roles*, **21**, 305–324.

Levy, G. D., Sadovsky, A. L., & Troseth, G. L. (2000). Aspects of young children's perceptions of gender-typed occupations. *Sex Roles*, **42**, 993–1006.

Lewkowicz, C. J. (1995). *Maternal predictors of deaf and hearing children's sex-role stereotypes.* Unpublished doctoral dissertation, Pennsylvania State University.

Liben, L. S. (1991). The Piagetian water-level task: Looking beneath the surface. In R. Vasta (Ed.), *Annals of Child Development* (Vol. 8, pp. 81–143). London: Jessica Kingsley.

Liben, L. S. (in press). The drama of sex differences in academic achievement: And the show goes on. *Issues in Education*.

Liben, L. S., & Bigler, R. S. (1987). Reformulating children's gender schemata. In L. S. Liben & M. L. Signorella (Eds.), *New directions for child development: Vol. 38. Children's gender schemata* (pp. 89–105). San Francisco: Jossey-Bass.

Liben, L. S., Bigler, R. S., & Krogh, H. R. (2001). Pink and blue collar jobs: Children's judgments of job status and job aspirations in relation to sex of worker. *Journal of Experimental Child Psychology*, **79**, 346–363.

Liben, L. S., Bigler, R. S., & Krogh, H. R. (2002). Language at work: Children's gendered interpretation of occupational titles. *Child Development*, **73**, 810–828.

Liben, L. S., & Signorella, M. L. (1980). Gender-related schemata and constructive memory in children. *Child Development*, **51**, 11–18.

Liben, L. S., & Signorella, M. L. (Eds.). (1987). *New directions for child development: Vol. 38. Children's gender schemata.* San Francisco: Jossey-Bass.

Liben, L. S., & Signorella, M. L. (1993). Gender-schematic processing in children: The role of initial interpretations of stimuli. *Developmental Psychology*, **29**, 141–149.

Liben, L. S., Susman, E. J., Finkelstein, J. W., Chinchilli, V. M., Kunselman, S. J., Schwab, J., et al. (2002). The effects of sex steroids on spatial performance: A review and an experimental clinical investigation. *Developmental Psychology*, **38**, 236–253.

Linn, M. C., & Petersen, A. C. (1985). Emergence and characterization of sex differences in spatial ability: A meta-analysis. *Child Development*, **56**, 1479–1498.

Lobel, T. E. (1994). Sex typing and the social perception of gender stereotypic and nonstereotypic behavior: The uniqueness of feminine males. *Journal of Personality and Social Psychology*, **66**, 379–385.

Lytton, H., & Romney, D. M. (1991). Parents' differential socialization of boys and girls: A meta-analysis. *Psychological Bulletin*, **109**, 267–296.

Maccoby, E. E. (1998). *The two sexes: Growing up apart, coming together.* Cambridge, MA: Harvard University Press.

Marcus, D. E., & Overton, W. F. (1978). The development of cognitive gender constancy and sex role preferences. *Child Development*, **49**, 434–444.

Marsh, H. W., Balla, J. R., & McDonald, R. P. (1988). Goodness-of-fit indexes in confirmatory factor analysis: The effect of sample size. *Psychological Bulletin*, **103**, 391–410.

Martin, C. L., Eisenbud, L., & Rose, H. (1995). Children's gender-based reasoning about toys. *Child Development*, **66**, 1453–1471.

Martin, C. L., & Halverson, C. (1981). A schematic processing model of sex typing and stereotyping in children. *Child Development*, **52**, 1119–1134.

Martin, C. L., & Halverson, C. F. (1983). The effects of sex-typing schemas on young children's memory. *Child Development*, **54**, 563–574.

Martin, C. L., Ruble, D., & Szkrybalo, J. (in press). Cognitive theories of early gender development. *Psychological Bulletin*.

Martin, C. L., Wood, C. H., & Little, J. K. (1990). The development of gender stereotype components. *Child Development*, **61**, 1891–1904.

McCandless, B. R. (1969). Instructions to authors. *Developmental Psychology*, **1**, i.

Mead, M. (1928). *Coming of age in Samoa*. New York: American Museum of Natural History.

Mischel, W. (1970). Sex typing and socialization. In P. H. Mussen (Ed.), *Carmichael's handbook of child psychology* (Vol. 2, pp. 3–72). New York: Wiley.

Morgen, S. (Ed.). (1989). *Gender and anthropology: Critical reviews for research and teaching*. Washington, DC: American Anthropological Association.

O'Heron, C. A., & Orlofsky, J. L. (1990). Stereotypic and nonstereotypic sex role trait and behavior orientations, gender identity, and psychological adjustment. *Journal of Personality and Social Psychology*, **58**, 134–143.

Overton, W. F. (1998). Developmental psychology: Philosophy, concepts, and methodology. In W. Damon (Series Ed.) & R. M. Lerner (Vol. Ed.), *Handbook of child psychology, Vol. 1. Theoretical models of human development*. (5th ed., pp. 107–188). New York: Wiley.

Pease, B., & Pease, A. (2000). *Why men don't listen & women can't read maps: How we're different and what to do about it*. New York: Welcome Rain.

Perry, D. G., & Bussey, K. (1979). The social learning theory of sex difference: Imitation is alive and well. *Journal of Personality and Social Psychology*, **37**, 1699–1712.

Powlishta, K. K., Serbin, L. A., Doyle, A., & White, D. R. (1994). Gender, ethnic, and body type biases: The generality of prejudice in childhood. *Developmental Psychology*, **30**, 526–536.

Reskin, B. F., & Hartmann, H. I. (Eds.). (1986). *Women's work, men's work: Sex segregation on the job*. Washington, DC: National Academy Press.

Resnick, S. M., Berenbaum, S. A., Gottesman, I. I., & Bouchard, T. J. (1986). Early hormonal influences on cognitive functioning in congenial adrenal hyperplasia. *Developmental Psychology*, **22**, 191–198.

Ridgeway, C. (Ed.). (1991). *Gender, interaction, and inequality*. New York: Springer-Verlag.

Riska, E. (2001). Towards gender balance: But will women physicians have an impact on medicine? *Social Science and Medicine*, **52**, 179–187.

Rosaldo, M. Z. (1974). Women, culture, and society: A theoretical overview. In M. Z. Rosaldo & L. Lamphere (Eds.), *Women, culture and society* (pp. 17–42). Stanford, CA: Stanford University Press.

Ruble, D. N., & Martin, C. L. (1998). Gender development. In W. Damon (Series Ed.) & N. Eisenberg (Vol. Ed.), *Handbook of child psychology, Vol. 3. Social, emotional, and personality development* (5th ed., pp. 933–1016). New York: Wiley.

Sanday, P. R., & Goodenough, R. G. (1990). *Beyond the second sex: New directions in the anthropology of gender*. Philadelphia: University of Pennsylvania.

Serbin, L. A., Powlishta, K. K., & Gulko, J. (1993). The development of sex typing in middle childhood. *Monographs of the Society for Research in Child Development*, **58** (2, Serial No. 232).

Serbin, L. A., Tonick, I. J., & Sternglanz, S. H. (1977). Shaping cooperative cross-sex play. *Child Development*, **48**, 924–929.

Serbin, L. A., & Unger, R. K. (1986). Social change: Introduction. *Sex Roles*, **14**, 561–566.

Shepard, W. O., & Hess, D. T. (1975). Attitudes in four age groups toward sex role division in adults' occupations and activities. *Journal of Vocational Behavior*, **6**, 27–39.

Sherman, J. (1978). *Sex-related cognitive differences*. Springfield, IL: Charles C. Thomas.

Signorella, M. L. (1987). Gender schemata: Individual differences and context effects. In L. S. Liben & M. L. Signorella (Eds.), *New directions for child development: Vol. 38. Children's gender schemata* (pp. 89–105). San Francisco: Jossey-Bass.

Signorella, M. L. (1999). Multidimensionality of gender schemas: Implications for the development of gender-related characteristics. In W. B. Swann, Jr., J. H. Langlois, &

L. A. Gilbert (Eds.), *Sexism and stereotypes in modern society: The gender science of Janet Taylor Spence* (pp. 107–126). Washington, DC: American Psychological Association.

Signorella, M. L., Bigler, R. S., & Liben, L. S. (1993). Developmental differences in children's gender schemata: A meta-analytic review. *Developmental Review, 13,* 147–183.

Signorella, M. L., Frieze, I. H., & Hershey, S. W. (1996). Single-sex versus mixed-sex classes and gender schemata in children and adolescents. *Psychology of Women Quarterly, 20,* 599–607.

Signorella, M. L., & Liben, L. S. (1984). Recall and reconstruction of gender-related pictures: Effects of attitude, task difficulty, and age. *Child Development, 55,* 393–405.

Signorella, M. L., & Liben, L. S. (1985). Assessing children's gender-stereotyped attitudes. *Psychological Documents, 15,* 7.

Signorielli, N., & Bacue, A. (1999). Recognition and respect: A content analysis of prime-time television characters across three decades. *Sex Role, 40,* 527–544.

Smetana, J. G. (1986). Preschool children's conceptions of sex-role transgressions. *Child Development, 57,* 862–871.

Snow, M. E., Jacklin, C. N., & Maccoby, E. E. (1983). Sex-of-child differences in father-child interaction at one year of age. *Child Development, 54,* 227–232.

Spence, J. T. (1984). Masculinity, femininity, and gender-related traits: A conceptual analysis and critique of current research. In B. A. Maher & W. B. Maher (Eds.), *Progress in experimental personality research* (Vol. 13, pp. 1–97). New York: Academic Press.

Spence, J. T. (1985). Gender identity and its implications for the concepts of masculinity and femininity. In T. B. Sonderegger (Ed.), *Psychology and gender: Nebraska Symposium on Motivation* (pp. 59–96). Lincoln: University of Nebraska Press.

Spence, J. T. (1993). Gender-related traits and gender ideology: Evidence for a multifactorial theory. *Journal of Personality and Social Psychology, 64,* 624–635.

Spence, J. T., & Buckner, C. E. (2000). Instrumental and expressive traits, trait stereotypes, and sexist attitudes. *Psychology of Women Quarterly, 24,* 44–62.

Spence, J. T., & Hall, S. K. (1996). Children's gender-related self-perceptions, activity preferences, and occupational stereotypes: A test of three models of gender constructs. *Sex Roles, 35,* 659–691.

Spence, J. T., & Helmreich, R. L. (1972). The Attitudes Toward Women Scale: An objective instrument to measure attitudes toward the rights and roles of women in contemporary society. *JSAS Catalog of Selected Documents in Psychology, 2,* 66–67.

Spence, J. T., & Helmreich, R. L. (1978). *Masculinity and femininity: Their psychological dimensions, correlates, and antecedents.* Austin: University of Texas Press.

Spence, J. T., Helmreich, R. L., & Stapp, J. (1974). The Personal Attributes Questionnaire: A measure of sex-role stereotypes and masculinity femininity. *JSAS Catalog of Selected Documents in Psychology, 4,* 43–44.

Stangor, C., & Ruble, D. N. (1987). Development of gender role knowledge and gender constancy. In L. S. Liben & M. L. Signorella (Eds.), *New directions for child development, Vol. 8. Children's gender schemata* (pp. 5–22). San Francisco: Jossey-Bass.

Szkrybalo, J., & Ruble, D. N. (1999). "God made me a girl": Sex-category constancy judgments and explanations revisited. *Developmental Psychology, 35,* 393–402.

Taylor, S. E., & Falcone, H. T. (1982). Cognitive bases of stereotyping: The relationship between categorization and prejudice. *Personality and Social Psychology Bulletin, 8,* 426–432.

Trautner, H. M., Helbing, N., Sahm, W. B., & Lohaus, A. (1989, April). *Beginning awareness-rigidity-flexibility: A longitudinal analysis of sex-role stereotyping in 4- to 10-year-old children.* Paper presented at the biennial meeting of the Society for Research in Child Development, Kansas City.

111

U.S. Department of Labor, Bureau of Labor Statistics. (1991). *Employment and earnings, February 1991*. Washington, DC: U.S. Government Printing Office.

Wicker, A. W. (1971). An examination of the "other variables" explanation of attitude-behavior inconsistency. *Journal of Personality and Social Psychology*, **19**, 18–30.

Williams, C. L. (Ed.). (1993). *Doing "Women's Work": Men in nontraditional occupations*. Newbury Park, CA: Sage.

Williams, J. E., Bennett, S. M., & Best, D. L. (1975). Awareness and expression of sex stereotypes in young children. *Developmental Psychology*, **11**, 635–642.

APPENDIX A
ITEMS ON COAT AND OAT MEASURES AND RATINGS OF THE DEGREE TO WHICH ITEMS ARE STEREOTYPED IN AMERICAN CULTURE

The six tables that follow present items on the occupation, activity, and trait domains of the COAT and OAT measures and mean ratings of the degree to which those items are stereotyped in American culture. Participants rated each item on a 7-point scale in which options were (1) *for males only*; (2) *much more likely for males*; (3) *somewhat more likely for males*; (4) *equally likely for males and females*; (5) *somewhat more likely for females*; (6) *much more likely for females*; (7) *for females only*. Items receiving a mean score of 3.4 or below were categorized as "Masculine," those receiving a mean score of 4.6 or above were categorized as "Feminine," and all others are listed under "Neutral." Items marked * were included on the short form of the relevant attitude measure. Items marked with + were included on the short form of the relevant personal measure. Items for the children's measures are listed in Tables A1–A3 and those for the adults' measures in Tables A4–A6.

TABLE A.1

Masculine		Feminine		Neutral	
airplane pilot	2.2	baby-sitter*	5.8	artist*+	4.0
architect*+	2.7	ballet dancer	5.7	baker*+	3.7
auto mechanic	1.6	cheerleader+	6.3	comedian*	3.5
band/orchestra leader	2.5	dental assistant*+	5.5	cook in a restaurant*+	3.5
banker+	2.9	elementary school teacher	5.3	dishwasher in a restaurant*	3.5
bus driver	3.0	florist*+	5.4	elevator operator+	3.5
chemist	2.8	hair stylist*+	5.6	writer+	3.8
computer builder*+	2.4	house cleaner*	6.4		
construction worker+	1.6	interior decorator	5.1		
dentist*	2.6	jewelry maker+	5.1		
doctor	2.9	librarian*+	6.1		
engineer	2.5	nurse*+	6.0		
factory owner*	2.2	perfume salesperson+	6.4		
farmer	1.9	secretary*+	6.0		
firefighter	1.7	supermarket clerk*+	5.4		
football broadcaster	1.8	telephone operator*	5.6		
garbage collector	1.8				
geographer+	3.4				
janitor	2.3				
jockey+	2.0				
lawyer+	3.2				
mail carrier	2.6				
mathematician	2.9				
parking lot attendant	2.5				
plumber*	2.0				
police officer*	2.6				
president of the U.S.	1.6				
professional athlete	2.3				
refrigerator salesperson	2.7				
school principal*	2.6				
scientist*+	2.8				
ship captain*+	1.8				
shoe repairer	2.6				
soldier	1.7				
spy*+	2.4				
supermarket owner	2.5				
Supreme Court judge	2.3				
telephone installer	2.1				
traffic director	2.8				
truck driver	1.7				
umpire	1.5				

TABLE A.2

Masculine		Feminine		Neutral	
build forts+	2.0	baby-sit*+	5.9	act in a play	4.1
build model airplanes*	2.1	bake cookies*+	6.1	do crossword puzzles*	4.2
build with tools*+	2.0	cook dinner+	5.4	go bowling	3.5
collect baseball cards	2.0	do gymnastics*+	5.3	go horseback riding*	4.2
draw/design buildings*	2.6	grocery shop*	5.4	go skating	4.5
draw/design cars or rockets*+	2.1	iron clothes*+	6.0	go to the beach*	4.1
fix bicycles*	2.2	jump rope+	5.4	go to the movies	4.1
fix a car+	1.8	knit a sweater	6.4	listen to music	4.0
fly a model plane*	2.1	make jewelry	4.6	paint pictures+	4.2
go fishing+	2.1	play hop scotch	5.7	play cards*	3.7
hunt+	1.6	practice cheerleading+	6.3	play checkers	3.6
play basketball*	2.4	set the table for dinner*	5.5	play hide & seek*+	4.1
play chess	3.0	sew from a pattern*	6.3	play marbles	3.5
play darts*+	2.8	sketch/design clothes*	5.4	play tag+	3.9
play dodgeball+	3.1	take ballet lessons	6.1	practice an instrument	4.1
shoot pool*+	2.4	twirl a baton	6.1	read books	4.3
play video games*	2.8	vacuum a house*+	5.8	ride a bicycle+	3.9
shoot a bow & arrow+	1.9	wash clothes*+	5.7	sing in a choir	4.1
use a chemistry set	2.8	wash dishes+	5.2	watch game/quiz shows+	4.3
use a microscope	3.1	watch soap operas	6.0	watch nature shows	3.6
use maps	3.4	write poems	4.9	work jigsaw puzzles	4.2
wash a car	3.2				
watch crime/detective shows	3.2				
watch televised sports	2.3				

TABLE A.3

Trait Items on the COAT-AM and COAT-PM and
Mean Ratings of Cultural Stereotypes

Masculine		Feminine		Neutral	
act as a leader*	2.9	affectionate*+	5.7	appreciative+	4.5
adventurous+	2.6	charming*+	4.6	creative*+	4.2
aggressive+	2.1	complain*	4.9	curious	4.1
ambitious+	3.4	cry a lot	6.0	enjoy art*	4.3
brag a lot*	2.7	dependent+	5.0	enjoy foreign languages	4.5
brave	2.5	emotional+	5.8	enjoy music*	4.2
competitive*	2.9	enjoy English	5.2	enjoy social studies	4.0
confident*+	3.2	excitable+	4.6	friendly	4.5
cruel	2.8	follow directions*	4.6	good at art*	4.4
dominant*+	2.4	gentle*+	5.5	good at foreign languages+	4.5
enjoy geography*+	2.9	good at English	5.3	good at music+	4.4
enjoy math	3.1	have good manners*+	5.2	good at social studies+	4.1
enjoy physical education+	2.6	helpful*+	5.0	happy	4.3
enjoy science	2.8	loving*+	5.3	jealous	4.3
good at geography+	3.1	neat*	5.3	secretive	4.4
good at math+	2.9	sentimental	5.8	study hard*	4.5
good at science	2.8	shy	4.8	truthful	4.5
good at physical education	2.6	talkative	5.4		
good at sports	2.6	try to look good*+	5.0		
independent	2.9	weak	5.8		
logical*+	3.4				
loud*	3.1				
misbehave*	2.8				
smart*	3.4				
strong	2.2				

TABLE A.4

Occupation Items on the OAT-AM and OAT-PM and
Mean Ratings of Cultural Stereotypes

Masculine		Feminine		Neutral	
airplane pilot[+]	2.2	baby-sitter[+]	5.8	artist*[+]	4.0
architect[+]	2.7	ballet dancer*	5.7	baker[+]	3.7
astronomer[+]	2.9	birth attendant[+]	5.5	comedian[+]	3.5
athletic director	2.4	cheerleader	6.3	cook in a restaurant*[+]	3.5
auto mechanic*	1.6	dental assistant*[+]	5.5	dishwasher in a restaurant*	3.5
band/orchestra leader	2.5	dietitian*[+]	5.3	elevator operator*	3.5
banker	2.9	elementary school teacher	5.3	physical therapist*	4.1
bus driver	3.0	florist*[+]	5.4	writer[+]	3.8
chemist	2.8	hair stylist*[+]	5.6		
computer builder	2.4	house cleaner	6.4		
construction worker[+]	1.6	interior decorator*	5.1		
dentist	2.6	jewelry maker	5.1		
dermatologist	3.4	librarian*	6.1		
disk jockey	2.9	manicurist*[+]	6.5		
doctor	2.9	nurse*[+]	6.0		
electrician*	2.0	perfume salesperson	6.4		
engineer*[+]	2.5	secretary*[+]	6.0		
factor owner[+]	2.2	social worker	5.2		
farmer	1.9	supermarket clerk	5.4		
firefighter	1.7	telephone operator[+]	5.6		
football broadcaster	1.8				
garbage collector	1.8				
geographer	3.4				
janitor	2.3				
jockey	2.0				
landscape architect[+]	2.9				
lawyer	3.2				
logger	1.9				
mail carrier	2.6				
mathematician	2.9				
parking lot attendant	2.5				
plumber*	2.0				
police officer*[+]	2.6				
president of the U.S.	1.6				
prison guard	1.8				
probation officer	2.5				
professional athlete	2.3				
refrigerator salesperson*	2.7				
school principal	2.6				
scientist	2.8				
security guard	2.0				
ship captain*[+]	1.8				
shoe repairer	2.6				
soldier	1.7				
spy	2.4				
supermarket owner[+]	2.5				
Supreme Court judge	2.3				
telephone installer*	2.1				
traffic director	2.8				
truck driver	1.7				
umpire*	1.5				
welder*	2.0				

TABLE A.5

Activity Items on the OAT-AM and OAT-PM and Mean Ratings of Cultural Stereotypes

Masculine		Feminine		Neutral	
build model airplanes*	2.1	baby-sit*+	5.9	act in a play	4.1
build with tools*+	2.0	bake cookies*+	6.1	dance	4.5
design computer programs	2.7	cook dinner+	5.4	do crossword puzzles	4.2
draw/design buildings	2.6	do aerobics	6.0	go bowling+	3.5
draw/design cars or rockets*	2.1	do gymnastics*+	5.3	go horseback riding	4.2
fix bicycles*	2.2	grocery shop*+	5.4	go skating	4.5
fix a car*	1.8	iron clothes+	6.0	go to bars	3.5
fly a model plane*	2.1	knit a sweater*	6.4	go to the beach*+	4.1
go fishing+	2.1	make jewelry	4.6	go to the movies+	4.1
hunt+	1.6	practice cheerleading	6.3	listen to music	4.0
lift weights	2.4	read romance novels*	6.1	paint pictures	4.2
play basketball	2.4	set the table+	5.5	participate in political	
play chess	3.0	sew from a pattern*	6.3	activities*	3.5
play darts+	2.8	sketch/design clothes*	5.4	participate in religious	
play Dungeons & Dragons	2.4	spend an hour on		activities	4.4
play video/computer games+	2.8	personal appearances	6.2	play cards*+	3.7
practice martial arts*	2.6	talk on the telephone	5.3	play checkers	3.6
read science fiction	3.0	vacuum a house+	5.8	practice a musical	
ride a motorcycle*+	2.4	volunteer for charity	5.4	instrument*	4.1
shoot a bow & arrow*+	1.9	wash clothes*+	5.7	ride a bicycle	3.9
shoot pool*+	2.4	wash dishes+	5.2	sing in a choir*	4.1
use a chemistry set	2.8	watch soap operas*	6.0	watch game/quiz shows+	4.4
use a microscope	3.1	write poems	4.9	watch nature shows	3.6
use maps	3.4			watch M.T.V.	3.9
wash a car+	3.2			work jigsaw puzzles	4.2
watch crime/detective shows+	3.2				
watch televised sports	2.3				

TABLE A.6

Trait Items on the OAT-AM and OAT-PM and Mean Ratings of Cultural Stereotypes

Masculine		Feminine		Neutral	
act as a leader*+	2.9	affectionate*+	5.7	appreciative*	4.5
adventurous	2.6	charming+	4.6	creative	4.2
aggressive+	2.1	complain*+	4.9	curious	4.1
ambitious	3.4	cry a lot*+	6.0	enjoy art*+	4.3
brag a lot	2.7	dependent+	5.0	enjoy foreign languages+	4.5
brave*	2.5	emotional*+	5.8	enjoy music	4.2
competitive	2.9	enjoy English*	5.2	enjoy social studies	4.0
confident	3.2	excitable	4.6	friendly	4.5
cruel*	2.8	follow directions	4.6	good at art+	4.4
dominant*	2.4	gentle*	5.5	good at foreign languages*+	4.5
enjoy geography+	2.9	good at English*	5.3	good at music*+	4.4
enjoy math*	3.1	have good manners+	5.2	good at social studies	4.0
enjoy physical education *+	2.6	helpful	5.0	happy	4.3
enjoy science*+	2.8	loving	5.3	jealous	4.3
good at geography+	3.1	neat*	5.3	secretive	4.4
good at math*	2.9	sentimental+	5.8	study hard*	4.5
good at science*+	2.8	shy	4.8	truthful	4.5
good at physical education*+	2.6	talkative*	5.4		
good at sports	2.6	try to look good*+	5.0		
independent	2.9	weak+	5.8		
logical	3.4				
loud	3.1				
misbehave+	2.8				
smart	3.4				
strong+	2.2				

SUMMARY RATINGS OF DEGREE TO WHICH MASCULINE, FEMININE, AND NEUTRAL ITEMS ON COAT AND OAT ARE STEREOTYPED IN AMERICAN CULTURE

TABLE B.1

MEAN RATINGS (AND STANDARD DEVIATIONS) OF DEGREE OF STEREOTYPING
OF ITEMS USED ON LONG FORMS OF COAT AND OAT

	COAT Long Form	OAT Long Form
Occupation items		
Masculine	1.65 (.44)	1.63 (.44)
Feminine	1.72 (.40)	1.72 (.40)
Neutral	0.38 (.39)	0.38 (.33)
Activity items		
Masculine	1.52 (.42)	1.51 (.42)
Feminine	1.69 (.52)	1.66 (.49)
Neutral	0.25 (.24)	0.27 (.23)
Trait items		
Masculine	1.15 (.49)	1.15 (.49)
Feminine	1.23 (.47)	1.23 (.47)
Neutral	0.35 (.42)	0.35 (.42)

Notes.—Scores range from 0 (representing the most neutral rating) to 3 (representing the maximum stereotyping rating). Ratings apply to both attitude and personal measures because the long forms of the scales contain the same items.

TABLE B.2

MEAN RATINGS (AND STANDARD DEVIATIONS) OF DEGREE OF STEREOTYPING
OF ITEMS USED ON SHORT FORMS OF COAT AND OAT

	COAT Short Form		OAT Short Form	
	Attitude Measure	Personal Measure	Attitude Measure	Personal Measure
Occupation items				
Masculine	1.60 (.54)	1.76 (.57)	1.64 (.55)	1.56 (.47)
Feminine	1.77 (.48)	1.78 (.41)	1.73 (.48)	1.62 (.60)
Neutral	0.37 (.44)	0.29 (.45)	0.27 (.34)	0.28 (.38)
Activity items				
Masculine	1.64 (.46)	1.80 (.57)	1.94 (.45)	1.61 (.51)
Feminine	1.74 (.58)	1.71 (.46)	1.70 (.50)	1.71 (.60)
Neutral	0.20 (.34)	0.18 (.30)	0.33 (.48)	0.30 (.46)
Trait items				
Masculine	0.97 (.54)	1.13 (.54)	1.25 (.58)	1.30 (.49)
Feminine	1.10 (.50)	1.15 (.54)	1.41 (.52)	1.36 (.50)
Neutral	0.34 (.61)	0.47 (.53)	0.46 (.48)	0.46 (.60)

Note.—Scores range from 0 (representing the most neutral rating) to 3 (representing the maximum stereotyping rating).

APPENDIX C
TEST ADMINISTRATION VERSIONS
OF SHORT COAT AND OAT SCALES

WHO SHOULD DO THESE JOBS?

Here is a list of jobs that people can do. We want you to tell us if you think each job should be done by men, by women, or by both men and women. There are no right or wrong answers. We just want to know who you think should do these jobs. If you think it should be done by only men, circle 1; if you think it should be done by only women, circle 2; if you think it should be done by both men and women, circle 3.

WHO SHOULD BE A(N):	Only Men 1	Only Women 2	Both Men & Women 3
1. dishwasher in a restaurant	1	2	3
2. supermarket check-out clerk	1	2	3
3. artist	1	2	3
4. house cleaner	1	2	3
5. telephone operator	1	2	3
6. school principal	1	2	3
7. librarian	1	2	3
8. cook in a restaurant	1	2	3
9. baby-sitter	1	2	3
10. secretary	1	2	3
11. plumber	1	2	3
12. nurse	1	2	3
13. factory owner	1	2	3
14. hair stylist	1	2	3
15. scientist	1	2	3
16. baker	1	2	3
17. police officer	1	2	3
18. computer builder	1	2	3
19. architect	1	2	3
20. dentist	1	2	3
21. comedian	1	2	3
22. dental assistant	1	2	3
23. ship captain	1	2	3
24. spy	1	2	3
25. florist (arrange & sell flowers)	1	2	3

FIGURE C1.—COAT-AM (short version)

WHO SHOULD DO THESE ACTIVITIES?

Here is a list of activities that people can do. We want you to tell us if you think each activity should be done by boys, by girls, or by both boys and girls. There are no right or wrong answers. We just want to know who you think should do these activities. If you think it should be done by only boys, circle 1; if you think it should be done by only girls, circle 2; if you think it should be done by both boys and girls, circle 3.

WHO SHOULD:	Only Boys 1	Only Girls 2	Both Boys & Girls 3
1. fly a model plane	1	2	3
2. iron clothes	1	2	3
3. sew from a pattern	1	2	3
4. vacuum a house	1	2	3
5. go to the beach	1	2	3
6. go horseback riding	1	2	3
7. wash clothes	1	2	3
8. build with tools	1	2	3
9. play cards	1	2	3
10. shoot pool	1	2	3
11. set the table for dinner	1	2	3
12. fix bicycles	1	2	3
13. play darts	1	2	3
14. do gymnastics	1	2	3
15. play hide and seek	1	2	3
16. baby-sit	1	2	3
17. play video games	1	2	3
18. draw (or design) buildings	1	2	3
19. bake cookies	1	2	3
20. sketch (or design) clothes	1	2	3
21. grocery shop	1	2	3
22. draw (or design) cars/rockets	1	2	3
23. play basketball	1	2	3
24. build model airplanes	1	2	3
25. do crossword puzzles	1	2	3

FIGURE C2.—COAT-AM (short version)

WHO SHOULD BE THIS WAY?

Here is a list of words that describe people. Please circle the number that shows who you think should be this way. There are no right or wrong answers. We want to know who you think should be this way. If you think only boys should be this way, circle 1; if you think only girls should be this way, circle 2; if you think both boys and girls should be this way, circle 3; and if you think neither boys nor girls should be this way, circle N.

WHO SHOULD:	Only Boys 1	Only Girls 2	Both Boys & Girls 3	Neither Boys nor Girls N
1. be affectionate	1	2	3	N
2. misbehave	1	2	3	N
3. be confident (sure of themselves)	1	2	3	N
4. be logical	1	2	3	N
5. be gentle	1	2	3	N
6. enjoy geography	1	2	3	N
7. complain	1	2	3	N
8. be dominant	1	2	3	N
9. be charming	1	2	3	N
10. brag a lot	1	2	3	N
11. be loud	1	2	3	N
12. be loving	1	2	3	N
13. have good manners	1	2	3	N
14. be neat	1	2	3	N
15. be good at art	1	2	3	N
16. enjoy art	1	2	3	N
17. act as a leader	1	2	3	N
18. try to look good	1	2	3	N
19. be helpful	1	2	3	N
20. be competitive	1	2	3	N
21. be creative	1	2	3	N
22. enjoy music	1	2	3	N
23. study hard	1	2	3	N
24. follow directions	1	2	3	N
25. be smart	1	2	3	N

Figure C3.—COAT-AM (short version)

WHAT I WANT TO BE

Here is a list of jobs that people can do. Please circle the number that shows how much you would want to do each of these jobs.

HOW MUCH WOULD YOU WANT TO BE A(N):	Not At All 1	Not Much 2	Some 3	Very Much 4
1. supermarket check-out clerk	1	2	3	4
2. artist	1	2	3	4
3. perfume salesperson	1	2	3	4
4. elevator operator	1	2	3	4
5. jockey (ride a horse in a race)	1	2	3	4
6. librarian	1	2	3	4
7. cheerleader	1	2	3	4
8. cook in a restaurant	1	2	3	4
9. secretary	1	2	3	4
10. nurse	1	2	3	4
11. banker	1	2	3	4
12. writer	1	2	3	4
13. geographer	1	2	3	4
14. lawyer	1	2	3	4
15. hair stylist	1	2	3	4
16. construction worker	1	2	3	4
17. scientist	1	2	3	4
18. baker	1	2	3	4
19. computer builder	1	2	3	4
20. architect	1	2	3	4
21. dental assistant	1	2	3	4
22. ship captain	1	2	3	4
23. spy	1	2	3	4
24. jewelry maker	1	2	3	4
25. florist (arrange & sell flowers)	1	2	3	4

FIGURE C4.—COAT-PM (short version)

WHAT I DO IN MY FREE TIME

Here is a list of activities that people do. Please circle the number that shows how often you do each of these activities.

HOW OFTEN DO YOU:	Never 1	Rarely 2	Sometimes 3	Often or Very often 4
1. wash the dishes	1	2	3	4
2. iron clothes	1	2	3	4
3. build forts	1	2	3	4
4. paint pictures	1	2	3	4
5. vacuum a house	1	2	3	4
6. go fishing	1	2	3	4
7. wash clothes	1	2	3	4
8. fix a car	1	2	3	4
9. practice cheerleading	1	2	3	4
10. build with tools	1	2	3	4
11. cook dinner	1	2	3	4
12. shoot pool	1	2	3	4
13. jump rope	1	2	3	4
14. play tag	1	2	3	4
15. play darts	1	2	3	4
16. do gymnastics	1	2	3	4
17. play dodgeball	1	2	3	4
18. ride a bicycle	1	2	3	4
19. play hide and seek	1	2	3	4
20. watch game/quiz shows	1	2	3	4
21. baby-sit	1	2	3	4
22. hunt	1	2	3	4
23. shoot a bow and arrow	1	2	3	4
24. bake cookies	1	2	3	4
25. draw (or design) cars/rockets	1	2	3	4

FIGURE C5.—COAT-PM (short version)

WHAT I AM LIKE

Here is a list of words and phrases that describe people. Please circle the number that shows how much each of the words or phrases describes you.

IS THIS LIKE YOU?	Not At All Like Me 1	Not Much Like Me 2	Somewhat Like Me 3	Very Much Like Me 4
1. emotional (express feelings)	1	2	3	4
2. aggressive	1	2	3	4
3. excitable	1	2	3	4
4. dependent	1	2	3	4
5. ambitious (work hard to get ahead)	1	2	3	4
6. affectionate	1	2	3	4
7. adventurous	1	2	3	4
8. enjoys geography	1	2	3	4
9. good at geography	1	2	3	4
10. confident (sure of yourself)	1	2	3	4
11. enjoys physical education (gym)	1	2	3	4
12. logical	1	2	3	4
13. good at math	1	2	3	4
14. dominant	1	2	3	4
15. charming	1	2	3	4
16. good at foreign languages	1	2	3	4
17. has good manners	1	2	3	4
18. creative	1	2	3	4
19. tries to look good	1	2	3	4
20. appreciative (thankful)	1	2	3	4
21. gentle	1	2	3	4
22. good at social studies	1	2	3	4
23. loving	1	2	3	4
24. helpful	1	2	3	4
25. good at music	1	2	3	4

FIGURE C6.—COAT-PM (short version)

WHO SHOULD DO THESE JOBS?

Here is a list of jobs. We want you to tell us if you think each job should be done by men, by women, or by both men and women. There are no right or wrong answers. We just want to know who you think should do these jobs. If you think it should be done by only men, circle 1; if you think it should be done by mostly men, some women, circle 2; if you think it should be done by both men and women, circle 3; if you think it should be done by mostly women, some men, circle 4; and if you think it should be done by only women, circle 5.

WHO SHOULD BE A(N):	Only Men 1	Mostly Men, Some Women 2	Both Men And Women 3	Mostly Women, Some Men 4	Only Women 5
1. dishwasher in a restaurant	1	2	3	4	5
2. refrigerator salesperson	1	2	3	4	5
3. artist	1	2	3	4	5
4. elevator operator	1	2	3	4	5
5. interior decorator	1	2	3	4	5
6. auto mechanic	1	2	3	4	5
7. telephone installer	1	2	3	4	5
8. librarian	1	2	3	4	5
9. cook in a restaurant	1	2	3	4	5
10. secretary	1	2	3	4	5
11. plumber	1	2	3	4	5
12. nurse	1	2	3	4	5
13. ballet dancer	1	2	3	4	5
14. hair stylist	1	2	3	4	5
15. engineer	1	2	3	4	5
16. police officer	1	2	3	4	5
17. umpire	1	2	3	4	5
18. dental assistant	1	2	3	4	5
19. ship captain	1	2	3	4	5
20. florist	1	2	3	4	5
21. welder	1	2	3	4	5
22. electrician	1	2	3	4	5
23. manicurist	1	2	3	4	5
24. dietician	1	2	3	4	5
25. physical therapist	1	2	3	4	5

FIGURE C7.—OAT-AM (short version)

WHO SHOULD DO THESE ACTIVITIES?

Here is a list of activities. We want you to tell us if you think each activity should be done by men, by women, or by both men and women. There are no right or wrong answers. We just want to know who you think should do these activities. If you think it should be done by only men, circle 1; if you think it should be done by mostly men, some women, circle 2; if you think it should be done by both men and women, circle 3; if you think it should be done by mostly women, some men, circle 4; and if you think it should be done by only women, circle 5.

WHO SHOULD:	Only Men	Mostly Men, Some Women	Both Men And Women	Mostly Women, Some Men	Only Women
	1	2	3	4	5
1. fly a model plane	1	2	3	4	5
2. knit a sweater	1	2	3	4	5
3. sew from a pattern	1	2	3	4	5
4. go to the beach	1	2	3	4	5
5. wash clothes	1	2	3	4	5
6. fix a car	1	2	3	4	5
7. build with tools	1	2	3	4	5
8. play cards	1	2	3	4	5
9. shoot pool	1	2	3	4	5
10. ride a motorcycle	1	2	3	4	5
11. fix bicycles	1	2	3	4	5
12. do gymnastics	1	2	3	4	5
13. practice a musical instrument	1	2	3	4	5
14. read romance novels	1	2	3	4	5
15. practice martial arts	1	2	3	4	5
16. watch soap operas	1	2	3	4	5
17. baby-sit	1	2	3	4	5
18. shoot a bow and arrow	1	2	3	4	5
19. bake cookies	1	2	3	4	5
20. sketch (or design) clothes	1	2	3	4	5
21. grocery shop	1	2	3	4	5
22. draw (or design) cars	1	2	3	4	5
23. build model airplanes	1	2	3	4	5
24. sing in a choir	1	2	3	4	5
25. participate in political activities	1	2	3	4	5

FIGURE C8.—OAT-AM (short version)

WHO SHOULD BE THIS WAY?

Here is a list of traits. Please circle the number that shows who you think should be this way. There are no right or wrong answers. We want to know who you think should be this way. If you think only men should be this way, circle 1; if you think mostly men, some women should be this way, circle 2; if you think both men and women should be this way, circle 3; if you think mostly women, some men should be this way, circle 4; and if you think only women should be this way, circle 5. If you think it should be neither, circle N.

WHO SHOULD:	Only Men 1	Mostly Men, Some Women 2	Both Men And Women 3	Mostly Women, Some Men 4	Only Women 5	Neither Men Nor Women N
1. be emotional	1	2	3	4	5	N
2. be affectionate	1	2	3	4	5	N
3. be good at English	1	2	3	4	5	N
4. enjoy English	1	2	3	4	5	N
5. be cruel	1	2	3	4	5	N
6. be talkative	1	2	3	4	5	N
7. be appreciative	1	2	3	4	5	N
8. be good at physical education	1	2	3	4	5	N
9. enjoy physical education	1	2	3	4	5	N
10. be gentle	1	2	3	4	5	N
11. be good at foreign languages	1	2	3	4	5	N
12. complain	1	2	3	4	5	N
13. enjoy math	1	2	3	4	5	N
14. be good at math	1	2	3	4	5	N
15. be dominant	1	2	3	4	5	N
16. cry a lot	1	2	3	4	5	N
17. be neat	1	2	3	4	5	N
18. enjoy art	1	2	3	4	5	N
19. act as a leader	1	2	3	4	5	N
20. try to look good	1	2	3	4	5	N
21. be good at science	1	2	3	4	5	N
22. enjoy science	1	2	3	4	5	N
23. be good at music	1	2	3	4	5	N
24. study hard	1	2	3	4	5	N
25. be brave	1	2	3	4	5	N

FIGURE C9.—OAT-AM (short version)

WHAT I WANT TO BE

Here is a list of jobs that people can do. Please circle the number that shows how much you would want to do each of these jobs.

HOW MUCH WOULD YOU WANT TO BE A(N):	Not At All 1	Not Much 2	Some 3	Very Much 4
1. airplane pilot	1	2	3	4
2. artist	1	2	3	4
3. telephone operator	1	2	3	4
4. cook in a restaurant	1	2	3	4
5. baby-sitter	1	2	3	4
6. secretary	1	2	3	4
7. supermarket owner	1	2	3	4
8. nurse	1	2	3	4
9. writer	1	2	3	4
10. factory owner	1	2	3	4
11. hair stylist	1	2	3	4
12. construction worker	1	2	3	4
13. engineer	1	2	3	4
14. baker	1	2	3	4
15. police officer	1	2	3	4
16. architect	1	2	3	4
17. comedian	1	2	3	4
18. dental assistant	1	2	3	4
19. ship captain	1	2	3	4
20. florist	1	2	3	4
21. landscape architect	1	2	3	4
22. manicurist	1	2	3	4
23. birth attendant	1	2	3	4
24. dietician	1	2	3	4
25. astronomer	1	2	3	4

FIGURE C10.—OAT-PM (short version)

WHAT I DO IN MY FREE TIME

Here is a list of activities that people do. Please circle the number that shows how often you do each of these activities.

HOW OFTEN DO YOU:	Never 1	Rarely 2	Sometimes 3	Often or Very Often 4
1. wash dishes	1	2	3	4
2. iron clothes	1	2	3	4
3. go bowling	1	2	3	4
4. vacuum a house	1	2	3	4
5. go fishing	1	2	3	4
6. go to the beach	1	2	3	4
7. wash clothes	1	2	3	4
8. build with tools	1	2	3	4
9. cook dinner	1	2	3	4
10. play cards	1	2	3	4
11. shoot pool	1	2	3	4
12. wash a car	1	2	3	4
13. ride a motorcycle	1	2	3	4
14. set the table	1	2	3	4
15. go to the movies	1	2	3	4
16. play darts	1	2	3	4
17. do gymnastics	1	2	3	4
18. watch crime/detective shows	1	2	3	4
19. watch game/quiz shows	1	2	3	4
20. baby-sit	1	2	3	4
21. play video/computer games	1	2	3	4
22. hunt	1	2	3	4
23. shoot a bow and arrow	1	2	3	4
24. bake cookies	1	2	3	4
25. grocery shop	1	2	3	4

FIGURE C11.—OAT-PM (short version)

WHAT I AM LIKE

Here is a list of words and phrases that describe people. Please circle the number that shows how much each of the words or phrases describes you.

IS THIS LIKE YOU?	Not At All Like Me 1	Not Much Like Me 2	Somewhat Like Me 3	Very Much Like Me 4
1. emotional	1	2	3	4
2. weak	1	2	3	4
3. aggressive	1	2	3	4
4. strong	1	2	3	4
5. dependent	1	2	3	4
6. affectionate	1	2	3	4
7. sentimental	1	2	3	4
8. enjoys geography	1	2	3	4
9. good at geography	1	2	3	4
10. enjoys physical education	1	2	3	4
11. good at physical education	1	2	3	4
12. complaining	1	2	3	4
13. charming	1	2	3	4
14. cries a lot	1	2	3	4
15. enjoys foreign languages	1	2	3	4
16. good at foreign languages	1	2	3	4
17. has good manners	1	2	3	4
18. good at art	1	2	3	4
19. enjoys art	1	2	3	4
20. acts as a leader	1	2	3	4
21. good at science	1	2	3	4
22. enjoys science	1	2	3	4
23. tries to look good	1	2	3	4
24. misbehaves	1	2	3	4
25. good at music	1	2	3	4

FIGURE C12.—OAT-PM (short version)

APPENDIX D
USE AND SCORING OF COAT AND OAT SCALES

Age Guidelines

The OAT scales (AM and PM) were developed using college student samples and are appropriate for individuals about 15 years of age or older. The COAT scales (AM and PM) were developed using 10- to 13-year-old samples, and are appropriate for individuals ages 14 years and younger. The COAT has been used successfully with children as young as 7 years of age, but should probably not be used with children younger than age 6 or 7. Pictorial versions of the scales (the POAT-AM and PM) are under development and are appropriate for children under age 6 or 7 and for individuals who may have difficulty with the spoken vocabulary needed for the COAT (e.g., older deaf children).

Scale Administration

The COAT-AM and PM and OAT-AM and PM scales may be administered to individuals or groups. If administering to groups of young children, it is important to prepare the scale in larger type with fewer items per page, and with alternating white and shaded lines. Instructions and items should be read aloud while children follow along. So, for example, the tester would say: "We are on number 3. It is a gray line. It says, 'Who can be a _____?'" It is important to have enough adults present to monitor children's progress and answer questions.

If scales are copied on the front and back of the same page, the phrase "PLEASE TURN PAGE OVER" should be added to the bottom of the first page of each subscale to ensure that individuals complete the entire questionnaire.

If participants are to be given both AM (attitude measures) and PM (personal measures), all PM scales should be given first to avoid making individuals' gender-related beliefs highly salient prior to their self-ratings.

Researchers may elect to give only one or all three of the subscales of OAT/COAT-AM or PM, and either the long or short versions of the scales, depending on their particular interests and logistical constraints. The short versions should not, however, be cut further because reliability would be reduced.

134

Scoring

The COAT-AM and PM and OAT-AM and PM were designed to provide flexibility to researchers in assessing children's and adults' gender schemata. Thus, there are several potential ways to derive scores as outlined below. The method of choice will depend on the researcher's particular theoretical interests, methodological design, and logistical constraints.

Attitude measures (COAT-AM and OAT-AM). Responses may be scored in one of two ways: (a) The dependent measure may be scored as the proportion of "both (neither) men and women" responses to stereotypic (i.e., masculine and feminine) scale items—in this case, higher scores indicate *greater flexibility* of gender attitudes; or (b) the dependent measure may be scored as the proportion of stereotypic responses—that is, the number of feminine items assigned to "only women," plus the number of masculine items assigned to "only men," divided by the total number of stereotypic items on the scale (e.g., 20 for the short version of the COAT-AM). In this case, higher scores indicate *greater stereotyping.*

Scores derived from these two methods are equivalent when respondents are highly knowledgeable about cultural stereotypes about gender. In other words, individuals with knowledge of cultural gender stereotypes very rarely attribute a sex-typed item to the culturally "incorrect" sex (e.g., individuals almost never say "Only men should be nurses"). Thus, the number of "both men and women" responses is usually equal to the total number of items minus the number of stereotyped responses.

It is also possible to use the AM items to measure *knowledge* of (rather than attitudes about) cultural stereotypes of gender. To do so, researchers should eliminate the "both men and women" response and ask "Who usually . . ." (rather than "Who should . . .") perform (or have) the occupation, activity, or trait. Discussion of the importance of question format may be found in Signorella et al. (1993).

For both the COAT-AM and OAT-AM, proportion scores are used because they allow for the handling of missing data and because differing numbers of masculine and feminine items appear on the long versions of the OAT-AM and COAT-AM scales. As described above, neutral items are not included when scoring the COAT-AM and OAT-AM measures.

Unless the researcher has some theoretical reason to be interested in masculine versus feminine attitudes, or attitudes about a particular domain (occupations, activities, and traits), it is unnecessary to create separate attitude scores for masculine and feminine items or for each domain because the subscale scores are highly correlated with one another and load together when factor analyzed.

135

Personal measures (COAT-PM and OAT-PM). For the PM scales it is important to create separate scores for the masculine and feminine items. This is because the two domains are not highly correlated with each other and load on separate factors. The dependent measures are thus the number of points awarded, separately, for masculine and for feminine items, divided by the total number of items of each type. This procedure may be followed for each domain separately (yielding six scores—three masculine and three feminine) or may collapse across domains to yield two scores, one masculine and one feminine. (The latter is possible because across domains, the three masculine subscales and the three feminine subscales load together.)

Item Categorization

For ease of scoring, the items that comprise each scale component are listed below. Item numbers are those of the administration versions of the scales provided in Appendix C.

Occupation subscale of COAT-AM.

Masculine: 6, 11, 13, 15, 17, 18, 19, 20, 23, 24

Feminine: 2, 4, 5, 7, 9, 10, 12, 14, 22, 25

Neutral: 1, 3, 8, 16, 21.

Activity subscale of COAT-AM.

Masculine: 1, 8, 10, 12, 13, 17, 18, 22, 23, 24

Feminine: 2, 3, 4, 7, 11, 14, 16, 19, 20, 21

Neutral: 5, 6, 9, 15, 25.

Trait subscale of COAT-AM.

Masculine: 2, 3, 4, 6, 8, 10, 11, 17, 20, 25

Feminine: 1, 5, 7, 9, 12, 13, 14, 18, 19, 24

Neutral: 15, 16, 21, 22, 23.

Occupation subscale of COAT-PM.

Masculine: 5, 11, 13, 14, 16, 17, 19, 20, 22, 23

Feminine: 1, 3, 6, 7, 9, 10, 15, 21, 24, 25

Neutral: 2, 4, 8, 12, 18.

Activity subscale of COAT-PM.

Masculine: 3, 6, 8, 10, 12, 15, 17, 22, 23, 25

Feminine: 1, 2, 5, 7, 9, 11, 13, 16, 21, 24

Neutral: 4, 14, 18, 19, 20.

Trait subscale of COAT-PM.

Masculine: 2, 5, 7, 8, 9, 10, 11, 12, 13, 14

Feminine: 1, 3, 4, 6, 15, 17, 19, 21, 23, 24

Neutral: 16, 18, 20, 22, 25.

Occupation subscale of OAT-AM.

Masculine: 2, 6, 7, 11, 15, 16, 17, 19, 21, 22

Feminine: 5, 8, 10, 12, 13, 14, 18, 20, 23, 24

Neutral: 1, 3, 4, 9, 25.

Activity subscale of OAT-AM.

Masculine: 1, 6, 7, 9, 10, 11, 15, 18, 22, 23

Feminine: 2, 3, 5, 12, 14, 16, 17, 19, 20, 21

Neutral: 4, 8, 13, 24, 25.

Trait subscale of OAT-AM.

Masculine: 5, 8, 9, 13, 14, 15, 19, 21, 22, 25

Feminine: 1, 2, 3, 4, 6, 10, 12, 16, 17, 20

Neutral: 7, 11, 18, 23, 24.

Occupation subscale of OAT-PM.

Masculine: 1, 7, 10, 12, 13, 15, 16, 19, 21, 25

Feminine: 3, 5, 6, 8, 11, 18, 20, 22, 23, 24

Neutral: 2, 4, 9, 14, 17.

Activity subscale of OAT-PM.

Masculine: 5, 8, 11, 12, 13, 16, 18, 21, 22, 23

Feminine: 1, 2, 4, 7, 9, 14, 17, 20, 24, 25

Neutral: 3, 6, 10, 15, 19.

Trait subscale of OAT-PM.

Masculine: 3, 4, 8, 9, 10, 11, 20, 21, 22, 24

Feminine: 1, 2, 5, 6, 7, 12, 13, 14, 17, 23

Neutral: 15, 16, 18, 19, 25.

APPENDIX E
CONTINGENCY TABLES RELATING RESPONSES TO
QUESTIONS ABOUT SELF AND OTHERS, BY INDIVIDUAL ITEM

CONTINGENT RELATION TABLES FOR COAT—ATTITUDINAL PATHWAY

	Percentages for Boys			Percentages for Girls		
Feminine Jobs	Sex-Typed Boys ("only women" should do job)	Sex-Typed Boys Interested in Job	Non-Sex-Typed Boys Interested in Job	Sex-Typed Girls ("only women" should do job)	Sex-Typed Girls Interested in Job	Non-Sex-Typed Girls Interested in Job
ballet dancer	74	3	0	62	21	53
cheerleader	85	6	17	82	75	57
dental assistant	38	0	4	56	23	18
florist	46	11	10	67	46	38
house cleaner	56	0	6	77	20	11
interior decorator	36	14	36	67	69	77
jewelry maker	64	0	7	41	56	39
librarian	72	4	9	82	34	29
nurse	69	4	0	72	57	45
perfume salesperson	80	0	0	85	15	33
secretary	72	4	9	82	62	29
supermarket check-out clerk	44	6	23	44	47	27
telephone operator	54	0	6	54	10	6
Masculine Jobs	Sex-Typed Boys ("only men" should do job)	Sex-Typed Boys Interested in Job	Non-Sex-Typed Boys Interested in Job	Sex-Typed Girls ("only men" should do job)	Sex-Typed Girls Interested in Job	Non-Sex-Typed Girls Interested in Job
auto mechanic	77	23	33	77	3	11
band/orchestra leader	36	0	12	36	14	20
banker	46	50	43	26	50	48
bus driver	23	11	10	38	0	13
chemist	44	29	55	44	17	33
computer builder	46	44	48	46	17	10
dentist	36	36	20	38	27	17
doctor	33	54	58	21	62	65
engineer	64	28	43	71	7	9
factory owner	38	20	13	41	0	17
farmer	62	38	13	67	3	23
firefighter	67	38	31	62	9	20
garbage collector	64	0	0	74	0	0
geographer	28	18	29	15	0	24
janitor	44	18	5	64	4	7
jockey	41	6	17	31	25	30
lawyer	26	30	62	18	43	63
mail carrier	33	15	4	36	0	12
mathematician	26	30	24	21	0	16
parking lot attendant	51	5	0	46	6	5
plumber	69	0	0	85	0	0
police officer	54	33	22	36	36	16
president of the U.S.	56	68	71	31	42	67
professional athlete	41	75	61	23	11	30
refrigerator salesperson	56	0	6	62	0	0
school principal	49	42	45	38	53	58
ship captain	59	39	13	80	3	25
shoe repairer	46	0	5	72	4	0
spy	49	68	55	39	13	39
supermarket owner	38	33	25	31	17	19
Supreme Court judge	26	50	45	28	18	54
telephone installer	54	4	6	80	0	0
traffic director	38	0	8	38	7	4
truck driver	64	24	43	72	7	27
umpire	85	30	33	74	3	10

TABLE E.2

Contingent Relation Tables for COAT—Personal Pathway

	Percentages for Boys			Percentages for Girls		
Feminine Jobs	Boys Interested in Job	Boys Interested in Job Who Have "Both" Attitude	Boys Not Interested in Job Who Have "Both" Attitude	Girls Interested in Job	Girls Interested in Job Who Have "Both" Attitude	Girls Not Interested in Job Who Have "Both" Attitude
ballet dancer	3	0	26	33	62	27
cheerleader	8	33	14	72	10	27
dental assistant	3	100	61	20	38	45
florist	10	50	54	44	29	36
house cleaner	3	100	42	18	14	25
interior decorator	28	82	57	72	36	27
jewelry maker	10	50	34	46	50	67
librarian	5	50	27	33	15	19
nurse	3	0	32	54	24	33
perfume salesperson	0	—	21	18	29	13
secretary	5	50	27	56	9	29
supermarket check-out clerk	17	83	52	36	43	64
telephone operator	3	100	45	8	33	47

	Boys Interested in Job	Boys Interested in Job Who Have "Both" Attitude	Boys Not Interested in Job Who Have "Both" Attitude	Girls Interested in Job	Girls Interested in Job Who Have "Both" Attitude	Girls Not Interested in Job Who Have "Both" Attitude
Masculine Jobs						
auto mechanic	26	30	21	6	50	22
band or orchestra leader	8	100	61	18	71	63
banker	46	50	57	49	74	75
bus driver	10	75	77	8	100	58
chemist	44	71	45	28	82	64
computer builder	46	56	52	13	40	56
dentist	26	50	69	8	50	65
doctor	56	68	65	64	80	79
engineer	33	46	31	8	33	29
factory owner	15	50	64	10	100	54
farmer	28	18	64	10	75	29
firefighter	36	29	36	13	60	35
garbage collector	0	—	36	0	—	26
geographer	26	80	69	21	100	81
janitor	10	25	60	5	50	35
jockey	13	80	56	28	73	68
lawyer	54	86	61	59	87	75
mail carrier	8	33	69	8	100	61
mathematician	26	70	76	13	100	76
parking lot attendant	3	0	50	5	50	54
plumber	0	—	31	0	—	15
police officer	28	36	50	23	44	70
president of the U.S.	69	44	42	59	78	56
professional athlete	67	54	69	26	90	72
refrigerator salesperson	3	100	42	0	—	38
school principal	44	53	50	56	64	59
ship captain	28	18	50	8	67	17
shoe repairer	3	100	53	3	0	29
spy	62	46	60	29	82	52
supermarket owner	28	54	64	18	71	69
Supreme Court judge	46	72	76	44	88	59
telephone installer	5	50	46	0	—	21
traffic director	5	100	59	6	50	62
truck driver	31	50	30	13	60	24
umpire	31	17	15	5	50	24

TABLE E.3

CONTINGENT RELATION TABLES FOR COAT—ATTITUDINAL PATHWAY

Feminine Activities	Percentages for Boys			Percentages for Girls		
	Sex-Typed Boys ("only girls" should do activity)	Sex-Typed Boys Who Engage in Activity	Non-Sex-Typed Boys Who Engage in Activity	Sex-Typed Girls ("only girls" should do activity)	Sex-Typed Girls Who Engage in Activity	Non-Sex-Typed Girls Who Engage in Activity
baby-sit	46	5	29	92	78	67
bake cookies	54	19	44	90	80	75
cook dinner	41	38	35	59	48	56
draw/design clothes	59	30	19	54	48	22
iron clothes	69	0	8	72	36	36
jump rope	31	0	11	69	37	33
knit a sweater	85	0	0	90	17	0
make jewelry	47	5	15	46	17	29
play hopscotch	54	0	6	51	15	32
practice cheerleading	79	3	13	87	53	40
set the table	36	14	32	43	71	59
sew from a pattern	82	3	0	85	39	17
take ballet lessons	69	11	0	87	9	40
twirl a baton	82	6	0	92	56	67
vacuum a house	54	19	22	67	54	23
wash clothes	51	0	11	69	30	33
wash dishes	56	14	18	41	31	48
watch soap operas	56	9	18	85	45	67
write poems	21	0	13	33	23	12

Masculine Activities	Sex-Typed Boys ("only boys" should do activity)	Sex-Typed Boys Who Engage in Activity	Non-Sex-Typed Boys Who Engage In Activity	Sex-Typed Girls ("only boys" should do activity)	Sex-Typed Girls Who Engage in Activity	Non-Sex-Typed Girls Who Engage in Activity
collect baseball cards	64	48	36	74	7	30
draw/design buildings	29	55	41	36	21	40
draw/design cars/rockets	39	60	65	59	22	31
fix a car	77	27	11	85	6	17
fix bicycles	56	59	47	74	10	10
fly a model plane	56	41	35	64	4	21
hunt	64	36	57	61	8	20
play basketball	41	69	74	28	45	46
play chess	23	22	37	21	0	23
play darts	44	35	45	46	33	38
shoot pool	31	67	56	26	30	48
use chemistry set	39	40	61	28	18	29
use a microscope	31	42	56	21	25	26
use maps	10	25	40	18	29	42
wash a car	33	23	38	34	23	52

TABLE E.4

CONTINGENT RELATION TABLES FOR COAT—PERSONAL PATHWAY

	Percentages for Boys			Percentages for Girls		
Feminine Activity	Boys Who Engage in Activity	Boys Who Engage in Activity With "Both" Attitude	Boys Who Do Not Engage in Activity With "Both" Attitude	Girls Who Engage in Activity	Girls Who Engage in Activity With "Both" Attitude	Girls Who Do Not Engage in Activity With "Both" Attitude
baby-sit	18	86	47	77	7	11
bake cookies	31	67	37	79	9	13
cook dinner	36	57	60	51	45	37
draw/design clothes	26	30	45	36	29	56
iron clothes	2	100	29	36	29	28
jump rope	8	100	67	36	29	32
knit a sweater	0	—	15	15	0	12
make jewelry	11	75	50	23	67	50
play hopscotch	2	100	45	23	67	43
practice cheerleading	5	50	19	51	10	16
set the table	26	80	59	64	52	64
sew from a pattern	2	0	18	36	7	20
take ballet lessons	8	0	33	13	40	9
twirl a baton	5	0	19	56	9	6
vacuum a house	21	50	45	43	17	45
wash clothes	5	100	46	31	33	30
wash dishes	15	50	42	41	69	52
watch soap operas	13	60	41	49	21	10
write poems	10	100	77	15	50	70

Masculine Activity	Boys Who Engage in Activity	Boys Who Engage in Activity With "Both" Attitude	Boys Who Do Not Engage in Activity With "Both" Attitude	Girls Who Engage in Activity	Birls Who Engage in Activity With "Both" Attitude	Girls Who Do Not Engage in Activity With "Both" Attitude
collect baseball cards	44	29	41	13	60	21
draw/design buildings	45	65	76	33	77	58
draw/design cars/rockets	63	62	57	26	50	38
fix a car	23	11	27	8	33	14
fix bicycles	54	38	50	10	25	26
fly a model plane	38	40	46	10	75	31
hunt	44	47	27	13	60	35
play basketball	72	61	55	46	72	71
play chess	33	85	73	18	100	75
play darts	41	62	52	36	57	52
shoot pool	59	65	75	44	82	68
use chemistry set	53	70	50	26	80	69
use a microscope	51	75	63	26	80	79
use maps	38	93	88	39	87	78
wash a car	33	77	62	42	81	55

TABLE E.5

CONTINGENT RELATION TABLES FOR COAT—ATTITUDINAL PATHWAY

	Percentages for Boys			Percentages for Girls		
Feminine Traits	Sex-Typed Boys ("only girls" should have trait)	Sex-Typed Boys Who Endorse Trait	Non-Sex-Typed Boys Who Endorse Trait	Sex-Typed Girls ("only girls" should have trait)	Sex-Typed Girls Who Endorse Trait	Non-Sex-Typed Girls Who Endorse Trait
affectionate	26	40	59	38	67	63
charming	31	50	74	41	50	65
complain	54	43	33	72	43	55
cry a lot	64	8	7	72	11	18
dependent	21	38	65	21	50	81
enjoy English	33	15	35	28	36	32
excitable	13	60	74	16	83	90
gentle	31	50	81	44	76	77
loving	23	89	83	33	92	92
neat	28	36	61	28	91	57
shy	56	27	41	69	33	33
talkative	31	67	85	41	75	91
try to look good	15	67	91	37	79	96
weak	72	7	18	67	12	15

Masculine Traits	Sex-Typed Boys ("only boys" should have trait)	Sex-Typed Boys Who Endorse Trait	Non-Sex-Typed Boys Who Endorse Trait	Sex-Typed Girls ("only boys" should have trait)	Sex-Typed Girls Who Endorse Trait	Non-Sex-Typed Girls Who Endorse Trait
act as a leader	26	50	45	41	31	52
adventurous	33	69	88	31	75	89
aggressive	41	75	61	67	15	23
ambitious	23	56	63	26	70	72
brag a lot	64	24	14	74	14	30
brave	36	100	84	28	54	75
competitive	24	78	83	31	50	67
cruel	66	12	15	82	16	0
dominant	46	44	62	33	31	35
enjoy geography	28	45	43	41	12	26
enjoy physical education	28	82	89	13	40	65
enjoy science	15	67	88	26	30	69
good at physical education	26	90	82	23	100	77
good at science	18	71	84	18	43	63
independent	28	36	71	28	55	61
logical	13	40	65	23	44	53
loud	59	39	63	72	43	73
misbehave	62	38	33	69	37	50
smart	18	86	94	24	67	83
strong	46	83	90	31	58	56

TABLE E.6

CONTINGENT RELATION TABLES FOR COA<u>T</u>—PERSONAL PATHWAY

	Percentages for Boys			Percentages for Girls		
Feminine Traits	Boys Who Endorse Trait for Self	Boys Who Endorse Trait With "Both" Attitude	Boys Who Do Not Endorse Trait With "Both" Attitude	Girls Who Endorse Trait for Self	Girls Who Endorse Trait With "Both" Attitude	Girls Who Do Not Endorse Trait With "Both" Attitude
affectionate	54	81	67	64	60	64
charming	67	77	54	59	65	50
complain	38	40	50	46	33	24
cry a lot	8	33	36	13	40	26
dependent	59	87	69	74	86	60
enjoy English	28	82	61	33	69	73
excitable	72	89	82	89	85	75
gentle	72	79	45	77	57	56
loving	85	76	83	92	67	67
neat	54	81	61	67	62	92
shy	33	54	38	33	31	31
talkative	79	74	50	85	64	33
try to look good	87	88	60	89	68	25
weak	10	50	26	13	40	32

Masculine Traits	Boys Who Endorse Trait for Self	Boys Who Endorse Trait With "Both" Attitude	Boys Who Do Not Endorse Trait With "Both" Attitude	Girls Who Endorse Trait for Self	Girls Who Endorse Trait With "Both" Attitude	Girls Who Do Not Endorse Trait With "Both" Attitude
act as a leader	46	72	76	44	71	50
adventurous	82	72	43	85	73	50
aggressive	67	54	69	18	43	31
ambitious	61	79	73	72	75	73
brag a lot	21	25	39	18	43	22
brave	90	60	100	69	78	58
competitive	82	77	71	62	75	60
cruel	13	40	33	13	0	21
dominant	54	62	44	33	69	65
enjoy geography	44	71	73	21	75	55
enjoy physical education	87	74	60	62	92	80
enjoy science	85	88	67	59	87	56
good at physical education	84	72	83	82	72	100
good at science	82	84	71	59	87	75
independent	62	83	53	59	74	69
logical	62	92	80	51	80	74
loud	49	53	30	51	40	16
misbehave	36	36	40	41	38	26
smart	92	83	67	79	80	63
strong	87	56	40	56	68	71

ACKNOWLEDGMENTS

This project would not have been possible without the children, adults, and school officials who gave generously of their time to make data collection a reality. We were aided immeasurably by the many undergraduate and graduate students who helped us in data collection and entry, and by two staff assistants at Penn State—Sandra Ranio and Tracey Kennedy—who tirelessly, repetitively, and yet cheerfully used their professional skills to help us prepare endless versions of the COAT and OAT scales, tables, text, and figures. Portions of the data were collected as part of the Replication and Extension of the Pennsylvania Early Adolescent Transitions Study (REPEATS), supported by a grant from the National Institute of Child Health and Human Development (HD23229) to Richard M. Lerner, Jacqueline V. Lerner, and Alexander von Eye. We thank the Principal Investigators and the many staff associated with REPEATS for graciously including our measures.

We owe a special debt to Willis F. Overton who motivated and guided the evolution of this publication into a far richer contribution than it would otherwise have been. In addition to his own insights, he assembled an outstanding set of reviewers. We are deeply grateful to Janet Spence and two additional anonymous reviewers who provided detailed and insightful comments on the initial submission of this manuscript. The Blackwell staff—particularly Maggie Walsh—has made the production process efficient, easy, and even enjoyable.

Throughout the entire project, our immediate and extended families have provided the personal supports for what appeared to be a Sisyphean task. They comprise the small group of people in the world who understand the verb "oating." We thank them deeply for their encouragement, patience, and their many practical contributions to this endeavor.

Finally, we give special thanks to two people who played particularly important roles in the research itself. At Penn State, Candice Yekel was a central colleague during early phases of data collection for this project. At Texas, Debbie Lobliner made extensive contributions to many aspects of data analysis. We are sad to report that during her graduate program in developmental psychology, Debbie died from Wilson's Disease, a rare genetic disorder. Her presence as both a scholar and a friend has been deeply missed, and we dedicate this *Monograph* to her memory.

Portions of this work were presented at the Biennial Meeting of the Society for Research in Child Development, Seattle, April 1991, at the Biennial Meeting of the International Society for the Study of Behavioral Development, Minneapolis, July 1991, and at the Annual Convention of the American Psychological Association in Washington, D.C., August 1992.

This manuscript represents a completely collaborative effort between the two authors, and thus order of authorship is arbitrary. Correspondence may be sent either to Lynn S. Liben, Department of Psychology, The Pennsylvania State University, University Park, PA 16802, liben@psu.edu; or to Rebecca S. Bigler, Department of Psychology, 1 University Station A8000, Austin, TX, bigler@psy.utexas.edu.

COMMENTARY

CONCEPTUALIZING, MEASURING, AND EVALUATING THE DEVELOPMENTAL
COURSE OF GENDER DIFFERENTIATION: COMPLIMENTS, QUERIES,
AND QUANDARIES

Diane N. Ruble and Carol Lynn Martin

The series of studies by Liben and Bigler, presenting a suite of measures of gender stereotyping and personal preferences and self-perceptions
(and their interrelations), advances the field of gender development in
several important respects. The measures they introduce have a number
of extremely attractive features that will be much welcomed by the field.
It might seem odd to herald another measure of gender stereotyping,
given the already large number of studies on this topic which have uti-
lized an array of existing measures (e.g., Edelbrock & Sugawara, 1978;
Williams & Best, 1982). What is significant about these new measures is
not their extensive list of items and their psychometric properties. Rather,
two features of these measures are particularly noteworthy. First, Liben
and Bigler have an impressive track record of research on gender stereotyping, and the present measures grow out of a systematic analysis of the
limitations of other measures and the studies that have used them. For
example, as Spence and her colleagues have argued (Spence & Buckner,
2000; Spence & Helmreich, 1978), sex typing of self and others is not
well assessed using measures of expressive and instrumental traits. Liben
and Bigler incorporate multiple domains (occupations, activities, and traits)
and are attentive to other problems that have plagued the field, such as
differing social desirability for males and females.

Second, and perhaps more significantly, the measures are the first to
allow a real examination of whether self and other sex typing are related,
and, if so, in which domains. The authors do an outstanding job in their
Introduction of explaining the history of research on this question and
why it is important theoretically and empirically. As they note, few prior
studies have examined the self-other relation for the same items. Thus,

148

when no relation is shown, it is not clear what to conclude. Do children who hold strong stereotypes truly not show higher levels of sex typing themselves? Or, is it perhaps that stereotyped beliefs about, for example, household chores may not affect children's own activity or occupational choices? By developing measures that ask participants to report their stereotyped beliefs and personal preferences and self-perceptions for exactly the same items, Liben and Bigler have made this limitation in prior research salient to the field and have optimized the possibilities of detecting self-other sex-typing relations that may exist.

Another substantial contribution of the paper is the theoretical account of the self-other relation. The common assumption in research looking at this relation (at least from a gender schema theoretical perspective, as discussed below) is that the strength of stereotypic beliefs influences the extent to which children develop or emphasize gender-typed personal orientations. Of course children may develop sex-typed interests for other reasons, such as availability, parent or peer pressure, and temperament, and it would seem that such personal inclinations, regardless of their sources, must affect children's emerging sex-typed attitudes (e.g., if I like it, it must be for girls). Indeed, this alternative direction about schema effects has been observed in previous studies (e.g., Martin, Eisenbud, & Rose, 1995). This bidirectionality of relations is developed and highlighted in a most intriguing way by Liben and Bigler, who suggest that the consideration of children's own interests, in addition to the influences of their gender schemas, makes a more satisfying and empirically supportable model of gender differentiation than has been explicitly made by previous models. The ideas underlying their model are strongly cognitive and constructive, with children being active forces in their own development. As a whole, the theoretical ideas outlined in this *Monograph* represent a rich blend of cognitive developmental and gender schema approaches, and they serve to highlight the inherent usefulness of cognitive approaches (also see Martin, Ruble, & Szkrybalo, in press). Even more important, these authors provide an elaboration and expansion of cognitive ideas about gender, consistent with but more explicit than those found in existing theories.

In addition to supplying researchers with a heuristic model that can enable us to think in novel ways about the course of gender differentiation, these authors extend constructivist accounts to better incorporate individual differences. Whereas most developmental theories about gender differentiation have acknowledged individual variations in pathways of development, little empirical attention has been directed toward understanding the various routes that gender development can take. Even in an earlier set of studies assessing *personal pathways* (as labeled by Liben and Bigler), in which we found that children's own preferences for novel toys were projected onto other children depending on their sex (Martin et al., 1995), we did not go nearly as far in integrating interest-related processing into gender schematic processing as has been done in here. This *Monograph* reminds us that variations in processing strategies are interesting and that even alternative routes—that is, nontraditional choices and preferences—can be better understood and incorporated within the larger picture of gender development using a broad-based and inclusive theoretical approach.

A Few Reservations (Questions)

Despite our overall very positive assessment of the contribution of the *Monograph*, we feel it is important to highlight a few potential limitations. In this section we raise certain questions about the measures and the interpretations of the findings.

Measurement issues. One potential limitation of the measures for some uses is that many of the items included as stereotypes are not highly stereotyped. A very lenient criterion was used to assign items to stereotyped versus neutral lists. An examination of Appendix A reveals that an item listed as stereotyped could differ from neutrality by as little as .1 on a 7-point scale. For example, geographer and lawyer are rated as masculine at 3.4 and 3.2, respectively, whereas elevator operator and comedian are rated as neutral at 3.5. The domain of traits is particularly problematic. There are six masculine items with ratings above 3 and five feminine items with rating less than 5. For example, charming (4.6) is listed as feminine, whereas friendly (4.5) is listed as neutral. This means that a substantial number of "stereotyped" items are on average seen as less than "somewhat more likely" for males or females. Moreover, Appendix E shows very low agreement on stereotyping of some items. For example, "excitable" is rated as "for girls only" by only 13% of the boys and only 16% of the girls. It is difficult, then, to consider "excitable" to be a stereotypically feminine item. Many other items show similarly low levels of stereotyping.

A second, related potential limitation is that, unlike the adults' stereotypes and unlike the self-ratings, children's stereotype ratings were not assessed in terms of degree or strength of stereotypes. Instead, children rated whether the item applied to only males, only females, or both males and females. This means that for children to indicate stereotyped attitudes, they need to take rather extreme positions—that only men should be doctors, that only women should be librarians, that only girls should be excitable, and so forth.

There are, of course, understandable reasons for these decisions. It would be quite time-consuming and tedious (and perhaps confusing) to ask children to rate so many items on the same 5-point scale used for adults. Moreover, having a number of items that are not highly stereotyped allows more of a response range. Nevertheless, when the measures are used by researchers, these features should be taken into account for they may affect both the interpretation of how stereotyped different samples are as well as the presence or absence of self-other relations.

For example, when children give a "both" response when asked who they think should do something, it need not imply a perception of equal access. Indeed, they may actually hold clear stereotypes about many items they give "both" responses to, believing that they are activities that should mostly, though not exclusively, be done by one sex. The fact that not all "both" responses are the same is likely to affect self-other relations, as well as estimates of stereotyping. Table 27 indicates that 59% of the boys felt that only men should be pilots, meaning that 41% gave "both" responses. No difference was found between these two groups of boys in their personal attraction to this job, but it may be that a high percentage of the 41% who gave "both" responses still felt that this was largely a job for men. Thus, by not allowing for an assessment of the strength of stereotyping, some true self-other relations may have been masked. This same concern also applies to some extent to the adult correlations (Studies 2 and 4), because although these measures did include an assessment of strength of stereotyping (5-point scale), the dependent measure was the proportion of "both" responses. Presumably, the decision not to take advantage of having the strength of stereotyping assessment was to allow greater comparability to the child data. It is important to note, however, that the dependent measure is perhaps less comparable to the child data than intended. This is because for adults, the responses "mostly men" or "mostly women" were not part of "both" responses. Thus, "both" responses were more truly egalitarian for adults than for children. This difference may partly explain some differences between adults and children in the relations between attitudes and personal endorsements noted below.

Similarly, if many of the items categorized as stereotypic are perceived as relatively neutral, such as "excitable," the absence of self-other relations may not be very meaningful. This is because if the majority of children give "both" responses to these items, indicating that it is all right to act in this way, their personal decisions are likely to be affected by factors other than stereotypes. As Liben and Bigler argue, endorsing a "both" option for counterstereotypic behavior provides the freedom to engage in a counterstereotypic activity or not, a freedom that individuals who view the item as only for the other sex presumably do not experience.

But, if very few participants feel that the behavior is counterstereotypic, it will be difficult to detect relations because of low power. We hasten to note that we are not implying that relations could not be observed with items that are fairly neutral. Indeed, the contingency tables in Study 5 reveal a number of interesting specific relations involving such items. For example, Table 31 shows significant chi-square results for several traits (e.g., helpful, confident) that received more than 80% "both" responses. Our suggestion is simply that the strength of overall relations may have been diluted with the inclusion of so many items that most participants do not view as stereotyped by gender.

Interpretational issues. Like many previous researchers interested in possible relations between self and other sex typing, Liben and Bigler emphasize the multidimensionality of gender constructs and the distinctions between attitudes and personal orientations. This emphasis is not unreasonable, as concurrent correlations between the two sets of variables were unimpressive and children's attitudes did not predict self-endorsements at subsequent times. Does this mean, as Liben and Bigler conclude, that "attitudinal schemata are distinct from sex-typed self characteristics and, thus, changes in an individual's attitudes concerning others should not be expected to affect an individual's sex-typed beliefs." We believe this conclusion is premature, in part for the reasons suggested above (i.e., that the dichotomous nature of the stereotyping measure and the high frequency of neutral items may have masked some relations). Futhermore, as we outline later, we think the item analyses show strong support for attitude-preference links. Even beyond that, however, are a number of other reasons why attitude–personal endorsement relations may be difficult to observe. Because we have addressed this issue in recent publications (Aubry, Ruble, & Silverman, 1999; Ruble & Martin, 1998; Martin et al., in press), we will highlight here only a few points particularly relevant to this set of studies.

First, stereotypes may have their maximal impact as children first select and try out new activities, rather than once their personal conclusions about them have already been drawn (Ruble, 1994). Thus, 6th grade may already be too late to detect relations, because children of that age already know that they would, for example, consider being a nurse or umpire but not a garbage collector or cheerleader, and current attitudes may no longer have much impact. This does not mean that stereotypes did not affect the original decisions, however. A very striking finding in this *Monograph* is that, for occupations and activities, very few children endorse counterstereotypic items. This observation in itself would seem to support the significance of stereotypes in general as influencing behaviors, at least in a normative sense.

Second, attitude-self links are not perfectly symmetrical, as Liben and Bigler point out. When a girl has the belief that an object, person, or event (OPE) is own-sex stereotyped, then this stereotype may encourage her to approach the OPE. Or, the stereotype may simply permit her to approach the OPE but not compel her to do so. Similarly, holding a flexible attitude may encourage or allow her to approach the OPE. In contrast, holding the other-sex stereotype (the counterstereotypic view)— that is, believing that this OPE is "for boys"—discourages further interaction. Violations of the stereotype occur only with the counterstereotypic items. Thus, we would not expect to find attitude-preference links in the same patterns across all possible comparisons.

Consider the item analyses. If own-sex stereotypes *encourage* an activity, then we might see that a child who holds own-sex stereotypes would be more likely to endorse an OPE than would a child who has a flexible attitude or a child with an other-sex stereotype. If an own-sex stereotype *allows or permits* an activity, then we would see children who hold own-sex stereotypes to be more likely to endorse an OPE than children who have an other-sex stereotype but may be similar to children with a flexible attitude. In contrast, holding an other-sex stereotype may discourage an activity as compared to holding an own-sex or flexible attitude.

The lack of symmetry has several implications for the data presented in the *Monograph*. One implication is that the item analyses may provide more support for attitude-preference links than Liben and Bigler conclude. Liben and Bigler report that only 26 COAT items showed significant chi-squares—a modest percentage of the 147 items. However, due to the lack of symmetry, of the 147 items tested, significant patterns are likely to occur in only half of them. Thus, finding 26 significant chi squares out of approximately 74 is more compelling evidence of stereotype influence than 26 out of 147. And, not surprisingly, most of the significant chi squares were found for the counterstereotypic cases (e.g., for boys on the culturally feminine activities).

Also, because relatively few children endorse counterstereotypic behaviors, it is difficult to assess current self-other relations. Liben and Bigler do note that this problem makes it difficult to find significant chi-squares in Study 5, but it seems important to highlight this limitation because it affects conclusions about the strength of these relations. If a small base of personal endorsement means that it would not have been possible to find significant relations for many items, this number of significant effects may be more impressive. For example, an examination of Tables 27 and 29 (which show significant chi-squares) and their corresponding tables in Appendix E (which show nonsignificant chi-squares) reveals that, on the counterstereotypic items (feminine for boys, masculine for girls), for boys, 13 of 16 occupations (81%) and 16 of 21 activities (76%) show effects in the predicted direction. Because so few of boys in either category endorsed these items, however, the chance of finding a significant effect is slim. For most (11/16; 69%) feminine jobs, for example, less than 25% of the boys endorsed the item. More boys personally endorsed feminine activities (relative to occupations), but still one finds a number of zeros in Table E3. The mean ratings for occupations and activities that forms the base for these chi-squares are 1.2 and 1.4, respectively, on a 1–4 scale. Although girls are, as expected, more likely to personally endorse counterstereotyped occupations and activities, the mean ratings are still quite low (1.4 and 1.8, respectively). In addition, as for the boys, most of the items for girls were also in the predicted direction: 32 of 41 occupations (78%) and 23 of 24 activities (69%). Moreover, several items that are same-sex-typed are endorsed by very few children because they are unattractive or an idiosyncratic interest (e.g., knit a sweater, take ballet lessons, write poems, band leader, bus driver, garbage collector, janitor, jockey). Thus, an alternative interpretation of the present data is that stereotypes, rather than having little effect on endorsements, as currently implied, actually have quite a strong effect, but that such effects are masked by the difficulty in finding any significant chi-squares at all. Moreover, the infrequency of endorsing cross-sex-typed or idiosyncratic activities and occupations affects the strength of observed correlations and regressions, as well as the chi-squares, and thus all of these findings may also be stronger than they appear.

It is also possible to consider whether the data fit the various expectations for stereotypic influence by examining the overall patterns somewhat differently than was done by Liben and Bigler. To get a general sense of the patterns, we averaged across the percentages for each category of significant and nonsignificant activities and occupations. We made a number of comparisons. To assess the viability of the explanation that other-sex stereotyping discourages endorsement, we examined whether the average percentage of children endorsing items while stereotyping them for the other sex was lower than the average percentage who endorsed while holding a flexible attitude. For every set of items (8/8), the percentages suggest that children do not endorse items that are counterstereotyped. We also considered whether own-sex stereotyping of an item encouraged or permitted endorsement relative to counterstereotypic or flexible attitudes. For these items, in two of eight cases, own-sex stereotyping seemed to encourage endorsement; for the remainder, own-sex stereotyping allowed endorsement but at similar levels to a flexible attitude. Overall, these patterns confirm but also strengthen the conclusions that Liben and Bigler drew about attitude-preference links being stronger for cross-sex items.

That said, Liben and Bigler are to be applauded for their careful and thorough analysis of whether there might be some self-other relations for some types of items and for some children. The conclusions they reach from their contingency analyses—that relations are likely to be stronger for high status (i.e., masculine) and cross-sex-typed items—are quite interesting and should be highlighted as promising directions for future research. These findings suggest that the likelihood of finding self-other relations depends on the specific items. That is, relations are less likely to be found when items are not desirable (and thus there are not enough children who want to do them to find relations) and when they are same-sex typed because such items do not have the same quality of norm violation that cross-sex-typed items do. As Liben and Bigler argue, even the nonendorsement of a stereotypic item is not a real violation (just not the strongest adherence to the stereotype). Violations of the norms really only occur when children endorse an item that they believe is for the other sex only.

These examples and findings raise a more general question about the nature of relations between stereotypic attitudes and personal orientations. Liben and Bigler were justifiably restricted to describing and interpreting only relations that were significant. Because such relations are expected to be small, for the reasons described above, we decided to explore the patterns in a bit more detail. Specifically, we examined the concurrent correlations in Studies 1–4 (Tables 4, 8, 12, and 18), as well as the regressions in Studies 3–5 (regressions were not performed in Studies 1 and 2). As described by Liben and Bigler, relatively few tables show a consistent pattern of significant correlations. We sought to determine whether a consistent directional pattern could be observed for any set of attitudes and/or personal endorsements. Their strongest prediction would be that egalitarian attitudes ("both" responses) should be positively associated with endorsing cross-sex items. In addition, if attitudes relate to endorsement of same-sex items, one would expect a negative relation with egalitarian attitudes (i.e., greater same-sex endorsement should be associated with greater stereotyping and thus fewer "both" responses).

For women (Tables 8 and 18), the expected pattern for cross-sex items (albeit quite weak) was shown for self-endorsement of masculine activities and, for Table 18 only, for self-endorsement of masculine traits. Stated differently, women who held more sex-typed beliefs were slightly more likely to avoid masculine activities and characteristics, and this pattern was significant in the regression analysis reported for Study 4.

In contrast, egalitarian attitudes were not positively associated with men's endorsement of feminine items. A cursory examination of Tables 8 and 18 reveals mostly negative correlations. Some of these correlations were even of moderate size, especially for the short scale (Table 18). Most notably, egalitarian men were less likely to endorse masculine activities, showing the expected direction for endorsement of same-sex items, as described above, and this pattern was also significant in the Study 4 regression analysis.

For girls (Tables 4 and 12), the predicted pattern for cross-sex items was shown for personal endorsement of masculine activities and traits and very weakly for endorsement of both feminine and masculine occupations, but only for the full scale (Table 4). For the short scale, where self and other items were not the same, correlations were weak and inconsistent. For boys, there was little indication of any predicted relations. Table 4 suggests that egalitarian boys were slightly more likely to endorse both masculine and feminine traits, a finding one might predict from the androgyny literature. The regression analysis of Study 3 revealed no significant effects, but the patterns in Study 1 (Table 4) seem reasonably clear. Thus, if a regression had been done for Study 1, it seems likely that significant relations would have been found, supporting the correlational patterns described above. Moreover, the regressions done for Study 5 do support these patterns. That is, for girls, egalitarian attitudes toward masculine activities predicted personal endorsement of masculine activities and occupations (concurrent relation only). For boys, personal endorsement of feminine traits at time 1 (the beginning of 6th grade) significantly predicted egalitarian attitudes at time 4.

In short, we believe that Liben and Bigler may have been too restrained in their conclusions about self-other relations. Some reasonably clear patterns emerged that warrant focused, direct testing in future research. First, gender-typed attitudes did relate to endorsement of cross-sex-typed items for girls and women. This relation was found reasonably consistently despite the large number of factors described above that act to constrain such relations. It is not clear, however, why it was not found in Study 3. Perhaps the lack of congruence between attitude and personal endorsement items on the short scale made a difference, or perhaps other features of these specific items limited the possibility of finding relations. It is also not clear why in Study 5 this relation was found only for concurrent and not longitudinal analyses. One possibility is that it may have been difficult to predict endorsements at time 4 because girls were even less likely to personally endorse either feminine or masculine occupations at this point than they were at time 1 (see Table 23).

The failure to find this cross-sex-typed pattern for males in any of the studies is also noteworthy. Liben and Bigler attribute this sex difference to social desirability/status factors—that is, female occupations and activities are of lower status such that even egalitarian attitudes may be insufficient reason for boys to endorse them. As we noted above, however, examination of the contingency tables in Study 5 reveals that personal endorsements were generally in the predicted direction for cross-sex-typed occupations and activities, but there were not enough boys who endorsed feminine items to provide an adequate chi-square test for a large number of the items. Moreover, and also as noted earlier, we interpret this observation as further indication of the strength of stereotypes: Because boys had already learned to avoid such items, there may have been insufficient numbers left to reveal individual differences in the relations between attitudes and personal endorsement.

Second, gender-related attitudes also showed some relation to endorsing same-sex-typed items, but only for men. It is not particularly surprising that few relations with same-sex items were found; it is acceptable to endorse an item believed either to be appropriate for one's own sex or for both sexes. Thus, in Liben and Bigler's terms, such items simply elicit an interest filter. Why this interest filter should lead men but not women, boys, or girls to endorse more same-sex items is unclear but is an interesting question for future research. One possibility relates to the difference in the assessment of attitudes for adults and children, as noted earlier. Because "both" responses were clearer indications of egalitarian attitudes for adults than for children (that is, they did not include "mostly men/women" responses), the difference between egalitarian and sex-typed attitudes may have been sharper for adults than for children. Thus, the adult data may have provided a stronger test of the effects of holding same-sex-typed attitudes on personal endorsements.

Third, boys who endorsed more feminine traits showed more egalitarian attitudes. The finding is interesting because it was the only one to show prediction over time in the longitudinal analysis of Study 5. Liben and Bigler interpret this relation in terms of greater restraints placed on boys' expression of counterstereotypic characteristics, and thus the need to bring their attitudes and self-perceptions in line by changing their attitudes. They further suggest that this finding is consistent with previous research using the Bem Sex Role Inventory (BSRI). This interpretation may prove valid, but other aspects of the present data suggest that it should remain tentative. That is, at time 1, boys' self-endorsements of feminine traits were highly correlated (.66) with endorsements of masculine traits (see Table 4). Moreover, as noted above, at time 1 egalitarian attitudes were positively and often significantly related to personal endorsements of masculine (range = .19–.28) as well as feminine traits (range = .24–.35). Thus, it is not clear that this finding does, in fact, represent an anxious or defensive response from boys who feel uncomfortable about their feminine characteristics because these boys were, if anything, also higher on masculine characteristics. Instead, this finding seems qualitatively different from the other relations; it may even not be gender-linked at all. It may be that boys who view themselves as possessing a wider range of characteristics are more flexible or charitable in their beliefs about others. That is, it may not be a defensive reaction at all but rather exactly the opposite.

Broader Theoretical Issues and Future Directions (Quandaries)

The fascinating data sets and ideas in the Liben and Bigler *Monograph* as well as the questions we raised above lead to a number of broader issues to be considered in future research. Three such issues struck us as particularly intriguing: (a) the interrelation between developmental processes and the bidirectional model; (b) the nature of links between stereotypes and personal endorsements; and (c) the intersection between social and developmental approaches to exploring these links.

Exploring development in relation to the bidirectional model. The ideas presented by Liben and Bigler suggest many topics that require further elaboration, as they themselves acknowledge. Within the personal pathway and attitude pathways models, using gender as a "first filter" is equivalent to being gender schematic. It is consistent with cognitive accounts of gender to suggest that gender schematic individuals are characterized by having gender at the top of the bin of processing strategies, but they are not the only individuals to use the gender filter early in processing. Any person can be induced to use gender for processing under certain circumstances. Situational pressures to use gender can induce this form of processing even in individuals who are not gender schematic. Furthermore, the reverse is likely also to be true: even gender schematic individuals may be induced to use an interest-first filter for processing under some circumstances. These cases imply that there are two ways to conceptualize the pathways Liben and Bigler proposed: one is a person-centered view in which the pathway describes a general orientation to processing information; another is a situational view in which the pathways represent what a person does in one particular situation.

When thinking about the pathways from the person-centered view, an obvious set of questions concerns developmental changes. How do developmental changes influence children's attitudes and their relations to behaviors/choices to OPE? Cognitive changes with age may influence children's recognition of inconsistencies between their interests and their gender attitudes. Liben and Bigler state that this could then lead to changing of their gender attitudes. Presumably, the implication is that inconsistencies would lead children to change gender attitudes to be less traditional. However, the increased cognitive dissonance of recognizing inconsistencies also could lead to a different type of change, namely, a change in the knowledge structure in which children develop subgroups within the stereotype, and these subgroups could then provide a basis for self-identification (Greenwald, Banaji, Rudman, Farnham, Nosek, & Mellott, 2002). Girls who are interested in male-stereotypic activities appear to develop these subgroups when they label themselves as tomboys. Interestingly, there also may exist in the minds of children and adults a subgroup of very traditional girls who exhibit high levels of interest in female-stereotypic activities, labeled as *girly-girls*. To understand the role of stereotypic attitudes on behavior, we need to have more extensive knowledge about the subgroups that are formed by a clustering of interests within a domain or by the adoption of a set of cross-sex activities, how these subgroups are evaluated by in-group members (and out-group members), and how these groups develop. If children use subgroups and their associated attitudes to guide their behavior, but these subgroups have different norms, then the attitude pathway may still be operating, albeit on a nontraditional set of standards.

The long-term developmental picture of the interrelation between attitude and interest pathways would be illuminating. Consider a young girl with interest in transportation toys. Her initial interest-driven activity has real consequences for her later behavior. She may develop less stereotypic attitudes about transportation toys, find herself playing with boys more frequently than girls because of this interest, and over time she may develop a broader set of cross-sex interests because of her exposure to boys. As stated above, this does not necessarily suggest that attitudes play no role in her behavior. She may come to view herself as a tomboy, and then use her knowledge of and attitudes toward tomboys to guide her behavior in new domains. In this case, her attitude is formed in part by an early interest in a nontraditional activity; but her attitude may still play an active role in directing and guiding her behavior. In this way, the links between attitude and interest pathways can be developmentally linked in a transactional way.

Other broad developmental issues are brought to mind in considering the two pathways outlined by Liben and Bigler. How do changes in the content and structure of gender schemas influence children's behaviors and choices? What happens when structural changes and developmental changes suggest different directions to take in information processing? As children grow older, their gender stereotypic knowledge base expands, which might increase reliance on gender schemas, but they also have a more highly developed sense of self and self-preferences, which might promote the use of interest schemas. In the case of competing trends, are they more or less likely to rely on gender schemas?

To more fully develop the role of individual differences in gender differentiation requires that we recognize the factors that promote the use of one type of filter over another, as well as those that promote consistency in behavior versus those that might encourage variability in behavior. Certain characteristics, such as a child's temperament, encouragement from parents and/or peers, societal valuing of certain behaviors, and so forth, might promote a more consistent use of one type of filter over the other. Children raised in nontraditional families may use interest filters more frequently than children from more traditional families. Children's exposure to same-sex peers likely contributes to the use of gender filters rather than interest filters.

Remember, too, that the use of an interest filter may not be discernible in children who have strong agreement between their gender schemas and their interests. When interests and gender filters coincide, their choices will simultaneously engage both filters. In contrast, other children may be particularly likely to develop interest filters that clash with traditional gender schemas. As described earlier, tomboys often have interests in certain sports or activities that other girls may not share (and which are not part of the female stereotype). Tomboys' interests may derive from a variety of sources including parental and/or sibling socialization, hormone levels, and temperament. Another group are girls with congenital adrenal hyperplasia (CAH), who have increased prenatal androgen exposure and show greater interest in toys traditionally stereotyped for boys (see Berenbaum & Hines, 1992). Both of these groups of girls provide unique opportunities to investigate the use of interest filters that likely clash with those typically associated with girls' gender schemas.

Cognitive approaches have long recognized that schema deployment is dependent on situational requirements. Presumably, situational pressures also moderate the processes described in this *Monograph*. What features of situations influence children to shift from one type of filter to another? Can a child shift away from consistently using one type of filter under certain circumstances? Shifts due to situations are not hard to imagine: A child who has many highly gender-stereotyped children in her class may quickly adopt a gender schema–first approach at school but the same child may revert to interest-first processing at home.

The nature of links between stereotypic attitudes and personal endorsements. Liben and Bigler suggest that the topic of how interests and gender schemas relate to one another is worthy of further investigation. For the purposes of the present investigation, Liben and Bigler maintained the idea that interests and gender attitudes are separable but they did acknowledge their likely interdependence. Considering interests as separate from gender influences mirrors a not uncommon view in the lay public (see Nosek, Banaji, & Greenwald, 2002). Nosek and colleagues provide the example of David Gelernter (1999), who argued that gender differences in science participation are not due to gender biases (e.g., against hiring women). According to Gelernter, "the real explanation is obvious: women are less drawn to science and engineering than men are" (p. 11). Nevertheless, the emergence of such interests is likely linked to gender at some point in development, as has been demonstrated in many areas of gender research. Interests may be related to gender through one's hormone levels as the research on CAH girls suggests. Interests may be shaped by gender socialization through the experiences that are rewarded by peers and families. And interests (as well as motivation and competence) may be directed by gender schemas as indicated by research in which children's preferences are influenced by the labeling of novel games as being "games for girls" or "games for boys" (e.g., Montemayor, 1974; see Martin & Dinella, 2002, for a review).

What about the few children who do endorse items that are stereotyped for the other sex? Remember that these cases are rare—most of the boys who endorse feminine activities or occupations and the girls who endorse masculine activities and occupations do so while believing that these are appropriate for both sexes to engage in. But, the rare cases of, for instance, girls who say they want to be spies but think this is for boys, are puzzling. How do constructivist theories explain violations of gender norms? Children's gender-discrepant behavior may encourage them to develop different types of knowledge and attitude structures. Several patterns may be apparent. One is that children may soften their attitudes by acknowledging flexibility of a stereotypic norm. In probabilistic terms, a girl who likes trucks may have to reconcile her interest in trucks by changing her probabilities about boys' and girls' preferences about trucks. Probabilities about boys' and girls' preferences could change and/or variability associated with these stereotypes could be acknowledged. Rather than thinking that few girls play with trucks, she may think that many girls like to play with trucks. Another possibility is that she may modify the evaluation associated with playing with things associated with the other sex by saying that it is okay for some girls, like herself, to play with boys' things. As discussed earlier, children may form subgroups within gender groups, and these subgroups may have their own set of expectations. A girl who likes trucks may come to develop stereotypes about a subgroup of girls who are tomboys, and the norms guiding tomboy behavior may then provide impetus and constraints for her behavior. For instance, a girl who sees herself as a tomboy may be interested in a novel toy that she thinks boys like but not one that she thinks girls like.

In data we have recently analyzed, there is evidence suggesting that girls may differ in their understanding of variability in stereotypes. We asked 7- to 12-year-old girls to describe the interests of girls and boys, their own interests, and their perceptions of variability in interests (Are there girls who do not like to play with dolls? Are there girls who like to play with tool sets?), and whether they were tomboys (Dinella & Martin, 2002). Tomboys and traditional girls did not differ much in their perceptions of girls' and boys' interests but they did differ in acknowledging variability in stereotypes for girls.

This discussion highlights several points that must be made. First, for a number of children, there will be no clash between their interests and gender schemas. Second, gender schemas influence children's interests and interests may influence children's gender schemas. Third, children who do not endorse stereotypic interests may still be abiding by personal stereotypes; therefore their attitudes may still color their behavior. Future research based on Liben and Bigler's account of gender differentiation would benefit from a more explicit accounting of the interrelation among interests and gender.

*Do attitudes predict behavior? The issue from a developmental versus social psychological perspective.*Since Huston (1983) first drew our attention to the question of whether there is a cognitive underpinning to children's gender behavior, controversy has ensued about whether there is a link between attitudes or stereotypes and behavior (see Ruble & Martin, 1998), and some question whether any such link exists at all (Bussey & Bandura, 1999). A positive outcome of this concern has been an influence on the underlying assumptions of gender researchers: Rather than assuming a unidimensional gender typing of individuals, we now presume that gender typing is multidimensional—that is, that the different domains may not be related to one another and that they may have different etiologies.

The multidimensionality concern is valid and complex. In a recent paper (Martin et al., in press), we outlined many of the issues that are relevant to this concern, and many of the methodological constraints that have precluded our ability to convincingly address the extent of multidimensionality in gender differentiation and development. To summarize these arguments briefly, gender researchers have not used methodologically sound instruments to assess congruence between domains of gender typing, comparisons between domains often have been inappropriate, and developmental changes in relations have been neglected. And finally, significant findings that do show congruence have been ignored or downplayed. Our point was not to reject the multidimensionality argument; instead, we suggested that researchers should hold in mind the possibility that relations among some domains may be stronger than currently assumed.

Although the controversy about attitudes/stereotypes and behaviors has yet to be resolved, many developmental researchers appear to have concluded that gender-related attitudes have little to do with behavior and preferences. This *Monograph* should effectively alert researchers to the possibility that the question has yet to be resolved. Indeed, as our earlier analysis of the present findings shows, we have yet to even resolve exactly how to interpret the data in this *Monograph*. Furthermore, the *Monograph* may reenergize debate about attitudes and behavior by providing new ways to consider potential relations among them. The overall effect may be to slow the swing of the "multidimensionality" pendulum, which may have moved too far in the direction of lack of coherence among domains. Thinking about attitude-behavior links will enable developmental researchers to move closer to their counterparts in social psychology.

A social psychologist reading a review about gender differentiation in children would be surprised at the conclusions being drawn by many developmental psychologists about the relation between stereotypes and behavior. Whereas few developmental scientists have shown interest in investigating attitudes and stereotypes, social psychologists have been very much enthralled by this topic. The different levels of interest were confirmed by a simple search of the Psycinfo database (1955–2002), which showed that approximately three times as many articles have been written about either stereotypes in general and about gender stereotypes in particular in adults as in children. Four times as many articles on attitudes and behavior have been conducted on adults than children. Furthermore, even though the study of stereotyping has always been popular in social psychology, the area has seen a resurgence of interest over the past 5 to 10 years, whereas the direction of interest in developmental psychology seems to have waned.

What is different in social psychology? Some of this excitement about the study of stereotyping in social psychology can be traced to three related strands of research. The first strand was the research done on the automatic versus controlled features of stereotyping (e.g., Devine, 1989). Devine's research set the stage for the recent interest in stereotyping by demonstrating that stereotyping is automatic, but that conscious control can play a role in modifying whether a stereotype becomes translated into behavior. Other researchers such as Bargh and colleagues (Bargh & Chartrand, 1999; Bargh, Chen, & Burrows, 1996), who have argued about the unconscious use of stereotypes to categorize others, have confirmed the role of unconscious forces in everyday life.

The second strand was Steele and Aronson's stereotype threat research (Steele, 1997; Steele & Aronson, 1995). This research illustrated the powerful influence that stereotypes have on performance: Achievement scores are adversely affected when a stereotype relevant to one's own group is made explicit (as compared to when it is not made explicit). It has been hypothesized that the threat of being perceived in a stereotyped manner hinders performance by increasing anxiety and by diverting attention away from the task, and the effect does not depend upon believing that the stereotype is true for one's group.

The third strand was the development of measures of implicit social cognition. The assumption is that these measures are able to detect the strength of the associations between person concepts (groups, self) and attributes. Implicit assessments of social cognition, such as the Implicit Association Test (IAT) (Greenwald, McGhee, & Schwartz, 1998), allow for examination of individual differences in the processing of information about how attributes relate to one another. Furthermore, these methods are very flexible; they allow for assessments of many forms of associations including self-other, self-attribute, self-valuation, attribute-valuation, and so forth. For example, it is possible to use this technique to assess a person's gender identity (associative links between self and males and females), self-esteem (links between self and positive and negative characteristics), and gender attitudes (links between gender groups and positive and negative characteristics) (see Greenwald et al., 2002).

Although it is beyond the scope of this commentary to review the literature, this new approach has allowed for intensive investigation of stereotype-behavior links, and some intriguing relationships have emerged. Implicit measures seem to relate to one another better than explicit ones, and in some cases, they predict behavior better than do explicit ones. For instance, prejudice against female job applicants is associated with implicit gender stereotypes (as assessed with the IAT) even though explicit stereotypes are not (Rudman & Glick, 2001). Also, implicit attitudes as well as explicit attitudes about gender have been found to relate to performance in mathematics on the SAT (Nosek et al., 2002).

Although we hesitate to speak for all social psychologists or to make sweeping statements about a whole area within social psychology, there seems to be an increased interest within social psychology in these topics, and social psychologists appear to accept that stereotypes influence behavior. In discussing the role of implicit social cognition in math performance, Nosek et al. (2002) stated:

> we can suggest that a fundamental categorization at birth into the groups *male* or *female* produces identification with one's social group and that such identification shapes and is shaped by experiences that are expected of that social group. From such experiences flow preferences and performance that can be enhancing or limiting insofar as they interfere with free access to modes of thinking and choices that make for a fulfilling and productive life.(p. 57)

It is interesting that this research, published in the *Journal of Personality and Social Psychology*, is entitled, "Math = Male, Me = Female, Therefore Math ($\neq$) Me," which is strikingly similar to the "trucks are for boys, I am a girl, therefore trucks are not for me" of gender schematic processing theory (Martin & Halverson, 1981). Social psychologists may be reinventing gender schematic processing theory but now shifting the emphasis to implicit social cognition.

Conclusion

Advances in the area of gender development have been hampered by the paucity of reliable and valid measures of aspects of gender typing, as well as insufficient theoretical attention to the specific processes linking children's attitudes and preferences. A notable contribution to the field and to theory development in particular is found in the new measures and theoretical models described in this *Monograph*. Even though some of the items on these new measures may be problematic and the relations between attitudes and personal endorsements may be stronger than implied, the systematic use of multiple domains in a coherent set of measures represents a significant advance. These new measures allow researchers to investigate more extensively the developmental changes, diversity, and patterns in gender differentiation. Just as a theory provides an important tool for directing research efforts, research also feeds theory development: With new lines of empirical evidence come theory building and refinement of existing theoretical notions. "Build it and they will come" can be framed in our scientific world as, "Measure it and they will test theories."

References

Aubry, S., Ruble, D. N., & Silverman, L. B. (1999). The role of gender knowledge in children's gender-typed preferences. In L. Balter & C. S. Tamis-LeMonda (Ed.), *Child psychology: A handbook of contemporary issues.* (pp. 363–390). Philadelphia: Psychology Press.

Bargh, J. A., & Chartrand, T. L. (1999). The unbearable automaticity of being. *American Psychologist*, **54**, 462–479.

Bargh, J. A., Chen, M., & Burrows, L. (1996). Automaticity of social behavior: Direct effects of trait construct and stereotype priming on action. *Journal of Personality and Social Psychology*, **71**, 230–244.

Berenbaum, S. A., & Hines, M. (1992). Early androgens are related to childhood toy preferences. *Psychological Science*, **3**, 203–206.

Bussey, K., & Bandura, A. (1999). Social cognitive theory of gender development and differentiation. *Psychological Review*, **106**, 676–713.

Devine, P. G. (1989). Stereotypes and prejudice: Their automatic and controlled components. *Journal of Personality and Social Psychology*, **56**, 5–18.

Dinella, L., & Martin, C. L. (2002). *Gender stereotypes, gender identity, and preferences of self-identified tomboys and traditional girls.* Paper submitted for the meetings of the Society for Research in Child Development, Tampa.

Edelbrock, C., & Sugawara, A. I. (1978). Acquisition of sex-typed preferences in preschool children. *Developmental Psychology,* **14**, 614–623.

Gelernter, D. (1999, June 21). Women and science at Yale. *The Weekly Standard,* 11–12.

Greenwald, A. G., Banaji, M. R., Rudman, L. A., Farnham, S. D., Nosek, B. A., & Mellott, D. S. (2002). A unified theory of implicit attitudes, stereotypes, self-esteem, and self-concept. *Psychological Review,* **109**, 3–25.

Greenwald, A. G., McGhee, D. E., & Schwartz, J. L. K. (1998). Measuring individual differences in implicit cognition: The Implicit Association Test. *Journal of Personality and Social Psychology,* **74**, 1464–1480.

Huston, A. C. (1983). Sex typing. In E. M. Hetherington (Ed.), *Handbook of child psychology: Socialization, personality, and social development* (4th ed., Vol. 4, pp. 387–467). New York: Wiley.

Martin, C. L., & Dinella, L. (2002). Children's gender cognitions, the social environment, and sex differences in the cognitive domain. In A. McGillicuddy-De Lisi & R. De Lisi (Eds.), *Biology, society, and behavior: The development of sex differences in cognition* (pp. 207–239). Westport, CO: Ablex.

Martin, C. L., Eisenbud, L., & Rose, H. (1995). Children's gender-based reasoning about toys. *Child Development,* **66**, 1453–1471.

Martin, C., & Halverson, C. (1981). A schematic processing model of sex typing and stereotyping in children. *Child Development,* **52**, 1119–1134.

Martin, C. L., Ruble, D.N., & Szkrybalo, J. (in press). Cognitive theories of early gender development *Psychological Bulletin.*

Montemayor, R. (1974). Children's performance in a game and their attraction to it as a function of sex-typed labels. *Child Development,* **45**, 152–156.

Nosek, B. A., Banaji, M., & Greenwald, A. G. (2002). Math = male, me = female, therefore math ≠ me. *Journal of Personality and Social Psychology,* **83**, 44–59.

Ruble, D. N. (1994). A phase model of transitions: Cognitive and motivational consequences. In M. Zanna (Ed.), *Advances in experimental social psychology* (Vol. 26, pp. 163–214). New York: Academic Press.

Ruble, D. N., & Martin, C. L. (1998). Gender development. In W. Damon (Series Ed.) & N. Eisenberg (Vol. Ed.), *Handbook of child psychology, Vol. 3: Social, emotional and personality development* (5th ed., pp. 933–1016). New York: Wiley.

Rudman, L. A., & Glick, P. (2001). Prescriptive gender stereotypes and backlash toward agentic women. *Journal of Social Issues,* **57**, 743–765.

Spence, J. T., & Buckner, C. E. (2000). Instrumental and expressive traits, trait stereotypes, and sexist attitudes. *Psychology of Women Quarterly,* **24**(1), 44–62.

Spence, J. T., & Helmreich, R. (1978). *Masculinity and femininity: Their psychological dimensions, correlates, and antecedents.* Austin: University of Texas Press.

Steele, C. M. (1997). A threat in the air: How stereotypes shape intellectual identity and performance. *American Psychologist,* **6**, 613–629.

Steele, C. M., & Aronson, J. A. (1995). Stereotype threat and the intellectual test performance of African Americans. *Journal of Personality and Social Psychology,* **69**, 797–811

Williams, J. E., & Best, D. L. (1982). *Measuring sex stereotypes: A thirty-nation study.* Beverly Hills: Sage.

COMMENTARY

MEASURES AND MODELS OF GENDER DIFFERENTIATION

Kimberly K. Powlishta

Even though there have been substantial changes over the past few decades in the sorts of occupations and activities that are performed by and considered appropriate for men and women in our society, children continue to hold stereotypical attitudes and preferences. Although attitudes typically become more flexible with age (Powlishta, Sen, Serbin, Poulin-Dubois, & Eichstedt, 2001), adults are prone to gender stereotyping as well. In fact, under some circumstances, adults' perceptions of others are *more* stereotypical than are children's (Powlishta, 2000). As Liben and Bigler point out in their intriguing and important *Monograph,* "popular American culture is filled with evidence that gender is a common and pervasive dimension on which human experience differs."

Despite this pervasiveness, and despite the fact that "psychologists have made the study of gender differences a major focus of the discipline," there remain gaps in our understanding of how and why gender differentiation develops. In particular, little is known about how children's development of gender-based attitudes concerning others is related to their own sex-typed development, particularly in later childhood—a limitation that Liben and Bigler attribute in large part to a lack of reliable and comparable measures of the relevant constructs. One of the major contributions of their *Monograph* is the introduction of new measures designed to assess both children's and adults' attitudes about others and conceptions of themselves across multiple domains of sex typing, including occupations, activities, and traits. The second major contribution comes from highlighting the fact that there are two potential ways in which gendered attitudes about others and sex typing of the self may be related: Either attitudes about others guide the individual's own selection of behaviors, consistent with most traditional cognitively oriented theories of gender-role development (and reflected in the proposed attitudinal pathway model), or one's own behaviors play a causal role in shaping attitudes about others (reflected in the personal pathway model).

The Measures of Sex-Typed Attitudes and Preferences

The sex-typing measures presented in the *Monograph* include both adult and child versions of instruments designed to assess sex-typed attitudes ("Who *should* . . . ?" —males, females, or both/neither) as well as sex-typed personal descriptions ("How much would you like to be a . . . ?" "How often do you . . . ?"), with both the attitude and personal versions covering the domains of occupations, activities, and traits. Long and short versions were developed, with the former assessing attitudes and personal descriptions concerning identical items, thus being ideally suited for an examination of relations between attitudes and behaviors/ preferences.

All of these measures showed good inter-item and test-retest reliability. The fact that attitudes about individual items were almost exclusively either traditional or egalitarian/flexible, but not counter-stereotypical, and the fact that these items were personally endorsed in a generally stereotypical fashion (i.e., that males gave higher ratings on the masculine items and lower ratings on the feminine items than did females) attests to their validity as measures of the stereotypicality of attitudes and preferences. The personal version also correlated with other measures of sex typing (the Bem Sex Role Inventory, the Children's Sex Role Inventory, the Personality Attributes Questionnaire, and the Childrens's PAQ) in predicted ways, further supporting the validity of the measures.

Although there were slight variations among the five studies presented in the *Monograph*, the attitudes of both adults and children generally were more flexible/egalitarian for masculine than for feminine items. In other words, it was considered more acceptable for females to have masculine characteristics than for males to have feminine characteristics. Furthermore, among adults, females tended to be more flexible/egalitarian than did males, consistent with previous findings among children (e.g., Serbin, Powlishta, & Gulko, 1993). These patterns support past research in suggesting that the male role is more binding than the female role; it is considered worse to be a "sissy" than a "tomboy" (e.g., Hort, Fagot, & Leinbach, 1990; Levy, Taylor, & Gelman, 1995; Martin, 1990; Powlishta, 2000). The status differences between males and females noted in the *Monograph* may account for these findings. Even fairly young children are aware of these status differences, at least implicitly and probably explicitly (David, Grace, & Ryan, in press; Glick & Hilt, 2000; Lockheed & Klein, 1985; Powlishta, in press). For example, the first trait stereotypes they learn in the preschool years portray males as powerful and females as fearful and helpless (Ruble & Martin, 1998). Similarly, masculine traits are considered more adultlike/less childlike than are feminine traits by both children and adults (Powlishta, 2000).

There were a few intriguing exceptions to this pattern of a more binding gender role for males. In particular, on the short form of the attitude measure for children, although both boys and girls were more flexible for masculine than for feminine occupations, only girls viewed the masculine activities as more flexible (i.e., as appropriate for both females and males) than the feminine activities. In fact, boys actually viewed the feminine activities as more flexible ("boys can do them too") than the masculine activities ("for boys only"). And in the longitudinal study (Study 5), boys gave more flexible responses than girls for the feminine items. That is, boys were more likely to indicate that the feminine characteristics were appropriate for both sexes, whereas girls were more likely to indicate they were appropriate for females only. Perhaps we are seeing here an out-group homogeneity effect, similar to the one seen in adults' gender attitudes (Park & Rothbart, 1982). Social psychological studies of adults have documented that when people are placed into social categories, even ones created artificially in a research setting, they often view their own group as more variable (i.e., less homogeneous) than other groups ("They're all alike, but we're individuals"; Brown, 2000; Quattrone, 1986). Very few studies have examined this phenomenon directly with children, however (Powlishta, 1995c).

The *Monograph* results also demonstrate that attitudes become more egalitarian with age, perhaps because greater cognitive maturity and experience allow for increased flexibility. In particular, children's gender stereotyping declined over the middle school years. Furthermore, adults were less stereotyped in their attitudes than were children. This latter pattern is inconsistent with one recent study, however, in which adults rated others more stereotypically than did children with respect to feminine traits (Powlishta, 2000). An important methodological difference between the two studies highlights the fact that "sex-typed attitudes" and "sex typing of others" are not necessarily synonymous phrases. In the *Monograph*, attitudes were assessed by asking participants to attribute characteristics to males, females, or both/neither. In the previous study that found elevated stereotyping among adults, participants instead were asked to attribute characteristics to unfamiliar individuals depicted in photographs, with gender not mentioned explicitly. Adults may be more aware that males and females *can* possess similar characteristics, and even believe that they *should* do so (or at least recognize the political incorrectness of advocating traditional gender stereotypes). But these flexible or egalitarian attitudes do not always translate into perceptions of individuals.

The fact that sex-typed attitudes and attitudes about others are not necessarily synonymous has implications for another major finding presented in the *Monograph*. A factor analysis of the various test subscales yielded three factors: one reflecting gender attitudes (containing both masculine and feminine occupation, activity, and trait items), one reflecting feminine self ratings, and one reflecting masculine self ratings. It is from these results that the conclusions "sex typing of others forms a cohesive construct that operates across domains" but "masculinity and femininity retain important differences with respect to the self" are drawn. However, the key distinction may not be self versus other. That is, there is an important difference between the self and other ratings in the current study, despite the use of matching items. As noted above, items on the attitude scale measure sex typing directly, in that participants are asked to assign each item to males, females, or both/neither. But for the self scale, each item does not, by itself, reflect stereotyping. For example, a high rating on a feminine item for a girl (e.g., saying that she "very often" bakes cookies) is stereotypical, but the identical rating from a boy is not. For a boy, going fishing "very often" is stereotypical. Given that each item is scored to reflect degree of self-endorsement rather than the stereotypicality of those endorsements, masculine and feminine items from the self scale would not be expected to load together on a single factor, even if they formed a cohesive construct. Furthermore, a girl who says she bakes "very often" may or may not be highly sex typed, depending on her pattern of responses to other items (e.g., does she just as often endorse masculine items?). Once again, because each rating reflects degree of stereotyping on the attitude scale but not on the personal scale, it is not surprising that the "other" items fall on a single factor but the self items do not. It would be interesting to see a factor analysis when self items were scored to reflect degree of sex typing or where ratings of others reflected the attribution of characteristics to target individuals rather than to males and females in general. Although the current methodology makes perfect sense for the intended goal of examining relations between attitudes and preferences/behaviors, it may be premature to conclude that the results of the factor analysis have deep theoretical implications for the ways in which our gendered beliefs about self versus others are constructed. Despite these reservations, the conclusion that "gender schemata are not unitary constructs, but are instead multifactorial and multidimensional" is likely to be upheld (Serbin et al., 1993).

Models of Sex Typing

The second major contribution of the studies reported in the *Monograph*, beyond the introduction of a suite of useful measures, is the proposal that there are two plausible ways in which gender attitudes and sex typing of the self might be related. Although traditional constructivist models have focused on one pathway—that children's beliefs about gender roles have a causal impact on the sorts of behaviors and characteristics they choose for themselves (the attitudinal pathway model)—it is also possible that the children's own behaviors and characteristics shape their gender attitudes or beliefs (the personal pathway model). Liben and Bigler note that although they present the models separately, the models are not meant to be understood as mutually exclusive. Indeed, it is likely that the two pathways could operate simultaneously in a reciprocal fashion, with beliefs shaping behaviors, and these, in turn leading to the reinforcement or modification of beliefs. An important goal for future work is to find ways to model the interactive nature of these processes, and to study empirically the conditions under which one or the other pathway has priority.

Common to both proposed models is the notion that a series of filters comes into play, in a hierarchical fashion, in the development of sex-typed attitudes and behaviors or preferences. According to the personal pathway model, the interest filter is activated first. If the child is not interested in a particular object, person, or event, it is ignored and processing stops. On the other hand, if the child is interested in the target, he or she will engage with it, and only then does the gender salience filter come into play. For children who tend to process information in a gender-based fashion (i.e., who are gender schematic), their gender attitudes will be reinforced or modified based on their behaviors. For children who are gender aschematic, their behavior will have no impact on their gender attitudes. On the other hand, according to the attitudinal pathway model, the first filter is the gender salience filter. For children who are gender aschematic, whether they engage with a particular object, person, or event depends solely on personal interests. For children who are gender schematic, interests come into play only if the target is considered to be gender appropriate; if the target is considered to be exclusively for the other sex, it is avoided, and the interest filter is not engaged.

Of course, some of the details of the models may need to be modified once more empirical data are available. For example, it is possible that the various filters operate additively rather than hierarchically. For instance, within the attitudinal pathway model as currently represented, a gender schematic child who believes that a particular target is only for the other sex has only one pathway available: avoid. It seems likely that this child might still engage with the target, though, if due to inherent aptitudes, encouragement from others, and/or past positive experiences, he or she had a very strong personal interest in the target. Although

Liben and Bigler acknowledge that this sort of exception may occur, if such exceptions are at all frequent they would warrant a redrawing of the model to one in which two separate filters (gender schema and interests) *additively* determine whether or not a child engages with a target, with the strength of the pathway leading from each filter to behaviors depending on whether or not the child is gender schematic (i.e., the gender salience filter). Modifications to the personal pathway model may also be warranted. For example, as currently drawn, if a child is not interested in a particular target, that child would not form or modify gender attitudes about that target, even if he or she is highly gender schematic, because processing stops at this point. The gender salience filter is only activated if the child *is* interested in the target. That is, interests influence attitudes, but lack of interest does not. In other words, there is no place in the model for the following kind of reasoning: "I'm a girl and I don't like this object, so the object must not be for girls." Although Liben and Bigler indicate that this latter sort of influence is possible, particularly among younger children, once again if such a pattern is common, it may warrant a redrawing of the model.

Despite these sorts of questions (and perhaps even because of them), the proposed models are important in that they should increase the interest of developmental researchers in examining links not only from attitudes to behaviors but vice versa. A further strength of both models is that they build in opportunities for individual differences in gender-based attitudes and personal preferences. The interest filter and the gender salience filter in both models are subject to many influences, including environmental, cognitive-developmental, and presumably biological factors. Thus the models, like most contemporary theories, acknowledge that there are multiple mechanisms of gender role development.

Evidence Concerning the Models

In general, evidence consistent with the proposed models of gender differentiation was mixed. Although the overall relation between attitudes and self-descriptions was significant for adults, this was not true of children. Liben and Bigler suggest that "adults' gender schemata may be less fragmented and more integrated than children's gender schemata." Interestingly, previous research has shown that individual differences in adults' prejudiced attitudes are fairly consistent across targets (e.g., women, homosexuals, the elderly, or various political, racial, ethnic, or religious groups; Bierly, 1985; Ficarrotto, 1990; Grossarth-Maticek, Eysenck, & Vetter, 1989; Hassan & Khalique, 1987; Ray & Lovejoy, 1986), but that children do not show such consistency (Powlishta, Serbin, Doyle, & White, 1994). It may be, then, that the increased consistency between attitudes and behaviors among adults in the current monograph reflects more than the development of integrated gender schemata. Adults' personalities generally may show less fragmentation than do children's.

Despite the lack of overall relations between attitudes and self-descriptions for children, when correlations were examined domain by domain (occupations, activities, traits) or item by item (e.g., elementary school teacher, builds forts, emotional), children's judgments about themselves and others were sometimes (but not always) related. For example, among girls in the longitudinal study (Study 5), egalitarian attitudes toward masculine activities were associated with higher concurrent endorsement of masculine activities and occupations for the self. At a group level, too, there were some consistencies between attitudes and behaviors. For example, both attitudes and self-endorsements were less stereotypical in the trait domain than they were for occupations and activities. For girls, attitudes became more egalitarian during the same time period (from the beginning of 6th grade to the end of 7th grade) that interests became somewhat less sex typed.

Only one finding from the longitudinal analysis provided clear support for either specific model of gender differentiation, however. In particular, consistent with the personal pathway model, boys' endorsement of feminine traits for the self at time 1 (the beginning of 6th grade) predicted more flexible attitudes about masculine and feminine occupations, activities, and traits at time 4 (the end of 7th grade). For girls, despite the concurrent relations noted above, attitudes and self-reported sex typing were not related across time.

Why were the predictive relations so modest, particularly for girls? First, it is important to keep in mind that according to both the attitudinal and personal pathway models, strong relations are predicted only for individuals who are highly gender schematic. In future research, having an independent measure of gender schematic processing (e.g., using a release from proactive interference paradigm; Perez & Kee, 2000) would allow for an even finer evaluation of the models. The stereotypicality of one's attitudes may be related to, but is not interchangeable with, gender salience. Second, it is possible that the longitudinal relations between attitudes and behaviors are stronger at either earlier or later developmental periods than were examined here. Future research along these lines with younger children and with older adolescents is warranted. Third, initial individual differences in sex typing, together with a general stability of these differences over time (Serbin et al., 1993) may have obscured longitudinal relations. That is, when one examines the extent to which one variable (e.g., attitudes) at time 1 predicts another variable (e.g., preferences) at some later time, it often is useful to hold constant initial levels of the outcome variable (time 1 preferences) statistically. In this way, one can examine the extent to which a time 1 predictor in essence promotes change in the outcome variable. Despite these open questions, the *Monograph* presents a unique and much-needed examination of longitudinal relations between sex-typed attitudes and personal descriptions.

Gender Salience and the Importance of Context

As currently outlined, perhaps for the sake of simplicity, the gender salience filter is depicted as yielding a dichotomous outcome: "yes" (gender schematic) or "no" (gender aschematic). It seems likely, though, that gender schematicity actually represents a continuum. Most younger children probably engage in at least some gender schematic processing; in our society, there may be no such thing as a truly gender aschematic child. Cognitively grouping people allows for the efficient handling of large amounts of information. Social categories, and the stereotypes that so often accompany them, simplify a complex world by helping us to make predictions, resolve ambiguities, and establish a self-identity. The perceptual salience of a person's sex, the actual differences in the roles and behaviors of males and females, the emphasis society places on gender, and the fact that sex is a stable, dichotomous, exhaustive, biological basis for categorization, all likely contribute to the nearly ubiquitous salience of gender for young children (Allport, 1954; Bigler, Jones, & Lobliner, 1997; Martin & Halverson, 1981; Powlishta, in press). Preschoolers sometimes seem so obsessed with mastering gender categories that they will invent counterfactual ways in which males and females are different (Powlishta, in press). For example, my 3-year-old nephew recently announced to me that he liked "boy songs" but not "girl songs"; when asked to describe boy songs, he looked puzzled and responded that they are "not girl songs."

Although the gender salience filter is described primarily as reflecting variance among individuals, Liben and Bigler acknowledge that there may be important contextual influences on gender salience as well. According to a social psychological perspective known as Self-Categorization Theory (Turner & Onorato, 1999), people categorize themselves differently depending on the social context, with some contexts heightening the salience of personal identity, wherein the self is defined in terms of idiosyncratic attributes, and other contexts heightening the salience of social identity, wherein the self is defined by membership in social categories (e.g., gender). Which social categories are salient can also vary with context. As Turner and Onorato put it, "People who are categorized and perceived as different in one context (e.g., biologists and physicists in a science faculty) can be recategorized and perceived as similar in another context (e.g., scientists rather than social scientists in a university) without any actual change in their own positions" (p. 23). Similar contextual effects apply to gender. Deaux and Major (1987) suggest that some events (e.g., having just watched the Miss America Pageant or participating in mixed-sex groups) may make gender particularly salient. Indeed, studies with both adults and children have revealed that the extent to which people see males and females as different from each other and use gender stereotypes to describe themselves and others is increased in contexts that enhance gender salience (Bigler, 1995; Hogg & Turner, 1987; McKillip, DiMiceli, & Luebke, 1977; Powlishta, 2002; Sani & Bennett, 2001; Turner & Onorato, 1999). An exciting direction for future research will be to determine how contextual effects fit into the proposed models.

When gender is salient, not only do people tend to see themselves and others in stereotypical terms, but they also tend to view their own sex as better than the other (Deschamps & Doise, 1978; Hogg & Turner, 1987; McKillip et al., 1977; Schmitt, Silvia, & Branscombe, 2000; Starer & Denmark, 1974; Todor, 1980). According to Social Identity Theory (Tajfel & Turner, 1979), once we have identified ourselves as members of a particular group (e.g., male vs. female), we seek to positively differentiate our own group from others in order to enhance self-esteem (i.e., achieve a positive social identity). The nearly universal pattern of own-sex favoritism seen in children could be at least partially accounted for by the proposed models. For example, children might seek out same-sex playmates, a phenomenon known as gender segregation (see Maccoby, 1998), because gender is so often salient and their gender schema filter indicates that same-sex playmates are "for me" (Martin, Fabes, Evans, & Wyman, 1999; Powlishta, 1995b). Alternatively, due to sex differences in play styles, the varying interests of boys and girls (the interest filter) may cause them to choose same-sex playmates, which in turn may lead children to develop attitudes that same-sex playmates are appropriate (Maccoby, 1998). However, the fact that children not only choose same-sex playmates, but also believe that their own sex has more positive and fewer negative characteristics and is generally better than the other sex (Deschamps & Doise, 1978; Glick & Hilt, 2000; Parish & Bryant, 1978; Powlishta, 1995a, in press; Powlishta et al., 1994; Powlishta & Vartanian, 1999; Serbin et al., 1993; Silvern, 1977; Yee & Brown, 1994) points out that gender attitudes contain more than a list indicating which objects, people, and events are appropriate for each sex. They also are affect-laden, containing information such as "boys have cooties."

In summary, the set of studies presented in this *Monograph* provide a good model of test construction that should be of benefit to researchers studying many different aspects of human development. The theoretical propositions also have implications beyond gender. For anyone interested in the developmental connections between attitudes and behaviors,

175

regardless of the content domain, it is important to keep in mind that relations between the two constructs may occur because attitudes influence behaviors, behaviors influence attitudes, or both. Although issues such as these often have been the topic of social psychological research, they frequently are neglected in the developmental literature. Finally, for researchers with specific interests in the development of gender differentiation, the monograph presents a set of useful measures for assessing many components of sex typing, together with unique longitudinal and cross-sectional data on relations among these components.

References

Allport, G. (1954). *The nature of prejudice.* Cambridge, MA: Addison-Wesley.

Bierly, M. M. (1985). Prejudice toward contemporary outgroups as a generalized attitude. *Journal of Applied Social Psychology,* **15,** 189–199.

Bigler, R. S. (1995). The role of classification skill in moderating environmental influences on children's gender stereotyping: A study of the functional use of gender in the classroom. *Child Development,* **66,** 1072–1087.

Bigler, R. S., Jones, L. C., & Lobliner, D. B. (1997). Social categorization and the formation of intergroup attitudes in children. *Child Development,* **68,** 530–543.

Brown, R. (2000). Social identity theory: Past achievements, current problems and future challenges. *European Journal of Social Psychology,* **30,** 745–778.

David, B., Grace, D., & Ryan, M. K. (in press). The gender wars: A self-categorization perspective on the development of gender identity. In M. Bennett & F. Sani (Eds.), *The development of the social self.* East Sussex, England: Psychology Press.

Deaux, K., & Major, B. (1987). Putting gender into context: An interactive model of gender-related behavior. *Psychological Review,* **94,** 369–389.

Deschamps, J. C., & Doise, W. (1978). Crossed category memberships in intergroup relations. In H. Tajfel (Ed.), *Differentiation between social groups* (pp. 141–158). London: Academic.

Ficarrotto, T. J. (1990). Racism, sexism, and erotophobia: Attitudes of heterosexuals toward homosexuals. *Journal of Homosexuality,* **19,** 111–116.

Glick, P., & Hilt, L. (2000). Combative children to ambivalent adults: The development of gender prejudice. In T. Eckes & H. M. Trautner (Eds.), *The developmental social psychology of gender* (pp. 243–272). Mahwah, NJ: Erlbaum.

Grossarth-Maticek, R., Eysenck, H. J., & Vetter, H. (1989). The causes and cures of prejudice: An empirical study of the frustration-aggression hypothesis. *Personality and Individual Differences,* **10,** 547–558.

Hassan, M. K., & Khalique, A. (1987). A study of prejudice in Hindu and Muslim college students. *Psychologia,* **30,** 80–84.

Hogg, M. A., & Turner, J. C. (1987). Intergroup behaviour, self-stereotyping and the salience of social categories. *British Journal of Social Psychology,* **26,** 325–340.

Hort, B. E., Fagot, B. I., & Leinbach, M. D. (1990). Are people's notions of maleness more stereotypically framed than their notions of femaleness? *Sex Roles,* **23,** 197–212.

Levy, G. D., Taylor, M. G., & Gelman, S. A. (1995). Traditional and evaluative aspects of flexibility in gender roles, social conventions, moral rules, and physical laws. *Child Development,* **66,** 515–531.

Lockheed, M., & Klein, S. (1985). Sex equity in classroom organization and climate. In S.

Klein (Ed.), *Handbook for achieving sex equity through education* (pp. 189–217). Baltimore: Johns Hopkins University Press.

Maccoby, E. E. (1998). *The two sexes: Growing up apart, coming together.* Cambridge, MA: Harvard University Press.

Martin, C. L. (1990). Attitudes and expectations about children with nontraditional and traditional gender roles. *Sex Roles*, **22**, 151–165.

Martin, C. L., Fabes, R. A., Evans, S. M., & Wyman, H. (1999). Social cognition on the playground: Children's beliefs about playing with girls versus boys and their relations to sex segregated play. *Journal of Social & Personal Relationships*, **16**, 751–771.

Martin, C. L., & Halverson, C. F., Jr. (1981). A schematic processing model of sex typing and stereotyping in children. *Child Development*, **52**, 1119–1134.

McKillip, J., DiMiceli, A. J., & Luebke, J. (1977). Group salience and stereotyping. *Social Behavior and Personality*, **5**, 81–85.

Parish, T. S., & Bryant, W. T. (1978). Mapping sex group stereotypes of elementary and high school students. *Sex Roles*, **4**, 135–140.

Park, B., & Rothbart, M. (1982). Perception of out-group homogeneity and levels of social categorization: Memory for the subordinate attributes of in-group and out-group members. *Journal of Personality and Social Psychology*, **42**, 1051–1068.

Perez, S. M., & Kee, D. W. (2000). Girls not boys show gender-connotation encoding from print. *Sex Roles*, **42**, 439–447.

Powlishta, K. K. (1995a). Gender bias in children's perception of personality traits. *Sex Roles*, **32**, 17–28.

Powlishta, K. K. (1995b). Gender segregation among children: Understanding the "cootie phenomenon." *Young Children*, May, 61–69.

Powlishta, K. K. (1995c). Intergroup processes in childhood: Social categorization and sex role development. *Developmental Psychology*, **31**, 781–788.

Powlishta, K. K. (2000). The effect of target age on the activation of gender stereotypes. *Sex Roles*, **42**, 271–282.

Powlishta, K. K. (2002). *Perceived similarity of boys and girls: Contextual variations in the salience of gender.* Manuscript submitted for publication.

Powlishta, K. K. (in press). Gender as a social category: Intergroup processes and gender-role development. In M. Bennett & F. Sani (Eds.), *The development of the social self.* East Sussex, England: Psychology Press.

Powlishta, K. K., Sen, M. G., Serbin, L. A., Poulin-Dubois, D., & Eichstedt, J. A. (2001). From infancy through middle childhood: The role of cognitive and social factors in becoming gendered. In R. K. Unger (Ed.), *Handbook of the psychology of women and gender* (pp. 116–132). New York: Wiley.

Powlishta, K. K., Serbin, L. A., Doyle, A., & White, D. C. (1994). Gender, ethnic, and body type biases: The generality of prejudice in childhood. *Developmental Psychology*, **30**, 526–536.

Powlishta, K. K., & Vartanian, L. R. (1999, April). *Self-esteem and own-sex favoritism in middle childhood and early adolescence.* Poster presented at the Biennial Meeting of the Society for Research in Child Development, Albuquerque, NM.

Quattrone, G. A. (1986). On the perception of a groups' variability. In S. Worchel & W. G. Austin (Eds.), *Psychology of intergroup relations* (pp. 25–48). Chicago: Nelson-Hall.

Ray, J. J., & Lovejoy, F. H. (1986). The generality of prejudice. *Journal of Social Psychology*, **126**, 563–564.

Ruble, D. N., & Martin, C. L. (1998). Gender development. In W. Damon (Series Editor) & N. Eisenberg (Vol. Ed.), *Handbook of child psychology, Vol. 3. Social, emotional and personality development* (5th ed., pp. 933–1016). New York: Wiley.

Sani, F., & Bennett, M. (2001). Contextual variability in young children's gender ingroup stereotype. *Social Development*, **10**, 221–229.

Schmitt, M. T., Silvia, P. J., & Branscombe, N. R. (2000). The intersection of self-evaluation maintenance and social identity theories: Intragroup judgment in intergroup and interpersonal contexts. *Personality & Social Psychology Bulletin*, **26**, 1598–1606.

Serbin, L. A., Powlishta, K. K., & Gulko, J. (1993). The development of sex-typing in middle childhood. *Monographs of the Society for Research in Child Development*, **58** (Serial No. 232).

Silvern, L. E. (1977). Children's sex-role preferences: Stronger among girls than boys. *Sex Roles*, **3**, 159–171.

Starer, R., & Denmark, F. (1974). Discrimination against aspiring women. *International Journal of Group Tensions*, **4**, 65–70.

Tajfel, H., & Turner, J. (1979). An integrative theory of intergroup conflict. In W. G. Austin & S. Worchel (Eds.), *The social psychology of intergroup relations* (pp. 33–47). Monterey, CA: Brooks/Cole.

Todor, N. L. (1980). The effect of the sexual composition of a group on discrimination against women and sex-role attitudes. *Psychology of Women Quarterly*, **5**, 292–310.

Turner, J. C., & Onorato, R. (1999). Social identity, personality, and the self-concept: A self-categorization perspective. In T. R. Tyler, R. M. Kramer, & O. P. John (Eds.), *The psychology of the social self* (pp. 11–46). Mahwah, NJ: Erlbaum.

Yee, M., & Brown, R. (1994). The development of gender differentiation in young children. *British Journal of Social Psychology*, **33**, 183–196.

EXTENDING THE STUDY OF GENDER DIFFERENTIATION

Lynn S. Liben and Rebecca S. Bigler

The two commentaries on our work are the kinds of essays about which *Monograph* authors dream. The authors—Ruble and Martin, and Powlishta—begin with praise for our COAT and OAT measures, sharing their judgment that the suite of measures provides a unique and valuable assessment tool for the study of gender development. Both are laudatory about the value of our having extended the theoretical and empirical focus beyond the traditional other-to-self (attitudinal) pathway to include a self-to-other (personal) pathway. Both offer rich links to other empirical and theoretical traditions that place our work in a broad context. And perhaps most excitingly, both provide a collection of fascinating ideas that speak to the generative nature of our work for theoretical and empirical purposes. Predictably, the authors have also raised a number of gently phrased concerns about some of the methodological and interpretive decisions we have made. Although their points are not offered as stark contrasts between "right" and "wrong," they do raise a number of interesting questions about the value of alternative methodological and interpretative decisions.

Given strict limitations on the space allotted for our reply, we regret that we cannot discuss all of the many intriguing issues that the commentaries raise. We therefore consider only a single methodological point, and comment on two of the many possible future directions that emerge from the collection of papers.

Methodological Issues

One of the key methodological points raised by Ruble and Martin concerns the character of the individual items included in the COAT and

OAT scales. In particular, they point out that "One potential limitation of the measures for some uses is that many of the items included as stereotypes are not highly stereotyped." They correctly go on to point out that the ratings of items found in two different categories (e.g., masculine vs. neutral) may differ "by as little as .1 on a 7-point scale."

Why do the OAT and COAT scales contain some items that are not strongly sex typed? As explained in the text, we first assembled a pool of masculine, feminine, and neutral items from earlier research, and then asked adults to rate them for cultural sex typing. Ratings fell along a continuum from highly masculine to highly feminine, with neutral items falling in the middle. We then established numerical criteria to categorize items into three categories. As is inevitable with such a system, the ratings of some sex-typed items were close to the ratings of items in the neutral category. One possibility would have been to omit borderline items from the scales altogether. We judged even these items as potentially valuable, however, for reasons that differed for the short and long scales.

For the short scales, we had an alternative, preferred basis for deciding which items to retain and which to omit. Specifically, items were selected for inclusion on the short scale based on item-total correlations obtained from new empirical data. Thus, a particular item was selected for the short scale if it showed itself to be a psychometrically good item for the age group and measure in question, irrespective of how adults had rated that item on cultural stereotyping. Interestingly, the best performing items selected in this way were generally those with ratings that placed them at moderate, not high, levels of stereotyping. This undoubtedly occurs because it is moderate items that elicit the response variability needed to detect individual differences.

For the long scales, we reasoned that weakly stereotyped items might be useful for particular purposes. Consider, for example, an investigator interested in gender differences in performance on the National Geographic Bee (Liben, in press). For this work, it is of interest to compare students' attitudinal sex typing of "geographer" to students' personal interests in the occupation, *even though* the item itself is not judged to be highly stereotyped by adults, and is considered to be masculine by only a modest percentage of children. We also reasoned that a scale with a broad range of sex-typing items would have greater ecological validity (a concern that also led us to retain both more and less desirable items) and, as Ruble and Martin acknowledge, would be better for detecting variability.

Thus, we agree completely that these small differences may indeed be problematic, but only, as Ruble and Martin put it, "for some uses." In our view, these are probably better labeled as "inappropriate uses." In particular, these small differences would be problematic if an investigator were to select some idiosyncratic subset of items from the long form of the scales, and use them to try to infer participants' general level of sex typing. When item parsimony is desired, it is the short forms of the scales that should be used.

Although the ratings of items do not in and of themselves pose problems for the reasons just explained, the comments about small differences in ratings offered by Ruble and Martin combined with the comments about "substantial changes over the past few decades" noted by Powlishta make the important point that cultural stereotypes are constantly evolving. We must acknowledge that this evolution means that some items selected for the short versions of the scales will undoubtedly lose their centrality in the years ahead, thus necessitating future revisions of the COAT and OAT scales. What should remain constant, however, is the general structure of the scales with respect to including multiple domains (i.e., occupations, activities, and traits) and targets (i.e., attitude and personal measures), and the approach of selecting items for a given scale (e.g., COAT, OAT, POAT) based on empirical data from respondents of the appropriate age.

The remaining methodological points raised by Ruble and Martin and by Powlishta highlight many important issues that we, too, had considered as we developed our scales (e.g., the best number of response options offered to children and adults; the ideal way to score and analyze responses). Although space constraints prohibit discussions of these specific issues, we note in passing that at the deepest level, many of these methodological points concern the general and pervasive problem in developmental work of establishing functional equivalence of measures for participants of different ages. It is for this reason that we pressed so strongly in the body of the *Monograph* for selecting items and evaluating reliability and validity separately for each age group.

Future Directions

At the heart of our own contribution to this *Monograph*, and evident in both commentaries, is an implicit affirmation of a developmental approach to the study of sex typing. A developmental approach is evident in our focus on designing age-appropriate measures, the formulation of pathways to describe and explain change, and in the use of longitudinal data to evaluate these models. Ruble, Martin, and Powlishta push developmental thinking further by arguing for the importance of extending our work downward to younger ages.

We concur completely that this is a critical direction for future work. Developmental pathways must be studied in younger children to permit us to understand the *establishment* of gender differentiation. Such work— much of it already well represented in the past research programs of

Ruble, Martin, and Powlishta—dovetails well with the work on the application, maintenance, and revision of gender differentiation during middle childhood that is the focus of the current *Monograph.* Our hope is that future work with younger children will be facilitated even further once appropriate versions of the C/OAT scales become available (see the discussion of the pictorial version of the scales [POAT] mentioned in the body of the *Monograph*).

We would add, however, that at the same time that we and others extend work on gender differentiation down to younger children, it is also important to extend it upward to study individuals as they leave the college years and establish families, begin careers, and enter later portions of the life span. Scales developed for older age groups would need to tap age-appropriate gender attitudes and behaviors that have been identified in the family- and adult-development literatures. For example, scale items might include activities such as changing diapers, arranging child care, attending PTA meetings, coaching basketball, making medical appointments for aging parents, investing money, and buying insurance. Interestingly, many of the contextual effects of the kind that Ruble, Martin, and Powlishta raise may be particularly powerful at later portions of the life span. For example, single parents may take on, by necessity, many gendered household tasks that would normally have fallen outside their self-defined interests or that conflict with their beliefs. These behaviors may, in turn, lead to modifications of their gender attitudes.

In addition to underscoring the need to extend our collective research to a fuller portion of the life span, the commentaries also raise some intriguing suggestions about developmental timing of effects. We point to one suggestion made by Ruble and Martin in particular because it contrasts sharply with a suggestion that we had made. Specifically, they write: "First, stereotypes may have their maximal impact as children first select and try out new activities, rather than once their personal conclusions about them have already been drawn (Ruble, 1994). Thus, 5th grade may already be too late to detect relations. . .". This is a perfectly reasonable suggestion, but interestingly, one that is exactly the opposite of what we had proposed in the final discussion section of the *Monograph.* There we had suggested that young children might be oblivious to a logical conflict between (a) holding a gender stereotype and (b) behaving in a way that conflicts with that stereotype (e.g., a young girl who simultaneously believes that trucks are for boys, knows that she is a girl, but nevertheless plays with trucks). Further, we had suggested that as cognitive skills develop, children would become increasingly sensitive to logical inconsistencies, and thus, with age, would be increasingly motivated to bring behaviors into line with attitudes (or the reverse). Fortunately, both are clear hypotheses that readily lend themselves to empirical study. More generally, we extol the many points about timing raised in both commentaries, and look forward to seeing an expanding body of relevant empirical work.

Concluding Thoughts

We end our reply with a public expression of appreciation for the care and depth with which Ruble, Martin, and Powlishta considered our conceptual and empirical work. Their commentaries have extended our own thinking already. We expect that their commentaries will have a similar impact on readers in broadening their attention to related theoretical and empirical work, and in shaping future research agendas. Our hope is that these commentaries, combined with the scales and ideas we presented initially, will prove useful to all who are interested in understanding, and perhaps modifying, gender differentiation.

References

Liben, L. S. (in press). The drama of sex differences in academic achievement: And the show goes on. *Issues in Education.*
Ruble, D. N. (1994). A phase model of transitions: Cognitive and motivational consequences. In M. Zanna (Ed.), *Advances in experimental social psychology* (Vol. 26, pp. 163–214). New York: Academic Press.

CONTRIBUTORS

Lynn S. Liben (Ph.D., The University of Michigan, 1972) is Distinguished Professor of Psychology at the Pennsylvania State University. Her research has focused on the development of gender and on the development of spatial-graphic representation. She has also studied the intersection of these topics, as in her work on sex-related differences in spatial cognition and on the gender gap in success on the National Geographic Bee.

Rebecca S. Bigler (Ph.D., The Pennsylvania State University, 1991) is Associate Professor of Psychology at the University of Texas at Austin. Her work has concerned the development of gender and racial stereotypes, including how contextual factors serve to exaggerate or diminish their growth. She has also been active in developing and evaluating interventions designed to discourage the establishment and maintenance of gender and racial stereotypes.

Diane N. Ruble (Ph.D., UCLA, 1973) is Professor of Psychology at New York University. She has applied her phase model of development to the study of gender development, especially gender constancy. Her current research involves early gender identification and rigidity and ethnic identity development.

Carol Lynn Martin (Ph.D., University of Georgia, 1981) is Professor in the Department of Family and Human Development at Arizona State University. She has formulated theories related to gender development, especially concerning the role of cognition in gender-related thinking and behavior. Her current research is addressed to the development and influence of sex segregation on children's social and academic development and to variations in gender development.

184

Kimberly K. Powlishta (Ph.D., Stanford University, 1989) is Assistant Professor of Psychology at Saint Louis University. Her current research focuses on the development of gender stereotyping and gender-based biases, with a particular interest in the contribution of generic intergroup processes (e.g., in-group favoritism, the exaggeration of differences between and similarities within groups) to gender-role development.

STATEMENT OF EDITORIAL POLICY

The *Monographs* series is devoted to publishing developmental research that generates authoritative new findings and uses these to foster fresh, better integrated, or more coherent perspectives on major developmental issues, problems, and controversies. The significance of the work in extending developmental theory and contributing definitive empirical information in support of a major conceptual advance is the most critical editorial consideration. Along with advancing knowledge on specialized topics, the series aims to enhance cross-fertilization among developmental disciplines and developmental sub fields. Therefore, clarity of the links between the specific issues under study and questions relating to general developmental processes is important. These links, as well as the manuscript as a whole, must be as clear to the general reader as to the specialist. The selection of manuscripts for editorial consideration, and the shaping of manuscripts through reviews-and-revisions, are processes dedicated to actualizing these ideals as closely as possible.

Typically *Monographs* entail programmatic large-scale investigations; sets of programmatic interlocking studies; or—in some cases—smaller studies with highly definitive and theoretically significant empirical findings. Multi-authored sets of studies that center on the same underlying question can also be appropriate; a critical requirement here is that all studies address common issues, and that the contribution arising from the set as a whole be unique, substantial, and well integrated. The needs of integration preclude having individual chapters identified by individual authors. In general, irrespective of how it may be framed, any work that is judged to significantly extend developmental thinking will be taken under editorial consideration.

To be considered, submissions should meet the editorial goals of *Monographs* and should be no briefer than a minimum of 80 pages (including references and tables). There is an upper limit of 175–200 pages. In exceptional circumstances this upper limit may be modified (please submit four copies). Because a *Monograph* is inevitable lengthy and usually substantively complex, it is particularly important that the text be well organized and written in clear, precise, and literate English. Note, however, that authors from non-English speaking countries should not be put off by this stricture. In accordance with the general aims of SRCD, this series is actively interested in promoting international exchange of developmental research. Neither membership in the Society nor affiliation with the academic discipline of psychology are relevant in considering a *Monographs* submission.

The corresponding author for any manuscript must, in the submission letter, warrant that all coauthors are in agreement with the content of the manuscript. The corresponding author also is responsible for informing all coauthors, in a timely manner, of manuscript submission, editorial decisions, reviews received, and any revisions recommended. Before publication, the corresponding author also must warrant in the submission letter that the study has been conducted according to the ethical guidelines of the Society for Research in Child Development.

Potential authors who may be unsure whether the manuscript they are planning would make an appropriate submission are invited to draft an outline of what they propose, and send it to the Editor for assessment. This mechanism, as well as a more detailed description of all editorial policies, evaluation processes, and format requirements can be found at the Editorial Office web site (http://astro.temple.edu/~overton/monosrcd.html) or by contacting the Editor, Willis F. Overton, Temple University-Psychology, 1701 North 13th St. – Rm 567, Philadelphia, PA 19122-6085 (e-mail: monosrcd@blue.temple.edu) (telephone: 1-215-204-7360).

Monographs of the Society for Research in Child Development (ISSN 0037-976X), one of three publications of the Society for Research in Child Development, is published four times a year by Blackwell Publishers, Inc., with offices at 350 Main Street, Malden, MA 02148, USA, and 108 Cowley Road, Oxford OX4 1JF, UK. Call US 1-800-835-6770, fax: (781) 388-8232, or e-mail: subscrip@blackwellpub.com. A subscription to *Monographs of the SRCD* comes with a subscription to *Child Development* (published six times a year in February, April, June, August, October, and December). A combined package rate is also available with the third SRCD publication, *Child Development Abstracts and Bibliography*, published three times a year.

INFORMATION FOR SUBSCRIBERS   For new orders, renewals, sample copy requests, claims, change of address, and all other subscription correspondence, please contact the Journals Subscription Department at the publisher's Malden office.

INSTITUTIONAL SUBSCRIPTION RATES FOR MONOGRAPHS OF THE SRCD/CHILD DEVELOPMENT 2002   The Americas $293, Rest of World £192. All orders must be paid by credit card, business check, or money order. Checks and money orders should be made payable to Blackwell Publishers. Canadian residents please add 7% GST.

INSTITUTIONAL SUBSCRIPTION RATES FOR MONOGRAPHS OF THE SRCD/CHILD DEVELOPMENT 2002   The Americas $328, Rest of World £232. All orders must be paid by credit card, business check, or money order. Checks and money orders should be made payable to Blackwell Publishers. Canadian residents please add 7% GST.

BACK ISSUES   Back issues are available from the publisher's Malden office.

MICROFORM   The journal is available on microfilm. For microfilm service, address inquiries to ProQuest Information and Learning, 300 North Zeeb Road, Ann Arbor, MI 48106-1346, USA. Bell and Howell Serials Customer Service Department: 1-800-521-0600 ×2873.

POSTMASTER   Periodicals class postage paid at Boston, MA, and additional offices. Send address changes to Blackwell Publishers, 350 Main Street, Malden, MA 02148, USA.

FORTHCOMING

Child Emotional Security and Interparental Conflict—*Patrick T. Davies, Gordon T. Harold, Marcie C. Goeke-Morey, and E. Mark Cummings* (SERIAL NO. 270, 2002)

How Children and Adolescents Evaluate Gender and Racial Exclusion— *Melanie Killen, Jennie Lee-Kim, Heidi McGlothlin, and Charles Stangor* (SERIAL NO. 271, 2002)

CURRENT

The Developmental Course of Gender Differentiation: Conceptualizing, Measuring, and Evaluating Constructs and Pathways—*Lynn S. Liben and Rebecca S. Bigler* (SERIAL NO. 269, 2002)

The Development of Mental Processing: Efficiency, Working Memory, and Thinking—*Andreas Demetriou, Constantinos Christou, George Spanoudis, and Maria Platsidou* (SERIAL NO. 268, 2002)

The Intentionality Model and Language Acquisition: Engagement, Effort, and the Essential Tension in Development—*Lois Bloom and Erin Tinker* (SERIAL NO. 267, 2001)

Children with Disabilities: A Longitudinal Study of Child Development and Parent Well-being—*Penny Hauser-Cram, Marji Erickson Warfield, Jack P. Shonkoff, and Marty Wyngaarden Krauss* (SERIAL NO. 266, 2001)

Rhythms of Dialogue in Infancy: Coordinated Timing in Development— *Joseph Jaffe, Beatrice Beebe, Stanley Feldstein, Cynthia L. Crown, and Michael D. Jasnow* (SERIAL NO. 265, 2001)

Early Television Viewing and Adolescent Behavior: The Recontact Study—*Daniel R. Anderson, Aletha C. Huston, Kelly Schmitt, Deborah Linebarger, and John C. Wright* (SERIAL NO. 264, 2001)

Parameters of Remembering and Forgetting in the Transition from Infancy to Early Childhood—*P. J. Bauer, J. A. Wenner, P. L. Dropik, and S. S. Wewerka* (SERIAL NO. 263, 2000)

Breaking the Language Barrier: An Emergentist Coalition Model for the Origins of Word Learning—*George J. Hollich, Kathy Hirsh-Pasek, Roberta Michnick Golinkoff* (SERIAL NO. 262, 2000)

Across the Great Divide: Bridging the Gap Between Understanding of Toddlers' and Other Children's Thinking—*Zhe Chen and Robert Siegler* (SERIAL NO. 261, 2000)

Making the Most of Summer School: A Meta-Analytic and Narrative Review—*Harris Cooper, Kelly Charlton, Jeff C. Valentine, and Laura Muhlenbruck* (SERIAL NO. 260, 2000)

Adolescent Siblings in Stepfamilies: Family Functioning and Adolescent Adjustment—*E. Mavis Hetherington, Sandra H. Henderson, and David Reiss* (SERIAL NO. 259, 1999)